# THE BASIC YI JING
## Oracle of Change

# THE BASIC YI JING
## Oracle of Change

Dany Chin & Budhy Chen

Olive Press

ISBN 9789077787182
NUR 739

Copyright © 2008 Denis Dutrieux & Budhy Wetters,
Amsterdam, The Netherlands
Revised Edition 2012

All rights reserved. No part of this book may be reproduced in any form or by any means, without written permission from the owners of the copyright, or Olive Press as their representative.

Olive Press, Leeuwerikstraat 4B, 1021 GL Amsterdam, The Netherlands
info@olive-press.eu
www.olive-press.eu

Cover design by the authors.
Printed by Lightning Source

Our gratitude goes to the late Dr. Herman Cohen for his support to manifest this book.

*This book is an offering
to the Yi's great spirit of wisdom*

*About the authors*

The authors, Dany Chin and Budhy Chen, living in The Netherlands, are originally from Indonesian-European descent, with only a few Chinese drops of blood in their veins.

They took their writer's name from the names of their specific life-hexagrams: hexagram 35, *Chin* and hexagram 51, *Chen* (in *Pinyin*, resp. *Jin* and *Zhen*).

Although in this present life they are not so much of a Chinese, they are convinced that in a past life they must have had a very close relationship with the *Yi*. This conviction is supported by the fact that they dedicated six precious years of their life to this new translation of the *Yi*.

The cover is made by the authors from a photograph of the *yin/yang* symbol that was naturally formed on the bottom of a waterpot.

The drawing on the title page, designed by the authors, is a stylised presentation of the pictographs of the Sun, *ri* ☉, and the Moon, *yue* ☾, found on ancient oracle bones, with a *yang* and *yin* line enclosed. The character *yi* of change, evolved from those pictographs.

*He who uses the* Yi *becomes wise.*
*He who is wise does not use the* Yi *unwisely.*

# Contents

vii   *About the authors*
xiii   *Preface*

     *Introduction*
xvii   Origin
xviii   Signs and omens
xxi   The inner structure of the *Yi Jing*
xxvii   Three main methods of consultation
xxxi   Inquiry and interpretation

1   *The Basic Yi Jing*

     *The Twelfth Wing*
333   Introduction
335   Eight main principles in the *Yi Jing*
340   The *Yi Jing* and the process of change
345   The *Yi Jing* and the concept of time
349   The *Yi Jing* and the theory of chance
353   Parallelity and the *Yi Jing*
358   Inconsistencies in the *Yi Jing*
366   The *Yi Jing*'s ways of wisdom
371   The order and sequence of the hexagrams
382   *Yi Jing* methodology
389   Consulting the *Yi Jing* with a die

392  *Yi Jing* numerology
396  A mandala of hexagrams

**Appendixes**
403  I. The working method
408  II. *Yi Jing* corrections
417  III. The trigrams
420  IV. Miscellaneous
422  V. Chart to identify the hexagrams

423  **Bibliography**

# Preface

Why another expression of the *Yi Jing* when there are so many of them already? The main reason is that the authors were not satisfied with any of them. Even the ones they considered good had their weak parts. That is why they decided to write a text that they could fully approve.

The main purpose of this translation was to create a version of the *Yi Jing* that is most suitable as a divination tool.

This new translation was not a matter of translating the text from the Chinese language into English, but rather transcribing the essence of the *Yi Jing* into concepts that are as close as possible to its actual meaning and purpose.

As this text is not a homogeneous text with fixed meanings – because it has gone through a long process of re-interpretation through the centuries – the authors decided to stay with its structure and attempted to construct what they see as **The Basic Yi Jing**. One that is simple and easy and comes as close as possible to the essence of the *Yi*-tradition.

While exploring the inner structure and workings of the *Yi Jing*, the abstract and philosophical aspect of the *Yi* was expressed in a supplement which the authors named *The Twelfth Wing*.

Their basic text is the *Zhou Yi*, ascribed to king *Wen* of the *Zhou* dynasty (c. 1122-221 BCE), one of the three traditional divination texts in China. The others are the *Gui Cang Yi* of *Tang*, the first emperor of the *Shang* dynasty (c. 1766-1122 BCE), and the *Lian Shan Yi* of the first emperor *Yu* of the *Xia* dynasty (c. 2205-1766 BCE), both of which are extinct.

This *Zhou Yi* text put together as a coherent text around the middle of the 9th century BCE is considered to be the basic *Yi Jing* text since the middle ages.

One of the authors Budhy Chen (a.k.a. B. Wetters) who did the preliminary work, stayed strictly with the old text and words, and the other one Dany Chin (a.k.a. D. Dutrieux) contributed to the text his long-time experience (36 years) of working with the *Yi Jing*.

Knowing that what they did can only be an attempt to create 'the perfect *Yi Jing*', they humbly offer their effort to its eternal spirit of wisdom.

Amsterdam, 28 August 2008


Sadly, my co-author and dear friend Dany Chin passed away in October 2010. Without his wisdom, patience, and loving care, this book could not be manifested.

Amsterdam, 2 February 2012					Budhy Chen

*Contemplation of the changes in Reality
inspired the creation of the Yi.
Contemplation of life's changes
decides the choice between advance or retreat.*

# Introduction

## Origin

The *Yi Jing* (lit. *Classic of Change*), is a composite work consisting of the *Zhou Yi*, the ancient core text, and later added commentaries. The text contains 64 hexagrams or six-line images, and was mainly used for divination or prediction of future events. This *Book of Change* can be regarded as the foundation of Chinese civilisation. Many decisions that decided the course of Chinese history, and many inventions that made a change in Chinese culture, have been made on the basis of consulting the *Yi Jing*. Its origin can be traced back to *Fu Xi*, a legendary sage who lived during the age of hunting and fishing about 4500 years ago.

*Fu Xi* is said to have created the *yang* (whole) line and *yin* (broken) line representing the duality in Reality: *yang* and *yin*, light and dark, sun and moon, heaven and earth, day and night, male and female, action and rest and so on. From these two lines he composed eight trigrams, each made of three lines, representing aspects of nature (elements), natural phenomena (mountain, lake), weather, seasons, directions, and family members. By observing nature he was inspired to arrange the order of the trigrams.

The order of the eight trigrams are said to be derived from the *He Tu* and *Lo Shu* patterns of dots found on sacred animals (see Huang, *The Numerology of the I Ching*, p. 21 ff), but they may well have been derived from natural phenomena such as the weather and the seasons.

The 'Early Heaven Arrangement' (EHA) of trigrams is based on the observation of the sequence of events in the sky: *heaven* (clear sky), *cloud*, *fire* (lightning), *thunder*, *wind*, *water* (rain), *mountain* and *earth*.

The 'Later Heaven Arrangement' (LHA) of trigrams was inspired by the order of the seasons on earth: *water* (rain, winter), *earth*, *thunder* (spring, growth), *wind* (wood, plants), *fire* (summer), *heaven*, *lake* (cloud, autumn), and *mountain* (winter). Here *fire* was placed at the end, and not after *wind* where it belongs in the sequence based on the seasons. (See diagram page xxiii).

Some time before the beginning of the *Zhou* Dynasty (c. 1122-221 BCE) king *Wen* is said to have created the 'original' version of the *Yi Jing* as we know it today. While he was imprisoned for seven years by the last *Shang* emperor *Zhou Xin*, king *Wen* composed and named the 64 hexagrams, each made of six lines, and wrote a commentary for each hexagram known as 'The Judgment'. After his death king *Wen*'s son, the duke of *Zhou* completed his work by adding commentaries to the individual lines of the hexagrams as well as a commentary on each Judgment. These commentaries compose the theoretical framework of the *Yi Jing*.

Five hundred years later *Kong Fu Zi* (Confucius) came in contact with the *Book of Change* and studied it extensively. He is said to have written a series of essays known as the 'Ten Wings' in which he described and explained the philosophical bases of the book. These include a discussion on the attributes of the eight trigrams, a commentary on the 'Images' (symbols of the hexagrams), and notes on the relationships of the lines.

After Confucius many scholars studied the *Yi Jing* and contributed commentaries, especially in the *Han* dynasty (206 BCE-220 CE), when much was written on prediction. The *Yi Jing* has always been considered a sacred book in China, and generations of rulers, scholars and military strategists have consulted it before making important decisions. Nowadays there are many translations and commentaries on the *Book of Change* in the West indicating that it is becoming as popular as it was and still is in China.

## Signs and omens

The *Yi Jing* is in the first place a book of divination, based on an elaborated system of signs and omens. These signs and omens are based on subjective physical sensations (itchings and twitchings), the movements of animals (birds and foxes), and natural phenomena (thunder, rain and stars). Signs are things perceived in the present, which indicate a future state or occurrence. Omens are occurrences or objects regarded as portending good or evil. Signs and omens are actually events occurring at a particular time (present or past), which may give an indication as to what may happen at another time (future). These events are only called signs and omens *if* there is a subject (human being) observing them, and giving a particular meaning to them.

As the signs and omens are *not* the causes of future events, it is not the principle of Causality, but the principle of Synchronicity we have to rely on to understand the workings of signs and omens.

According to the principle of Synchronicity, two events occurring at a certain time are related to each other – in the sense that meaning is perceived from their occurrence – *only* if there is a subject observing them. That two events in Reality (the great Reality, Reality as a whole) are related to each other, is based on the idea of the One Reality. Because Reality is basically One, everything in Reality is related to everything else.

This relation between two events goes beyond the concept of Time, because time is an illusion and apparent only within the realm of the ordinary reality (the small reality, reality as an aspect of that great Reality) where everything is continuously changing. Time is noticed mainly because of the perception that everything is changing continuously, and Change is perceived also due to the indication of Time. *Change is Time and Time is Change*. Within the realm of Duality, Time manifests as past, present and future, but in the One Reality there is actually only the present that contains both past and future.

In the Oneness of Reality, where everything is related to everything else certain events acquire meaning only because an observing subject attaches it to them. Without the subject noticing the signs or omens, and giving meaning to them, everything in Reality is just related to everything else and has no significance attached to it. So, if a subject observes two events in Reality at different times, the meaning of their relation can still be noticed but only if the subject is open to the information.

Thus by looking at the early morning sky some farmers are still able to predict the weather of the coming day. By having noticed the sayings and actions of people who have died unexpectedly while there was no special reason for it, one could have known that death was imminent. By observing things and events carefully (seeing the signs and omens) one can be warned about things to come.

The signs and omens the *Book of Change* is composed of, are firstly signs and omens derived from the observation of natural phenomena.

In the EHA (see diagram, page xxiii), the sequence of the trigrams is consistent with the sequence of events in the sky when weather phenomena are observed:

1. *heaven* (a clear summer sky) – 2. *cloud* (due to heat, hot air rises and clouds are formed) – 3. *fire* (heavy clouds bring forth lightning) – 4. *thunder* (after lightning, thunder always follows) – 5. *wind* (wind follows thunder) – 6. *water* (after the wind comes the rain) – 7. *mountain* (the rain falls first on the mountain) – 8. *earth* (the rain falls on the earth).

*This sequence of the eight trigrams is a sequence of events related to the natural pattern of the weather, and can be considered a natural pattern of change.*

The eight trigrams are connected with the five elements or states of change: Earth, Water, Fire, Wood (Western element Air), and Metal (Western element Ether). Taking the relationships between the five states of change (producing, injuring, destroying, and exhausting), and other meanings (attributes) given to the trigrams as an underlying structure, various events occurring in nature and culture (sounds, animal behaviour, fishing, hunting, travelling, offering, sacrifices, etc.) were ordered as signs and omens in the book.

In the *Yi Jing* the idea of signs and omens is worked out extensively. While, ordinarily, omens have a positive or negative meaning in themselves, within the system of prediction in this old book the meanings of all kinds of signs and omens are described in a more sophisticated way. For example in hexagram 14, line 1 and line 5, and in hexagram 17, line 1, we can see that omens of crossing animals or persons (captives) are positive or negative depending on the position of the line in the hexagram.

The meanings of the omens are described in 64 hexagrams, as the 64 stages in a process of continuous change, and in 6 phases of change (6 lines) within each hexagram. With the help of the book, one event (throwing stalks, coins or dice) at a particular time (the present), can reveal meaning in relation to other events which will happen at another time (the future).

With the help of the *Yi Jing* human beings are able to open themselves to the meanings of the events happening around them. They can become receptive to signs and omens which may help them to make better choices as to advance or retreat in certain situations. Only if they have a choice can they exercise their inherent free will. With the help of the *Yi Jing* human beings will know which possible patterns of fate may manifest, and are then able to make a real choice. In this way they can influence their own fate, and not only to improve it, but mainly to grow in the wisdom of the *Dao*, or doing the right thing at the right time and in the right place.

## The inner structure of the *Yi Jing*

The inner structure of the *Yi Jing* is the basis for the whole of its theoretical framework and meanings. The root of the structure is the simple *yin-yang* division in Reality and its development into more complex structures as the trigrams and hexagrams. The meaning of the *yin-yang* division and the attributes and order of the trigrams are again the foundation of the 64 hexagrams and their 384 lines. The 64 hexagrams can be regarded as the 64 stages in an ongoing process of change in Reality. Each hexagram can also be seen as a different aspect of that great process of transformation. The sequence of the hexagrams and their relationship to each other may also give an indication about the incredible complexity of the inner structure of the *Yi Jing*.

The inner structure contains four parts: *yin-yang*, the order and attributes of the trigrams, the sequence and order of the hexagrams, the positions and relationships of the lines.

### *Yin-Yang*

In the Chinese theory of Reality everything is divided into *yin* and *yang*. This is not an ordinary dichotomy, because *yin* and *yang* are complementary to each other. The image symbolising *yin-yang* is a circle, *Tai Ji* (the Whole, lit. the Great Ultimate), with a black and white section in it, and in each section there is a small dot of the opposite quality ☯. This indicates that both 'opposites' are complementary to each other because there is always something of *yin* in the *yang* and vice versa. This may also be the reason that if one makes a list of the qualities of *yang* and *yin*, one may begin with certain qualities such as, light and dark, hot and cold, sun and moon, heaven and earth, day and night, fire and water, energy and matter, spirit and body, action and rest, life and death, etc., and if one continues, one may end with its opposite meanings. For example, if one takes the *yang* and *yin* style in martial arts – hard and soft, angular and round movements, and thus square and circular: earth and heaven, *yin* and *yang*, instead of *yang* and *yin*.

The presence of some *yang* in the *yin* and some *yin* in the *yang* implies that no quality, event or object is only of one kind, because there is always something of its opposite in it. In the *Yi Jing* this is specifically the case with the good fortune and misfortune division, for in every good fortune there is always some misfortune, and in every misfortune there is always some good fortune.

In the *Book of Change yin* and *yang* are expressed in lines: a broken line is *yin* and a straight line is *yang*. Two of these lines on top of each other make a bigram, and three lines create a trigram.

There are eight trigrams representing the five elements: Earth (*earth* and *mountain*), Water (*water/rain* and *lake/cloud*), Fire (*fire*), Wood (*wind* and *thunder*), and Metal (*heaven*). These 'elements' are actually *states of transformation or change*. Two trigrams make a hexagram or six-line image and combinations of the eight trigrams make up the 64 hexagrams that together represent the 64 stages in a continuous process of change in Reality. And within the hexagram structure of six lines, the *yin* and *yang* lines are related to each other in very specific ways, and represent its six phases of change.

## *The order and attributes of the trigrams*

The trigrams are three-line images formed by combining *yang* (whole, straight) lines, and *yin* (broken) lines. Some of the trigrams represent the so-called Western elements such as: Earth, Water, Fire, Air (Wood), and Ether (Metal), but in the *Yi Jing* they are actually regarded as *states of change or transformation*. The eight trigrams are formed out of the five trigrams representing the 'elements': Earth (*earth* and *mountain*), Water (*water/rain* and *lake/cloud*), Fire (*fire*), Wood (*wind* and *thunder*), and Metal (*heaven*).

The order of the eight trigrams are said to be derived from the *He Tu* and *Lo Shu* patterns of dots found on sacred animals (see Huang, *The Numerology of the I Ching*), but they can also be derived from natural phenomena such as the weather and the seasons. In the 'Early Heaven Arrangement' (EHA) of trigrams the sequence of events in the sky (heaven) was taken as the ideal and in the so called 'Later Heaven Arrangement' (LHA) the order of the seasons on earth served as the model.

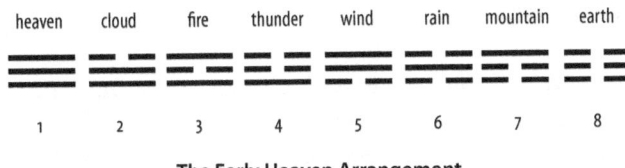

The Early Heaven Arrangement

In the EHA the sequence of the trigrams follows the sequence of events in the sky related to weather phenomena: 1. *heaven* (a clear summer sky) – 2. *cloud* (due to heat, hot air rises, and clouds are formed) – 3. *fire* (heavy clouds bring forth lightning) – 4. *thunder* (after lightning thunder always follows) – 5. *wind* (wind follows thunder) – 6. *water* (after the wind comes the rain) – 7. *mountain* (the rain falls first on the mountain) – 8. *earth* (the rain falls on the earth).

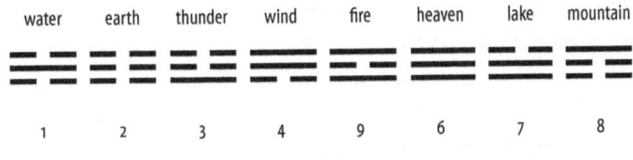

The Later Heaven Arrangement

In the LHA the sequence of trigrams follows the sequence of events on earth in relation to the seasons: 1. *water* (rain) and 2. *earth* (rain falls on the earth mainly in the winter) represent the winter – 3. *thunder* and 4. *wind* (thunder and wind stand for growth of plants) represent the spring – number 5 is missing; it should be followed by *fire* (but this trigram has number 9) representing the summer – 6. *heaven* and 7. *lake/cloud* represent autumn – 8. *mountain* (stillness is also an attribute of the winter).

In the course of time, besides the elements and natural phenomena, many other attributes were attached to the eight trigrams such as, family members (father, mother, daughter, son), numbers, characteristics, material things, shapes, colours, sounds, tastes, animals, body parts, places, directions, months, hours, and even foods. The various attributes of the trigrams play an important role in the meaning of the hexagrams, which are composed of the different trigrams.

Besides the attributes of the trigrams, the relationships of the trigrams as elements also play a role in the meanings of the hexagrams. These relationships are:

- *producing*: Wood produces Fire, Fire produces Earth, Earth produces Metal, Metal produces Water, Water produces Wood;
- *exhausting* (the opposite of producing): Wood exhausts Water, Water exhausts Metal, Metal exhausts Earth, Earth exhausts Fire, Fire exhausts Wood;
- *injuring*: Fire injures Water, Water injures Earth, Earth injures Wood, Wood injures Metal, Metal injures Fire;
- *destroying*: Water destroys Fire, Fire destroys Metal, Metal destroys Wood, Wood destroys Earth, Earth destroys Water.

These relationships of the elements help decide the good fortune or the misfortune aspects within each hexagram.

Each hexagram is composed of two *primary trigrams*, the upper and the lower. The upper trigram (lines 4, 5 and 6) is considered to be above and outside. The lower trigram (lines 1, 2 and 3) to be below and inside.

Inside the hexagram there are also two *inner trigrams* (see also page xxxiii). The second, third and fourth lines constitute the lower inner trigram. The third, fourth and fifth lines constitute the upper inner trigram.

These inner trigrams form an *inner hexagram*. They also play an important role in the composition of the meanings of the hexagrams.

## *The positions and relationships of the lines*

Each hexagram is composed of six lines. Whole lines are *yang* and broken lines are *yin*. A whole line is called 'strong' and a broken line 'yielding' or 'compliant'.

In general each hexagram has six phases of development in accordance with the six lines or phases of change of the first hexagram:

- the *first* or *base line* stands for the beginning of a situation where things have not appeared yet. Together with the sixth or top line, the first line usually stands somewhat outside the actual situation described in the hexagram;
- the *second line* stands for the appearance in the open of the subject of the hexagram;
- the *third line* stands for consolidation, preparation and development, but also for a condition of crisis;
- the *fourth line* stands for an attempt to take action or the uncertain beginning of an external manifestation;
- the *fifth line* stands for the fully developed situation coming into its powerful position;
- the *sixth* or *top line* marks the end of the process where the situation comes to an extreme or a condition of overdevelopment: it starts to crumble and is therefore ready to change into another situation.

These six phases of development can be compared to the phases in a human life. First one is in the womb and not yet in manifestation (line 1). Then there is birth (appearing in the world) (line 2), followed by growing up, which is always accompanied by crises (line 3). Then one tries to manifest something in life (line 4), followed by attaining one's position (line 5). At the end there is old age and death (line 6).
Within a hexagram the first (base), third and fifth lines are in *yang* positions and the second, fourth and sixth (top) lines are in *yin* positions.
When a *yang* (whole) line is in a *yang* position (first, third or fifth), or a *yin* (broken) line is in a *yin* position (second, fourth or sixth), that line is said to be 'correct' (*zheng*).
The second and fifth lines are said to be 'central' (*zhong*) to the trigrams of the hexagram. Hence a broken second line or a whole fifth line is said to be 'central and correct', and is specifically auspicious.
The first (base) and fourth line, the second and fifth, and the third and sixth (top) line are said to 'correspond' or 'answer' (*ying*) each other if one is whole and the other is broken. This is also an auspicious circumstance, especially in the thirty-two hexagrams where the second and fifth lines correspond in this way.

When a whole line stands above a broken one, the upper is said to 'ride' (*cheng*) the lower, and the lower to 'receive' or 'support' (*cheng*, a different Chinese character) the upper. This too is auspicious.

As the attributes of the trigrams and the relationships of the elements compose the general meanings of a hexagram, the positions and relationships of the lines express their specific meanings.

## *The origin of the* Yi Jing's *structure*

Change or Impermanence as an aspect of Reality is the basis of the *Book of Change*. The structure of the *Yi Jing*, namely the eight trigrams and the 64 hexagrams, is a sophisticated structure that can be regarded as the foundation of the Law of Change. The origin of this structure is said to have come from *Fu Xi*, a legendary Chinese sage who lived during the age of hunting and fishing (about 4500 years ago), and king *Wen* of the *Zhou* dynasty (c. 1122-221 BCE). But as we do not know how this structure actually came into existence the question is how did this structure come into being?

Did it come into existence in a gradual way, as is suggested by all the archæological findings of the cracked tortoise shell and bones? That out of the collected experiences of many fortune-tellers – who used to burn tortoise shell and bones, and used the patterns of cracks for their prediction – one or more persons have composed the structure of the eight trigrams and 64 hexagrams? Or was the structure suddenly available, in the sense that someone has received the whole structure by means of inspiration?

As the answer to this question may remain a matter of discussion, because we cannot really know it, the only way was to ask the *Yi Jing* itself.

The question asked was: did the structure of the eight trigrams and 64 hexagrams develop gradually or was it instantly available at some point? The *Yi Jing's* answer was hexagram 11, line 1, changing into hexagram 46. Hexagram 11 (Peace, The Great) is composed of the trigrams *heaven* and *earth* conjoined, indicating that it came out of the great harmony of heaven and earth, and could be received by means of an inspiration. Hexagram 11, line 1, reads that some grass was pulled out with shoot and root, indicating that something is done instantaneously, and this means that the structure was *suddenly available*. If we look at the bottom trigram of the changed hexagram 46, it shows us the trigram *wind* which stands for penetration.

Someone (*Fu Xi* or king *Wen*?) must have received a deep insight (penetration) into the nature of Reality, and that insight uncovered the whole structure of the *Yi Jing* at once.

## Three main methods of consultation

In China there were two systems of prediction, symbolic and numerical. The symbolic is older and made use of tortoise shells, and later of bones. The shells were exposed to fire until different patterns of cracks appeared like broken jade, like roof tiles, and like the cracks in dry land. From these patterns good fortune and misfortune were predicted. The patterns of cracks lead to the *yin-yang* lines, the images of the trigrams and hexagrams.

The numerical system is the basis of all the methods of consultation in the *Yi Jing*, and the ancient one made use of yarrow stalks. Later on, during the time of the Warring States (c. 480-221 BCE) the coin method was developed because the elaborate method with the yarrow stalks was too time consuming. This method is not as adequate as the stalks because the different lines of a hexagram do not have the same chance to appear as with the yarrow stalks (see diagram p. 351). In our modern times when everything seems to go even faster, the use of dice has been developed. This method is as good as the use of coins, but the yarrow stalks are still the best.

### *Yarrow stalks*

Yarrow or milfoil (*Achillea millefolium*) is a herb that grows in the north-temperate regions of China and is common in temperate zones of Europe. As it was allowed to grow old to gain its special quality, it was hard to find. As bamboo is readily available, already in ancient times bamboo was used as a substitute for the yarrow stalks. This method is lengthy and time consuming therefore it is a method suitable for people who consult the *Yi Jing* only once in a while.

In approaching the *Yi Jing* one should begin by praying. In the prayer one says who one is and what the question is. Then one may light some incense and pass the stalks through the smoke, all the time concentrating on the question.

One starts with a bundle of fifty yarrow stalks or bamboo sticks, but only forty-nine are actually used. From the fifty, one is taken and put aside and is not used again. On a flat surface the forty-nine stalks are separated into two groups. Throughout the process the right hand does the separating, picking up and counting, while the left hand does the holding. From the pile on the right, one takes one stalk with the right hand and puts it between the ring finger and little finger of the left hand. Now with the right hand one counts through the left bunch of stalks by fours until there is a remainder of just one, two, three or four stalks. The remainder is put between the ring and middle fingers of the left hand. Then one counts through the bunch of stalks on the right in the same way and puts that remainder between the middle and index fingers of the left hand. Now one counts the total of stalks one is holding in the left hand. It will be either five or nine. One writes this number down, puts these stalks aside and then one puts the two groups of the remainder stalks together again.

Now one repeats the process. Separating the stalks at random, one takes from the right, puts it between the little and ring fingers, and proceeds to count through the two bunches by four as before, first left and then right putting the remainders in the left hand.

This time one will have a total of four or eight. One writes this number down, puts these stalks aside and repeats the process one more time with the stalks that remain. Again the total of stalks in the left hand will be eight or four. The three processes complete the manipulations necessary to arrive at the bottom or base line of the hexagram.

A hexagram is constructed from bottom to top.

To compute the bottom line: of the totals obtained, nine and eight are assigned the number two; five and four are assigned the number three. After changing the three separate totals to their assigned numbers and adding them, a new total of six, seven, eight or nine will appear. Six stands for 'old *yin*' (a changing broken line ▬x▬), seven stands for 'young *yang*' (a whole line ▬▬▬ ), eight stands for 'young *yin*' ( ▬ ▬ a broken line) and nine stands for 'old *yang*' (a changing whole line ▬o▬ ). To obtain the other five lines of the hexagram one has to repeat the whole procedure five times.

When a hexagram has one or more changing lines, a new, resultant, hexagram is constructed by changing these lines into their opposites. This hexagram can be found in the chart to identify the hexagrams (see Appendix v).

## Coins

The coin method was developed to predict events faster. Of the many kinds of coin prediction the one with the three coins was found to be most appropriate and popular in the course of time. The basis for the coins is numerical but they were developed from the symbolic system. The symbolic associations of the ancient Chinese coins used for prediction are derived from the *Yi Jing* itself.

The Chinese coins are round with a square hole in the middle; the round outer shape stands for *qian*, heaven and the square hole represents *kun*, earth. One side has four characters; this is the *yang* side. The other side originally had no characters, later however, two were added, the *Man Chu* characters. This represents the *yin* side. The two added to the four characters stand for the six lines of the hexagram, and the three coins stand for heaven, earth and man, as well as for the three lines of the trigram. Actually any kind of coins can be used for prediction, as long as they are of the same kind. The 'heads' side is *yang* and the 'tails' side *yin*. Whatever coins are used, the procedure followed should be the same.

The person consulting the *Yi Jing* for prediction should first burn incense and then he should do some prayer, telling his name and what he wants. The three coins should be kept in clasped hands and shaken in the smoke of the incense and be thrown on a flat surface. The ritual will help to quiet the mind and keep concentrated on the question.

The hexagram is constructed from the base to the top; each throw of the coins determines one line. To obtain a hexagram the coins are thrown six times, the first throw determines the base line and the sixth throw the top line. For each toss of the coins there are four possible combinations:

a. one head (*yang*) and two tails (*yin*) stand for 'young *yang*' (a whole line ——— );

b. one tail (*yin*) and two heads (*yang*) stand for 'young *yin*' (a broken line — — );

c. three heads (*yang*) stand for 'old *yang*' (a changing whole line —●— );

d. three tails (*yin*) stand for 'old *yin*' (a changing broken line —x—). The obtained hexagram can be found in the chart to identify the hexagrams (see Appendix v).

Combinations *a* and *b* are based on what is called the 'minority rule': one head or one tail becomes a *yang* or a *yin* line. This is based on the nature of the trigrams, where three *yang* trigrams (*water, thunder* and *mountain*) have more dark lines (one *yang* line and two *yin* lines), and three *yin* trigrams (*fire, wind* and *lake* or *cloud*) have more light lines (one *yin* and two *yang* lines).

People also use combinations based on what is called the 'majority rule' where two tails give a *yin* line and two heads a *yang* line. Although both systems can be used, the one based on the 'minority rule' has a more adequate foundation. To transcend the choice for one or the other system the method using a ten-sided die is recommended.

## Dice

The die used for consultation is a *ten-sided die* (decahedron) with numbers 0 to 9 on it. The even numbers are *yin* and the odd numbers are *yang*:

a. 1, 3, 5, 7 = 'young *yang*' (a whole line ▬▬ );
b. 0, 2, 4, 8 = 'young *yin*' (a broken line ▬ ▬ );
c. 9 = 'old *yang*' (a changing whole line ▬●▬ );
d. 6 = 'old *yin*' (a changing broken line ▬x▬ ).

One has to throw six times to obtain a hexagram, and starts with the base line. This hexagram can be looked up in the chart to identify the hexagrams (see Appendix v).

This method is the most simple and easy to perform, it has only one object instead of fifty stalks or three coins, and one can see the correct line immediately. Because numerology is at the basis of the *Yi Jing* methods of consultation, this dice method is the most appropriate one to consult the *Yi Jing*. The only problem is that, because it is a faster method, one could become less attentive during the consultation.

The methods of consulting the *Yi Jing* differ in their quality because they give different chances of appearance to the stable or changing lines. The best method of the three main methods, yarrow stalks, coins or dice, is the one with the stalks. (See also the diagram on p. 351.)

## Inquiry and interpretation

### Framing the question

Based on the principle of Oneness, the question is the answer. By throwing the stalks, tossing the coins or dice, in a way one directs the question to the answer. Therefore framing the right question is already a good part of the answer.

The clearer the question, the better is the answer. Only when we clearly and definitely have in our mind what we want to know, the *Yi Jing* could give us a clear and definite answer. Any yes-or-no, or either/or type of question should be avoided.

Sometimes it is also advisable to place the question in a time frame so that the interpretation will be clearer.

Some appropriate questions are:
- Please comment on this situation, what does it really mean?
- What would be the best thing to do in this situation?
- How is this to be accomplished?
- If this is done, what will be the result?
- Considering the circumstances, should this action be performed?
- What is likely to happen to this person, object, people, project, etc., during such and such time (days, weeks, months, or years)?

### Interpretation of the answer

The *Yi Jing* can be regarded as a book of codes with which one is able to understand any event occurring in Reality by translating that event into meaningful information. It contains 64 categories of codes, or images representing specific situations (the hexagrams), each again containing six specifications (the lines), which may cover all aspects of the process of Change. In a way one could say that these codes are the indications and expressions of Impermanence itself – the detailed faces and phases of Change – all are related to each other through the Law of Change. The 64 hexagrams are symbols, or basic images, representing aspects of change in different stages that could be interpreted in various ways. As each hexagram represents a distinct face of change they are all related to each other and follow each other perfectly. The lines can be seen as specific phases of each particular aspect of change. With its number of symbols (hexagrams) the *Yi Jing* can provide 64 x 6 (lines) + 64 x 1 (hexagram without a changing line) = 448 possible answers to questions. As there is the possibility to interpret these answers in various ways, they may cover the whole of Reality.

Because the answers of the *Yi Jing* are multi-interpretable, interpreting an answer from the *Yi Jing* can be suited to any purpose. It is possible to disclaim its predictive power by finding several different interpretations that could all fit the question. But this is not the purpose of the book.

The *Yi Jing* is a tool to deal with Reality by means of knowing how to act at the right time. This is of course only an attempt to do the right thing at the right time and place, because one cannot fully control Reality. Still it is better to go with the flow of things than to have a destiny based on bad effects of acts performed out of ignorance.

After having completed throwing the stalks, tossing the coins or dice, one may refer to the chart of hexagrams to find the particular hexagram and receive an answer to the question (see Appendix v). The hexagram obtained usually has one or more changing lines. When these lines are changed into their opposites (a changing *yin* line changes into a whole line and a changing *yang* line into a broken line), one obtains another hexagram. Thus one may receive two hexagrams in respond to a single question.
Basically the first hexagram and its lines are about the present situation, and the second hexagram and its lines are about the future.

*In interpreting the answers there are some rules to keep in mind*

### 1. The significance of each answer

Any answer of the *Yi Jing* is significant and should be taken seriously. Even if one does not understand it immediately, one may later on. The answer may point to something one does not expect at all, because one cannot even imagine it. The *Yi Jing* will go into whatever it thinks is important, significant or necessary for that moment.

### 2. Staying with the question

In the interpretation it is advisable to stay close to the question, and not to wander off to all kinds of associations. Although these associations can be very useful sometimes, and enrich the answer, it may also create more confusion because of the archaic language of the *Yi Jing*.

### 3. Reading the text
First one reads about the *Image* (symbol), then about the *Judgment and commentary,* and the information of the specific *changing lines of the first hexagram*. After changing the changing lines into their opposites, and having obtained the second hexagram, one does the same, *including reading the transformed lines.*

In reading the text one should pay attention only to *that which connects to the question* and leaves the rest for what it is. The prediction may be interpreted according to any part of the text that relates to or sheds light on the situation, event, person or question one is concerned with.

### 4. The hexagrams and lines
The hexagram describes the general situation or condition of the present state of change and the lines are specifications of it. The second hexagram obtained when the changing lines have been changed into their opposites gives an indication of the situation or condition that may come out of it, and shows the possible future development of the situation. And the same lines belonging to the new hexagram give some tendencies to where it may lead to in the future.

As the first hexagram, the lines, and the second hexagram (and its lines) can be seen as belonging to one whole, the meanings of the lines of the second hexagram may also refer to the meanings of the lines of the first hexagram.

### 5. The inner hexagram
If it is necessary and one wants to know more about the situation, one could look at the inner hexagram (see also page xxiv) and its lines. This may give some information about the essence or hidden parts of the subject of enquiry.

### 6. The preceding hexagram
As the hexagrams are related to one another and follow each other in

a specific sequence, it is advisable to look at the preceding hexagram to see where the present situation came from.

### 7. No changing line

If one obtains a hexagram without a changing line, this means that, for the present moment, either there is no change in the situation inquired about or the *Yi Jing* does not want to give an answer because the person is not ready or prepared to receive the answer. Here one should read only the Image and the Judgment.

### 8. The context and meaning

The interpretation of the prediction depends on the situation and the level of reality. The same text may have a different meaning in a different context. With more knowledge of the background and context of the question, the better the answer will be. The interpretation of the prediction also depends on the skill and experience of the interpreter. A personal interpretation may be right but an impersonal (detached) one is better.

### 9. Specific subjects

In the *Yi Jing* there are a number of hexagrams related to specific subjects:

a. *Hexagrams about relationships.* In the *Yi Jing* there are six hexagrams about the relationship (engagement, marriage) between male and female: hexagram 31, Feeling, Sensation, Attraction, is about the beginning of a relationship; hexagram 32, Lasting, Enduring, Constancy, is about a long-enduring marriage; hexagram 42, Gain, Increase, is about a marriage which will bring material gain; hexagram 44, Meeting, Contact, Encounter is about a woman who has relationships with many men (one *yin* line and five *yang* lines); hexagram 53, Gradual Advance, Wild Goose, is about a marriage which improves gradually; hexagram 54, Marrying Maiden, is about a marriageable woman who marries as a second wife.

b. *Hexagrams about spiritual development.* In the *Yi Jing* there are six hexagrams about spiritual development: hexagram 20, Observing, View, Contemplation, is also about a method of meditation (observation of whatever appears in consciousness) related to the Daoist and Buddhist tradition; hexagram 30, Fire, Light, is also about the different stages of

Enlightenment; hexagram 40, Release, Liberation, is also about the different stages of Liberation after the attainment of Enlightenment; hexagram 49 Radical Change, Revolution, is also about the radical changes during a spiritual process; hexagram 50, The Cauldron, Transformation, is also about the process of spiritual transformation; hexagram 52, Mountain, Stilling, is also about the Daoist and Buddhist meditation where both body and mind activities are stilled.

### Notes on the structure of the Yi Jing text

Trying to construct the *Yi Jing* as close as possible to the essence of the *Yi*-tradition, the hexagrams in *The Basic Yi Jing* are structured as follows:

- The *Image* of the hexagram, composed of two trigrams, expresses the idea of the hexagram. The idea of the hexagram is explored through the specific meanings of the trigrams in a general way. The idea also expresses an attitude of the noble person based on the meanings of the trigrams of the hexagrams.
- The *Judgment* expresses the signs and omens related to the idea of the hexagram. In their basic text the authors decided where necessary to have two expressions of the Judgment (the main part of the text): *a*) and *b*) – where *a*) is the litteral text on the basis of the Chinese words, and *b*) is a clarification of that particular part. The same holds for the separate lines.
- The *Commentary* on the Judgment explores the meaning of the signs and omens expressed in the Judgment on the basis of the various meanings of the composing outside (upper) and inside (lower) trigrams of the hexagram.
- Each of the *Six Lines* of the hexagram expresses the idea of the hexagram specifically. These lines indicate the different stages of the idea of the hexagram in six successive moments in time. At the beginning of each line, on the right side, there is the image of the resultant hexagram when this particular line has changed into its opposite. This hexagram can provide some extra information on the subject matter.
- In the *Summary* the meaning of the hexagram and the lines is again described in more explanatory ways. Here the Chinese cultural

phenomena are translated in such a way that their universal meanings become apparent.

This description of each hexagram in the book – where the meanings of the hexagram and lines are expressed in successive stages of explanation – is done with the intention that the reader will have an easier understanding and a good overview of the hexagram as a whole.

In the text *square* [ ] *brackets* are used to indicate the authors' addition to the core text of the *Yi Jing*, because they found that a particular passage is lacking something or is not clear enough.

*Round* ( ) *brackets* are used as additional explanations, information or comment.

## *Some frequently used phrases in the text and commentaries*

In the text and commentaries there are a number of words and phrases that appear often enough to mention, for they keep their specific meaning throughout the book. Some examples of them are:

- *The noble person.* This connotes a man or woman of the highest moral worth and of great wisdom. In many passages where he is mentioned the implication is that the best course for the inquirer to take is the one attributed to him in that passage. This noble person could be a leader or a sage.
- *It is favourable to see a great man.* This indicates that it will be beneficial for us to approach someone of moral worth or great wisdom for advice or assistance.
- *Favourable to cross the great river or sea.* This usually means that it is beneficial to go on a journey in connection with our plans.
- *Favourable when there is somewhere or some place to go or it is advantageous to have a goal or destination.* This means that when we advance or undertake something, it will be better to have a clear objective.
- *Benefit in perseverance or persistence brings reward.* This means that we may safely continue with our plans, provided that they involve no harm to anyone.

- *Persistence or perseverance or determination brings misfortune.* This indicates that it will be better to stop with our plan.
- *Ominous or auspicious for an attack.* This means that advancing, moving forward or taking action will bring bad or good fortune.
- *Fulfilment of what is willed.* This means that we shall achieve our objective provided that it is a worthy one.
- *No error.* This indicates that if results do not accord with our wishes, it is not our fault; they are due to circumstances beyond our control.
- *Nothing brings advantage.* This means that we should desist what we were intended to do.
- *Shame.* This indicates disgrace in our own eyes when we review our conduct.
- *Blame.* This indicates disgrace in the eyes of others; we are regarded as guilty for a mistake made.
- *Regret or remorse.* This indicates that our troubles are due to our own conduct or lack of foresight.
- *The timely occurrence is of great importance.* This means that in this hexagram the timing of the recommended actions is crucial.
- *Blessing.* This indicates unexpected or unsought good fortune or benefit.
- *Blessings from Heaven.* This means that one receives help as a matter of course *if* one remains in the *Dao* (the Way).
- *Rainfall.* In general rainfall is representing a good omen (see hexagram 9, Judgment, 9.6, 38.6, 50.3 and 62.5). Only in hexagram 43.3 it is seen as an annoyance.

There are also a number of words and phrases that only appear in specific lines or hexagrams and need some more explanation, because they are very much connected with the old Chinese culture. These words and phrases are explained at the specific hexagrams or lines.

# THE BASIC YI JING

*In a dream
a large, folded, white and thick cloth
in which all the sixty-four hexagrams were woven
appeared.
Diagonally draped over it
was a red sash
with the eight trigrams painted in gold.
The cloth was offered by two hands
coming out of the Unmanifested.*

# 1. *Qian* / Heaven, The Creative

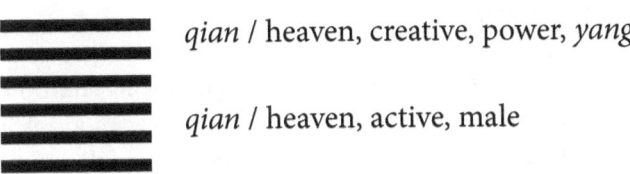

*qian* / heaven, creative, power, *yang*

*qian* / heaven, active, male

### • *Image*

Double Heaven.
Heaven proceeds: The Creative, Power.
A noble person strives without ceasing.

### • *Judgment*

a) Great offering.
   Favourable augury.

b) Sublime accomplishment.
   Determination is beneficial.

*Commentary*

Power is the fundamental nature of the Creative, pervading heaven, and the myriad things owe their beginning to it. As clouds move and rain falls, all things flow into forms. Clear and bright from beginning to end, the six lines are placed at the right time. The sage rides the six dragons through the heavens. The way of the Creative changes and transforms everything in its proper nature and destiny, in accord with the Great Harmony. The sage raises his head above the crowd, and the ten thousand states are at peace. Greatness is the leader of goodness; success is the fruit of excellence; beneficence brings together all that is right and just; determination and firmness are the main principles for action.

The great person, embodying goodness, is fit to be a leader of men; excellent, he is expressing perfect conduct; benefiting all beings, he manifests righteousness; being determined and persistent, he is able to carry out all actions. A noble person should exercise the four virtues: greatness, success, beneficence, and determination.

The Creative is the source of everything. It brings about the nature and essence of all things, and manifests through accomplishment. From the beginning the Creative benefits all under heaven; there is no word for such quality but 'great.' How great is the Creative: firm and powerful, central and correct, pure and essential. The six lines lay bare the meaning of the hexagram, explaining the heart of all matters. When the sage drives the six dragons through the heavens, clouds move, rain falls, and peace comes to the whole world.

Note. 'Dragons' in this hexagram refer to a constellation of stars as seen by the ancient Chinese.

## • *Base Line, 9*    44

a) *A submerged dragon.*
   *Do not act.*

b) *A hidden dragon.*
   *Do not act.*

### Commentary

*A submerged dragon. Do not act*: the Master said: 'The power of the dragon lies hidden. This refers to a noble person who has dragon-like virtues, but yet remains hidden. He neither changes himself to suit the world, nor does he seek fame. Withdrawn from the world, he does not regret it. Not being recognised, he is not sad. In favourable circumstances he is active; when times are unfavourable he retires. Indeed, he cannot be uprooted: such is a submerged dragon.'

- *Second line, 9*                                      ▬▬▬ 13

    *See a dragon in the field.*
    *Favourable to meet a great person.*

### Commentary

*See a dragon in the field:* the Master said: 'The power of the dragon appears in the open. A noble person who has the character of a dragon appears in the open. His speech is reliable and his actions are careful. Warding off falsehood, he keeps his integrity. He works for the good in the world without boasting. His influence spreads wide and effects change in man. This refers to one who has the qualities of a ruler or leader.'
*Favourable to meet a great person:* it is beneficial to see someone who accumulates knowledge by studying, raises questions for the sake of discrimination, is generous in attitude and benevolent in his conduct. This second line also indicates that the time for action has arrived.

- *Third line, 9*                                        10

    *The noble person is active all day long*
    *and at night still stays alert.*
    *Danger.*
    *No misfortune.*

### Commentary

The Master said: 'The noble person develops his powers, fosters his virtue, and cultivates his task. He fosters his virtue by being loyal and trustworthy. He tends his task by being upright and careful with words. He advances his powers by knowing how to handle a problem, and goes into the heart of the matter. Knowing how to achieve something, he accomplishes it with righteousness. Thus he is able to hold a high rank without boasting, and a low rank without distress. Because he stays alert and is active as the occasion requires, though things are dangerous, he does not make a mistake, and therefore suffers no misfortune.'

### • *Fourth line, 9*

*A dragon leaps above the depths.*
*No misfortune.*

#### Commentary

*A dragon leaps above the depths:* hesitation and uncertainty, but there is no misfortune. The Master said: 'In rising or falling there is no fixed rule except that one does not commit evil. Advance and retreat are not lasting; for that reason one does not go away on one's own and leave others behind. A noble person develops his powers, cultivates his task, and seizes the right opportunity. Therefore there is no error.'

### • *Fifth line, 9*

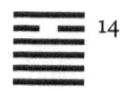

*A dragon flies through the heavens.*
*It is favourable and beneficial*
*to meet a great person.*

#### Commentary

*A dragon flies through the heavens:* the Master said: 'Similar sounds resonate together: people with similar natures seek one another. Water flows where it is wet, fire goes where it is dry. Like clouds follow the dragon, wind follows the tiger. When a sage rises, all beings look at him. What comes from heaven draws close to what is above; what comes from earth draws close to what is below. Each follows its own kind.'
The great person is in harmony with the powers of heaven, with the brilliance of sun and moon, with the regularity of the four seasons, and with the spirits in divining good and evil omens. When he acts in advance of heaven,

heaven does not oppose him; when he follows heaven, he keeps to heaven's timing. If heaven does not resist him, how can man, gods, and spirits do so? It is favourable and beneficial to meet a great person.

- ***Top line, 9***

    a) *A high-flying dragon. Regret.*

    b) *An arrogant dragon. There is remorse.*

*Commentary*

*A high-flying dragon. Regret*: the climax of the fifth line cannot last. The Master said: 'Although he is noble, he is without position; although in a high place, he has no following. There are able men below him, but he has no support. In this situation any action gives cause for regret.'

*A high-flying dragon*: one knows how to advance, but not how to retreat; how to win, but not how to lose; how to live, but not how to die. Only a sage knows how to go forward and to go back, to live and to die, and not to lose his integrity. Only a sage can do this.

- ***All lines, 9***

    a) *A flock of dragons without a head. Auspicious.*

    b) *A group of dragons appears without one at the head. Good fortune.*

9

*Commentary*

Not one dragon can take precedence over the others. Heaven's law, controlling everything under heaven, is made manifest. Heaven is fully supporting the subject. Good fortune.

## • *Summary*

Double Heaven. The Creative is the source of everything. Power is the fundamental nature of the Creative, pervading heaven. The way of the Creative changes and transforms everything in its proper nature and destiny. Sublime success. Determination is beneficial.

The first hexagram is about creativity, activity, power, clarity, and brightness. It is expressing the development of creative power (action and doing) in six stages:

In the first line the creative power has not yet appeared. One should not act.

In the second line the creative power comes into the open. It is time to act. It is beneficial to see a person of wisdom.

In the third line the power prepares, develops, and consolidates. If one stays alert in dangerous situations, one does not make a mistake, and therefore suffers no misfortune.

In the fourth line the creative power takes a leap and makes an attempt to take action. Seeing the right opportunity, one takes the challenge. There is hesitation and uncertainty, but there will be no misfortune.

In the fifth line the creative comes into its powerful position. One's actions are in harmony with the time and the way of Heaven.

In the sixth line the power of action (doing) comes to an extreme and starts to crumble. In this situation any action gives cause for regret.

In general the lines of each hexagram follow this pattern of change.

## 2. *Kun* / Earth, The Receptive

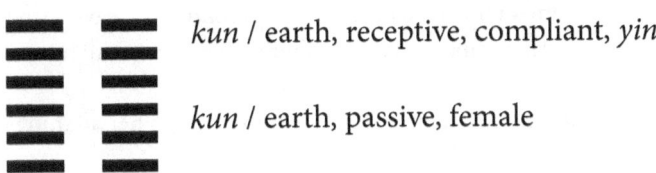

*kun* / earth, receptive, compliant, *yin*

*kun* / earth, passive, female

- *Image*

    Double Earth.
    Earth accepts: the Receptive, Compliant.
    A noble person bears with all things.

- *Judgment*

    a) Great offering.
    Favourable augury for a mare.
    A noble person who has some place to go,
    first goes astray, but later finds her way.
    Favourable in the southwest to gain a friend,
    in the northeast to lose a friend.
    Augury for safety: auspicious.

    b) Sublime accomplishment.
    Beneficial in persevering like a mare.
    A noble person who is going somewhere,
    first goes astray, but later finds her way.
    Beneficial in the southwest to gain a friend,
    in the northeast to lose a friend.
    Quiet perseverance brings good fortune.

*Commentary*

Receptivity is the fundamental nature of Earth, responding to Heaven, and giving birth to all the myriad things. As earth's abundance sustains all things, her all-embracing strength is boundless.

Her capacity to accommodate is great and bright, and through her all things prosper.

A mare is a creature of the earth; she roams the earth without bound: great is her strength; success is gained through her yielding; beneficence is due to her genuineness and reliability; perseverance and steadfastness are her main principles for action.

*A noble person who is going somewhere, first goes astray, but later finds her way:* if she takes the lead, she will lose her way; by following she will find her rightful place. In the southwest she gains friends by travelling with her own kind; in the northeast she loses friends. Peaceful perseverance will bring good fortune, because she is in harmony with the qualities of earth.

## • *Base line, 6*

*When one steps on frost,
solid ice is coming.*

*Commentary*

*When one steps on frost, solid ice is coming:* this is about acquiescence (staying passive) in circumstances, foreboding difficult times. This attitude causes trouble. A household that accumulates goodness will abound in blessings; a household that accumulates bad deeds will abound in misery.

The murder of a ruler by his subject, the murder of a father by his son: these affairs are not the result of events of a single day and night. They have accumulated for some time and not been dealt with at an early stage.

- *Second line, 6*  7

    Straight, square and great, without action.
    There is nothing not beneficial.

### Commentary

*Straight, square and great:* 'straight' means upright, and 'square' means just. A noble person is concerned about rectitude within herself, and righteousness in relation to others. Not doing anything, everything prospers.

- *Third line, 6*  15

    a) Hold a jade talisman in the mouth.
    Possible augury.
    If someone pursues the king's service,
    there will be no completion,
    there will be an end.

    b) Concealment of talent or beauty.
    One can be persevering.
    Undertaking public affairs will not be successful
    but this situation will come to an end.

### Commentary

One's good qualities are hidden. If someone pursues a public office, it will not be successful, but it will end well.

The way of Earth is the way of a wife. The way of Earth is not to claim success but to bring things to a conclusion in service of another. One should have no doubt how to proceed, because when the time is ripe everything comes naturally.

- *Fourth line, 6*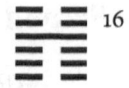

    Tied-up sacks.
    There is no misfortune and no honour.

#### Commentary

Heaven and earth will make plants and trees grow luxuriantly. If heaven and earth are inactive, worthy people hide.
*Tied-up sacks. There is no misfortune and no honour*: this is a warning. Carefulness will prevent injury.

Note. 'Tied-up sacks' is a reference to the autumn harvest of grain.

- *Fifth line, 6*

    A yellow skirt.
    Most auspicious.

#### Commentary

The noble person, clad in yellow, is in a central position. (Yellow is the colour of earth, and its qualities of genuineness and reliability.) She understands life's principles. In the correct position, she remains secure. Excellence is within her, and appearing in her deeds, she is the pinnacle of the great virtues of earth.

- *Top line, 6*

    Dragons fight above the wilds.
    Their blood is black and yellow.

*Commentary*

*Dragons fight above the wilds:* the way of Earth is running out (an unfavourable omen is implied). When yin competes with yang, struggle will ensure. Black and yellow mean that heaven and earth are in discord. The way of Earth (passivity and inaction) comes to an end.

- *All lines, 6*

  a) *Favourable in a long-term augury.*

  b) *Prolonged perseverance is beneficial.*

*Commentary*

*Favourable in a long-term augury:* this indicates that perseverance is a means for attaining great ends.

- *Summary*

Double Earth. Receptivity is the fundamental nature of Earth, responding to Heaven, and giving birth to all the myriad things. Earth's abundance sustains all things, her all-embracing strength is boundless. Her capacity to accommodate is great and bright, and through her all things prosper.

Sublime success. If she takes the lead, she will lose her way; by following she will find her rightful place. In the southwest she gains friends by travelling with her own kind; in the northeast she loses friends. Peaceful perseverance will bring good fortune, because she is in harmony with the qualities of earth.

The second hexagram is about receptivity, passivity, inaction, non-doing and openness. But also about the qualities of Earth: greatness, strength, squareness, genuineness, and reliability.

Earth is necessary for manifestation and is expressing receptivity, passivity, inaction, and non-doing in six stages:

In the first line passivity causes trouble. Staying passive is not appropriate. There is a need for caution.

In the second line, without doing anything, everything prospers. This line is about non-doing (*wu wei*), meaning that everything goes by itself. Without acting, everything will prosper.

In the third line everything will come with time. This line is about inaction. It is *not* about non-doing (*wu wei*), but about not taking any action at all. If one pursues something (a public office) now, one will not be successful but when the time is ripe, it will come.

The fourth line is about inactivity without respect (honour). With care one will escape trouble. No misfortune.

The fifth line is the culmination of receptivity, genuineness, reliability and the other qualities of Earth. Being in the correct position, she remains secure. It is a time of supreme good fortune.

In the sixth line the way of Earth (passivity, inaction) is fading. Passivity struggles with activity. Not acting is unfavourable, because it is inappropriate now.

# 3. *Zhun* / Beginning, Difficulty

*kan* / moving water, rain, danger

*zhen* / thunder, shock, moving, growth

- *Image*

    Thunder below Water.
    Thunder and rain: Difficulty in the beginning.
    A noble person establishes order.

- *Judgment*

    a) Great offering.
    Favourable augury.
    Do not use this in having somewhere to go.
    Favourable to establish a lord.

    b) Sublime accomplishment.
    Determination is beneficial.
    Do not use this hexagram
    as an encouragement to undertake something.
    Beneficial to establish order.

### Commentary

Thunder and rain make things grow prolifically. Sublime accomplishment. Determination is beneficial.
The lower trigram is 'moving' (Thunder), and the upper is 'danger' (Water). When Heaven, the Creative, and Earth, the Receptive begin to interact they bring to birth a new beginning which is always accompanied with difficulty.

This hexagram is not favourable for undertaking something. But *if* one has to go somewhere or undertake something, one should proceed with caution (upper trigram Water, danger).
Favourable to appoint a leader who is able to establish order.

### • *Base line, 9*

*To and fro.*
*Favourable augury for a dwelling.*
*Beneficial to obtain a master.*

#### Commentary

*To and fro:* going back and forth. It is favourable to stay where we are. It is beneficial to appoint a leader to set things in order.

### • *Second line, 6*

*Gathering together, but delayed.*
*Cars and horses arrayed.*
*Not bandits, but fetching a bride.*
*Augury for a woman who has not conceived:*
*she will conceive in ten years.*

#### Commentary

*Not bandits, but fetching a bride:* it is not an obstacle, but a matter of betrothal which causes delay.
Conceiving a child in ten years means that after a long time normal conditions will return.

Note. This refers to a marriage custom in which the groom's party pretends to abduct the bride as a testimonial to her desirability.

- **Third line, 6**

  *Stalking a deer
  without a woodsman (guide).
  Entering deep in a forest,
  the noble person considers giving up the chase.
  Going leads to great trouble.*

  *Commentary*

  *Stalking a deer without a woodsman:* rather than pursuing quarry in this way, the noble person refrains from action. Going on leads to trouble and he would find himself in dire straits.

- **Fourth line, 6**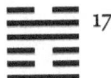

  *Cars and horses arrayed.
  Fetching a bride.
  To go is auspicious.
  There is nothing for which this is unfavourable.*

  *Commentary*

  After hesitation (first line), and delay (second line), moving forward will bring good fortune.

- **Fifth line, 9**

  *Hoarding fat meat.
  Small determination is auspicious.
  Great determination is ominous.*

*Commentary*

Fertility and growth are not easily brought about. In small matters, good fortune; in great matters, disaster.

Note. Meat was a delicacy reserved almost exclusively for the nobility. Fat meat was apparently considered the best.

## • *Top line, 6*

Cars and horses arrayed.
Streaming tears and blood.

*Commentary*

Weeping tears and shedding blood, but how can this last long?

## • *Summary*

Thunder below Water. Thunder and Rain. This hexagram is about the chaos (thunder and rainstorm) that creates something new when Heaven and Earth unite. A difficult beginning. Sublime success. Determination will be beneficial. Do not undertake something. If one has to go somewhere or undertake something, it should be done with caution and care. It will be beneficial to appoint someone to establish order.

The hexagram story is about a group of people setting out to travel with a marriage party.

When Heaven (hexagram 1) and Earth (hexagram 2) come together there is a new beginning, the birth of something new, which is always accompanied with difficulties (hexagram 3).

The chaos will be ordered in different stages:

The first line is about the call for an authority to set things in order. Hesitation: it is best to stay where we are.

The second line is about things that have to be set in order first. A matter of betrothal will cause delay. After a long time things return to their normal condition.

The third line is about entering a situation without a guide, which could lead to great trouble. It is advisable to refrain from action.

In the fourth line things are in order. Moving forward will bring good fortune. Nothing is unfavourable.

The fifth line is about fertility and growth, which cannot easily be attained. Only in small matters will there be good fortune; in great matters, disaster.

In the sixth line there will be great difficulties in the end, but they will not last long.

# 4. *Meng* / Growing, Immaturity, Dodder

 *gen* / mountain, standing still, stilling, stopping

*kan* / moving water, stream, danger

- ## *Image*

    Water below Mountain.
    Water springs at the foot of the mountain: Immaturity.
    A noble person acts with resolution
    and cultivates his virtue.

- ## *Judgment*

    a) *Offering.*
    We do not seek the dodder, the dodder seeks us.
    The first yarrow divination is auspicious,
    the second or third is insulting.
    Since it is insulting, they do not tell.
    Favourable augury.

    b) *Success.*
    We do not seek immaturity, immaturity seeks us.
    The first manipulation of the yarrow stalks
    gives the answer, the second or third is insulting.
    Since it is insulting, they give no answer.
    Determination is beneficial.

*Commentary*

Water (danger) and Mountain (youngest son): Immaturity. Going forward will lead to success when one acts in accordance with the proper time.
*We do not seek immaturity, immaturity seeks us:* the intention and attitude towards the oracle should be one of respect.
The hexagram is an apt image for an ignorant or inexperienced youth. Immaturity can be corrected by cultivation. This is a meritorious task.
One consultation receives a reply. Repetition is irreverent, receiving no reply because irreverence is immaturity. Experience teaches, that if the *Book of Change* is disrespectfully consulted more than once about a specific subject most of the time the outcome will be hexagram 4.

Note. A dodder (Cuscuta) *is a twining, parasitic flowering plant with no roots or leaves, growing easily and spreading everywhere. The ancients saw it on the roofs of huts and houses. Like other parasites, it attracts superstitious respect. To ward off evil spells, a young boy (immaturity) was sent to collect dodder plants.*

- *Base line, 6*  41

   a) Pulling dodder.
   Favourable for punishing someone,
   not using shackles and fetters.
   Going somewhere is distressing.

   b) Discarding immaturity.
   Beneficial to use discipline
   but do not use shackles and fetters.
   Undertaking something will bring distress.

*Commentary*

Favourable for discipline. Punishment should be given according to just rules. Undertaking something will be distressful.

- *Second line, 9*

    a) *Wrapping dodder. Auspicious.*
       *Bringing in a wife. Auspicious.*
       *A son can take on a family.*

    b) *Containing immaturity. Auspicious.*
       *Auspicious to take a wife.*
       *A son will take care of his family.*

*Commentary*

By taking a wife the son can become responsible and mature. Good fortune.

- *Third line, 6*

    a) *[Taking dodder.]*
       *Not for taking a wife.*
       *Seeing the metal fellow, she will lose her body.*
       *Nothing is favourable.*

    b) *Do not choose a wife,*
       *who, when seeing a powerful man, cannot contain herself.*
       *A marriage is unfavourable.*

*Commentary*

Do not take a wife whose conduct is improper. Proceeding is not beneficial.

- *Fourth line, 6*  64

    a) *Dodder in bundles.
    Distress.*

    b) *Bound by immaturity.
    Distress.*

### Commentary

Distress for the immature person who is entangled: alone and far from stable.


- *Fifth line, 6*  59

    a) *[Flowering] dodder.
    Auspicious.*

    b) *Immaturity.
    Auspicious.*

### Commentary

Auspiciousness of an immature lad: innocent, childlike. Good fortune.


- *Top line, 9*  7

    a) *Beating the dodder.
    Unfavourable for raiding;
    favourable for fending off bandits.*

    b) *Striking at immaturity.
    Unfavourable for harassment;
    favourable to guard against harassment.*

*Commentary*

Instead of dealing harshly with immaturity, it is better to prevent mischief.

## • *Summary*

Water below Mountain. Water (danger) springs at the foot of the mountain (youngest son), symbolising Immaturity.

This hexagram is about immaturity, symbolised by the dodder plant. It is a parable about an ignorant and inexperienced youth.

If the *Book of Change* is disrespectfully consulted more than once about a subject, the outcome will be hexagram 4. It is beneficial to stay determined.

After a new beginning and birth (hexagram 3), hexagram 4, growth and immaturity follows naturally.

It is expressed in six stages of dealing with the dodder:

In the first line the dodder is pulled out: punishment should be given according to just rules. Discipline should not be overdone. Going somewhere or undertaking something may bring distress.

The second line is about wrapping the dodder. By marrying, the youth becomes a responsible person. Good fortune.

Line three is about taking the dodder. Because the third line is in most cases negative, one should *not* take a woman whose behaviour is disorderly (immature). It is not advisable to continue with this.

Line four is about bundles of dodder. One is bound by immaturity: entangled in his own folly. Distress.

The fifth line is about the flowering dodder. It symbolises the good qualities of youth, such as innocence, and being like a child (childlike). Good fortune.

Line six is about beating the dodder: punishing the immature is not advised. It is better to prevent mischief.

# 5. *Xu* / Waiting, Getting Wet, Inaction

 *kan* / moving water, rain, danger

*qian* / heaven, creative, power, *yang*, active, male

- **Image**

    Water above Heaven.
    Rain in the sky: Waiting, Getting Wet, Inaction.
    A noble person eats, feasts and enjoys pleasure.

- **Judgment**

    a) There is a captive.
    Glory. Offering.
    Favourable augury.
    Auspicious for fording the great river.

    b) Have confidence.
    Glorious success.
    Perseverance (in waiting) is beneficial.
    Good fortune to go on a journey.

    *Commentary*

What lies ahead is dangerous (Water), but strength (power, Heaven) prevents any falling into danger. This means, by being firm and strong, and through inaction (waiting), one does not get involved in danger. Have confidence. Brilliant success. Perseverance in waiting is beneficial. To go on a journey will be rewarding. Proceeding will bring good fortune.

- *Base line, 9*  48

  a) Getting wet at the suburban altar.
  Favourable for a heng ceremony.
  No misfortune.

  b) Waiting at the outskirts.
  Beneficial to use constancy.
  No misfortune.

*Commentary*

Staying on the outskirts one avoids action. Constancy prevents harm. Do not do anything out of the ordinary.

Note. The suburban altar was a mound outside the city where large crowds attend rituals. A heng ceremony was a rite for fixing (perpetuating) an omen like a mordant fixes dye. It may be as simple as burying an oracle bone or drawing a circle round a place.

- *Second line, 9*  63

  a) Getting wet on the sands.
  There will be small talk.
  In the end auspicious.

  b) Waiting on the sands.
  There will be some gossip.
  Ultimately good fortune.

*Commentary*

Waiting on the sands: though there will be some gossip and complaints, all will be well in the end.

- **Third line, 9**  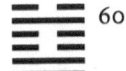 60

    a) Getting wet in the mud
       makes robbers come.

    b) Waiting in the mud
       brings on the arrival of bandits.

*Commentary*

Waiting (stuck) in the mud one attracts robbers. Danger lies ahead, but with careful precautions one avoids trouble.

- **Fourth line, 6**   43

    a) Getting wet in blood.
       One comes out of the hole.

    b) Waiting in blood.
       One comes out of the pit.

*Commentary*

*Waiting in blood:* being in a dangerous situation, through inaction (waiting) one comes out of it.

- **Fifth line, 9**   11

    a) Getting wet with wine and food.
       Augury: auspicious.

    b) Waiting with liquor and food.
       Perseverance brings good fortune.

*Commentary*

*Waiting with liquor and food:* being in a safe position, one may enjoy oneself. Perseverance brings good fortune.

## • *Top line, 6*

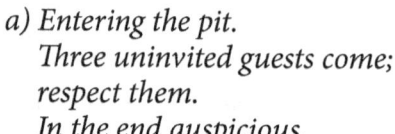

a) *Entering the pit.*
*Three uninvited guests come;*
*respect them.*
*In the end auspicious.*

b) *Entering a pit-house.*
*Three uninvited guests are arriving;*
*treat them with respect.*
*Ultimately auspicious.*

*Commentary*

Uninvited guests arrive. Treat them courteously. Ultimately auspicious. Showing respect will bring good fortune.

Note. Pit-houses, with floors lower than the ground outside, were dwellings of the common folk.

## • *Summary*

Water above Heaven. Water (rain) in the sky. The hexagram is about waiting and getting wet, because it refers to rain that makes everything damp and wet. Because it is raining one has to wait. (See hexagram 9, Judgment, and hexagram 62, line 5, where it is going to rain, but *not yet.*)

By being firm and strong (Heaven), and through inaction (waiting), one may not get involved in danger (Water). Have confidence. Brilliant success. It is beneficial to wait patiently. To go on a journey will bring good fortune.

As hexagram 4 is about youth and immaturity, it is followed by hexagram 5, Waiting, because youth is often depicted in situations of idle waiting (hanging around and waiting for something to happen).

This hexagram has six stages of waiting, in the sense of inactivity or not-doing:

In the first line, through inactivity and not doing anything out of the ordinary, one avoids misfortune.

In the second line there is some gossip or criticism, but in the end there will be good fortune.

In the third line danger lies ahead, but with careful precautions one may avoid trouble.

In the fourth line, being in a dangerous situation, by waiting patiently one can come out of it.

In the fifth line, waiting in a safe situation, one may enjoy oneself. Perseverance brings good fortune.

In the sixth line there is waiting for something unexpected (uninvited guests). With the right attitude (showing respect), there will be good fortune in the end.

# 6. *Song* / Conflict, Dispute, Lawsuit

qian / heaven, creative, power, *yang*, active, male

kan / moving water, rain, danger

- **Image**

    Water below Heaven.
    Heavy rain threatening in the sky: Conflict.
    In his affairs a noble person
    carefully considers how things begin.

- **Judgment**

    a) There are captives. They tremble in fear.
       In the middle auspicious, but ultimately ominous.
       Favourable to see a great man.
       Not favourable to cross the great river.

    b) There is confidence, but it is blocked by fear.
       Auspicious for part of the way, but in the end disaster.
       Beneficial to see a great person.
       Not beneficial to go on a journey.

*Commentary*

The upper trigram (Heaven) is strong, the lower (Water) is dangerous. Heaven and Water are parting company. Strength and danger often lead to conflict, dispute and lawsuit.

Some success in the course of the conflict, but ultimately it will be disastrous because the conflict cannot be resolved.

*Favourable to see a great man:* it will be beneficial to see a person of wisdom.
*Not favourable to cross the great river:* this is not the time to go on a journey.

### • Base line, 6

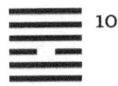

Not continuing the affair.
There will be little talk.
In the end auspicious.

#### Commentary

*Not continuing the affair:* the dispute should not go on for long. Though there is some grumbling, the argument is clear. Good fortune in the end.

### • Second line, 9

Not successful in a conflict.
Fleeing and returning to his town
of three hundred households.
No disaster.

#### Commentary

Failed in the dispute. Fleeing and returning home safely, one remains free from calamity.

### • Third line, 6

a) Eating old virtue.
   Augury of danger, but ultimately auspicious
   If someone pursues the king's service,
   there will be no completion.

b) *Nourished by ancient virtues.*
   *Perseverance in the face of danger,*
   *will bring good fortune in the end.*
   *Undertaking public affairs will not be successful.*

*Commentary*

*Nourished by ancient virtues:* holding on to them in dealing with conflicts will bring good fortune. Undertaking public affairs will not be successful.

- **Fourth line, 9**

a) *No success in a conflict.*
   *One returns for orders.*
   *Things change for the worse.*
   *Augury for safety: auspicious.*

b) *Not successful at the lawsuit.*
   *One returns to submit to fate.*
   *Matters change for the worse.*
   *Quiet determination brings good fortune.*

*Commentary*

Returning and submitting to one's destiny. Although matters get worse, with peaceful determination, there will be no failure. Good fortune.

- **Fifth line, 9**

   64

   *Most auspicious in a conflict.*

*Commentary*

Great good fortune in a conflict.

- *Top line, 9*

    One is rewarded with a great leather belt.
    By the end of the morning
    one is stripped of it three times.

    *Commentary*

Receiving distinction through dispute: not worthy of respect. This is a discouraging omen for honour.

Note. Great leather belts were emblems of rank and authority.

- *Summary*

Water below Heaven. Heavy rain is threatening in the sky. Strength (Heaven) and danger (Water) may lead to conflict. This hexagram is about a situation of conflict, dispute or lawsuit of a local ruler (of a 'town of three hundred households') with the king. There is some success in the course of the conflict, but ultimately it will end in disaster, because the conflict cannot be resolved.

It is beneficial to see a person of wisdom. This is not a time to go on a journey.

Hexagram 6 is about conflict, because one can imagine, that in a situation of idle waiting and doing nothing (hexagram 5), conflicts can arise.

This hexagram has six stages of conflict or dispute:

In the first line one should not speak too much about the conflict, then it will end well. Good fortune.

In the second line one loses the conflict or dispute, but returns home safely, and remains free from calamity.

In the third line, if one holds on to ancient virtues, it will be helpful to deal with the conflict. Good fortune. Doing something in public will not succeed.

In the fourth line one accepts the situation of conflict, and submits to destiny (fate). With peaceful determination there will be no failure. Good fortune.

In the fifth line one will have great good fortune in the conflict with one's superior or authority.

In the sixth line one will win a dispute, but the honour will not last because it will not be worthy of respect.

# 7. *Shi* / Army, Multitude

*kun* / earth, receptive, *yin*, passive, female

*kan* / moving water, rain, stream, danger

- *Image*

    Water below Earth.
    Water collects in the earth: Multitude, Army.
    The noble person cares for the people
    and strengthens the masses.

- *Judgment*

    a) Augury auspicious for a great man.
       No misfortune.

    b) Persistence for the respected (elder) man
       brings good fortune.
       No misfortune.

*Commentary*

Danger (Water) and compliant (Earth). The army means a multitude, a crowd. Though there could be trouble (Water, danger) among the crowd, the people will obey (Earth, compliant). A leader is able to control the multitude. Persistence also means perseverance. This being auspicious, how can there be misfortune?

- **Base line, 6**

   a) *The army goes forth,
   encouraged by the pitch-pipes.
   If it is not good: ominous.*

   b) *The multitude should move in ordered ranks.
   Without it, disaster will occur.*

### Commentary

Troops move in formations: lack of discipline means disaster.

*Note. Pitch-pipes were used to give signals and to encourage the soldiers, much as trumpets and drums were elsewhere. If there is anything wrong with the music when an army sets out, it is seen as a bad omen for the battle.*

- **Second line, 9**

   *Being amidst the troops.
   Auspicious. No misfortune.
   The king bestows a threefold award [on the general].*

### Commentary

In the midst of the multitude, the person who practices or abides in the Mean, will have good fortune, receiving heaven's grace.
The king confers a threefold award on the leader, thinking of the welfare of all the states.

*Note. The first award is a* jue *(a bronze ceremonial vessel, an emblem of noble rank). The second award is clothing, and the third is a carriage with horses.*

- **Third line, 6**

    The army carts corpses.
    Ominous.

    *Commentary*

The army carries corpses. Defeat. Disaster.


- **Fourth line, 6**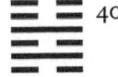

    The army makes camp to the left.
    No misfortune.

    *Commentary*

The army makes camp to the left bank of the river, or east side. The army halts and retreats. No error. This does not deviate from the army's way.


- **Fifth line, 6**

    a) There will be game for the hunt.
       Favourable to seize captives.
       No misfortune.
       An elder son commands the troops,
       a younger son carts the corpses.
       Augury: disaster.

    b) There is game in the fields.
       Beneficial to catch it.
       No error.
       The eldest son commands the army,
       the younger son carts the corpses.
       Persistence brings disaster.

#### Commentary

There is confidence to win a battle. No error.
The eldest son (lower inner trigram Thunder) should lead the troops. If the younger, inexperienced son (bottom trigram Water) insists on leading it will bring disaster ('carts the corpses').

### • Top line, 6

*A great ruler gives a mandate
to establish a state and a lineage.
The petty man should not be employed.*

#### Commentary

*A great ruler gives a mandate:* he shows his gratitude towards the meritorious general.
*The petty man should not be employed:* one should be careful not to appoint a petty man, otherwise turmoil in the state would be inevitable.

### • Summary

Water below Earth. Water collecting in the earth can be fertile, but there is also a danger of erosion, damage, overflowing. Earth also stands for masses of people, multitudes or crowds.

Water (danger) and Earth (compliant): though there could be trouble among the crowd, the people will obey. There is one strong, yang line (leader), and all the weak, yin lines (crowd) follow.

A leader is able to control the multitude. Persistence brings good fortune for an older man.

When conflict arises (hexagram 6), the army is put into action (hexagram 7).

In this hexagram there are six stages of an army in action:

In the first line there is a need for discipline, otherwise there will be disaster.

In the second line a strong leader, able to control the masses, is awarded. Good fortune.

In the third line the army meets with defeat. Disaster.

In the fourth line the army retreats and halts. One stops now in order to move on later. No error.

In the fifth line there is opportunity to win a battle, but the eldest son (experienced one) should be in command; if the younger (inexperienced one) is, there will be disaster.

In the sixth line a ruler gives a mandate to the strong leader to establish a state and a lineage. He should be careful not to appoint a petty man (incompetent person).

# 8. *Bi* / Joining, Union, Alliance

kan / moving water, rain, stream, danger

kun / earth, receptive, *yin*, compliant, female

- ## *Image*

    Water above Earth.
    Water moistens the earth: Joining, Union, Alliance.
    Kings established states
    and maintained good relations with underlords.

- ## *Judgment*

    a) Auspicious.
       Original divination: supreme offering.
       Long-range augury: no misfortune.
       Coming from not peaceful lands,
       for those who arrive late: ominous.

    b) Good fortune.
       Manipulation of the stalks brings supreme success.
       Long-term perseverance: no misfortune.
       Those in places not at peace will come
       but the latecomer faces disaster.

*Commentary*

Water (rain) moistens the earth: Joining, Union. Good fortune. Union means joining, helping. Those below are compliant and subordinate (lower trigram Earth). In a long-term perseverance there is no misfortune because the high and low correspond to each other.

*Those in places not at peace will come:* those who have not (security), seek out those who can give (protection).

*The latecomer faces disaster:* one who finds himself at the end of the process of union misses the opportunity to join. Disaster (Water, danger).

## • Base line, 6

a) There are captives.
   Join them.
   No misfortune.
   Booty filling earthenware jars.
   In the end auspicious.

b) There is sincerity.
   Alliance will not lead to error.
   Confidence like a filled earthenware pot.
   In the end it will bring good fortune.

### Commentary

Joining with sincerity and confidence will be auspicious. In the end there will be good fortune.

Note. Large pottery jars were used to store wine and grain.

## • Second line, 6

a) Join someone from inside.
   Augury: auspicious.

b) Alliance with those within.
   Perseverance brings good fortune.

*Commentary*

Joining those within one's own state or circle will lead to good fortune. Union from within means not failing (or neglecting) one's own kind.

## • Third line, 6

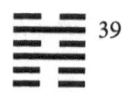

a) *Joining the wrong people.*
*[Danger.]*

b) *Joining unworthy persons.*
*[Danger.]*

*Commentary*

Joining undesirable people: will this not bring harm?

## • Fourth line, 6

a) *Join someone from outside.*
*Augury: auspicious.*

b) *Alliance with those outside.*
*Perseverance brings good fortune.*

*Commentary*

Joining those from outside one's own state or circle will lead to good fortune.

- *Fifth line, 9*

    a) *Joining a girth.*
       *The king uses three mounted beaters*
       *but misses the front game.*
       *The townspeople did not frighten it [into the trap].*
       *Auspicious.*

    b) *A glorious union.*
       *The king drives the game from three sides*
       *but leaving the front side open.*
       *The city folk are not warned [of his intentions].*
       *Good fortune.*

*Commentary*

A glorious union.
*Misses the front game*: the ruler seizes the compliant ones (tribes), and leaves those that back away alone.
The citizens need no warning, because the ruler adheres to the Mean, and does not force everyone to join. Good fortune.

*Note. By girth is meant a strap around a horse's belly. When hunting, the king used mounted beaters on three sides, leaving one side open so some animals could escape.*

- *Top line, 6*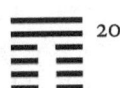

    a) *Joining them without a chief.*
       *Misfortune.*

    b) *Alliance without a ruler.*
       *Misfortune.*

*Commentary*

Union without a leader. There cannot be a result. Misfortune.

## • *Summary*

Water above Earth. Water (rain) moistens the earth, and earth receives the water: Joining, Union, Alliance. Supreme success. In a long-term perseverance there will be no misfortune. If one arrives at the end of the process of union, one may not be able to join. Disaster.

While both hexagrams 7 and 8 have Water and Earth, the name of this hexagram is 'Joining' and not 'Army', because in hexagram 8 Water and Earth join, and in hexagram 7 they do not.

In various translations the Judgment of hexagram 8 mentions a second consultation. Because in the Judgment it also says that the original divination (the first manipulation of the yarrow stalks) brings sublime success, there is no reason for a second consultation. Therefore, in this translation the recommendation is left out, but if the answer is not yet clear, then, in this case, a second consultation may be done.

After hexagram 7, the Army, Multitude, follows hexagram 8, Joining, Union, because it is about a ruler who (after a war) tries to create a greater union.

In this hexagram a ruler tries to persuade tribes and states around him to join him in six stages:

The first line, when joining with others, one should have confidence and sincerity. In the end good fortune.

In the second line union should be made with those from within one's own circle. Perseverance brings good fortune.

In the third line one joins unworthy partners. This may lead to harm.

In the fourth line one joins with those from outside one's own circle. Perseverance brings good fortune.

In the fifth line there is a glorious union, because the leader wants everyone to join him, but does not force them. Good fortune.

In the last line there is no leader to create union among the different people. This will lead to misfortune.

# 9. *Xiao Xu* / Small Cultivation

*xun* / wind, gentle, penetrating

*qian* / heaven, creative, power, *yang*, active, male

- ## *Image*

    Wind above Heaven.
    Wind blows across the sky: Small Cultivation.
    A noble person cultivates his civil virtues.

- ## *Judgment*

    a) Offering.
    Thick clouds, no rain, from our western town fields.

    b) Success.
    Dense clouds, but no rain, from the western outskirts.

*Commentary*

Wind (gentle) and Heaven (power). Success.

*Dense clouds, but no rain*: there will be progress, but no result yet.

*From the western outskirts*: some good fortune comes from a western direction. One will obtain an appropriate position, because those above and below respond. Since there are five strong lines, one's intention should be to go forward.

- **Base line, 9**

    *Back on the road.*
    *How can this be misfortune?*
    *Auspicious.*

*Commentary*

Returning to the way of virtue: this means good fortune.

- **Second line, 9**

    *Drawn along, one returns.*
    *Auspicious.*

*Commentary*

*Drawn along, one returns:* one does not get lost or one does not lose oneself. Good fortune.

- **Third line, 9**

    *The carriage loses wheel spokes.*
    *Husband and wife glare at each other.*

*Commentary*

Husband and wife are not in harmony. There is disorder in the house.

- *Fourth line, 6*

  a) *There is a capture.
  Blood departs.
  Go out warily.
  No misfortune.*

  b) *If there is confidence blood will be kept away.
  Going out with caution.
  No trouble.*

  #### Commentary

  With confidence and caution, one can avoid trouble. One's intentions agree with one's superior.

- *Fifth line, 9*

  a) *There are captives bound together.
  Riches shared with the neighbours.*

  b) *Sincerity and loyalty are binding.
  Wealth is shared with the neighbours.*

  #### Commentary

  Having confidence and cooperating with others, means not keeping wealth to oneself.

- **Top line, 9**

   a) It rains. It stops.
   Planting can still be finished.
   Augury for a wife: danger.
   Almost full moon:
   for a noble person going on a campaign: ominous.

   b) Rain may fall or stop.
   Virtues are still being cultivated.
   Determination for a woman is dangerous.
   The moon is almost full:
   for a noble person going out on a venture: disaster.

*Commentary*

Now it rains, now it stops. One still cultivates one's virtue, because the way of virtue is not yet 'full'. Determination will bring trouble to women. For a noble person to go forth and act: disaster.

- **Summary**

Wind above Heaven. The wind blows across the sky, and clouds (Lake, lower inner trigram) accumulate, covering up the sun (Fire, upper inner trigram). It is going to rain, but not yet, because, according to the Early Heaven Arrangement of the trigrams, rain comes after the wind (see p. xxii, *The Order and Attributes of the Trigrams*).

There will be some good fortune coming from the west, but it is not yet manifested. Success.

Hexagram 8, the creation of an alliance of states, is followed by hexagram 9, the cultivation of virtue, because here the values and norms of the great state are established.

This hexagram is about the cultivation of virtues in six stages:
In line one one returns to the way of virtue. Good fortune.

In line two one is drawn firmly on the way of virtue. One does not lose oneself. Good fortune.

In line three the cultivation of virtue meets with a setback. There will be disorder in relationships.

In line four confidence and caution prevent the occurrence of trouble. One's aims and goals are in accord with one's superior.

In the fifth line, which is the culmination of virtue, the virtues of sincerity and loyalty make one share wealth with others.

In line six, although the way of virtue is almost 'full', there is still danger and doubt. Determination will bring trouble to women. If one ventures out or takes some risky action at the time of the full moon, it can be disastrous.

# 10. *Lü* / Treading, Conduct

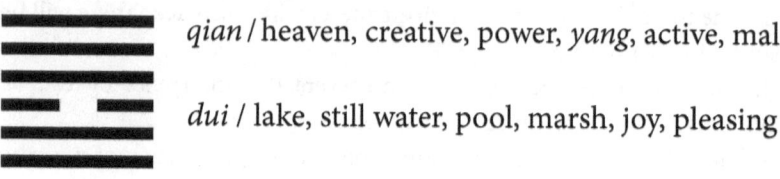

*qian* / heaven, creative, power, *yang*, active, male

*dui* / lake, still water, pool, marsh, joy, pleasing

- *Image*

    Lake below Heaven.
    A lake below the sky: Treading, Conduct.
    A noble person distinguishes between the high and the low and thereby provides a rule for the people's conduct.

- *Judgment*

    a) Treading on the tiger's tail.
    It won't bite the person.
    Offering.

    b) One steps on the tiger's tail, but is not bitten.
    Success.

*Commentary*

Joy (Lake) responds to the powerful (Heaven).
*One steps on the tiger's tail, but is not bitten. Success:* one treads in the place (territory) of the ruler, with no anxiety, luminous and clear.

- **Base line, 9**

    a) *Treading in plain white shoes.*
       *Going: no misfortune.*

    b) *Simply walking.*
       *There is no error in going forth.*

*Commentary*

*Treading in plain white shoes:* wanting to proceed alone in carrying out one's wishes.

- **Second line, 9**

    a) *Treading along a smooth flat road.*
       *Augury for a person in confinement:*
       *auspicious.*

    b) *Walking the way with ease.*
       *Perseverance for the secluded person brings good fortune.*

*Commentary*

*Perseverance for the secluded person brings good fortune:* if he keeps to the middle way, he will not be confused.

- **Third line, 6**

    *The one-eyed is able to see,*
    *the lame is able to walk.*
    *Treading on the tiger's tail, the person is bitten: disaster.*
    *A warrior acts as if he is a great ruler.*

*Commentary*

The one with failing eyes is able to see, but not sufficiently. The lame is able to walk, but unable to keep up with others. The disaster of being bitten is due to the third line being in an unsuitable position. If a warrior acts as if he is a great ruler, his conduct will result in disaster.

- ***Fourth line, 9***  61

  a) *Stepping on a tiger's tail.*
  *He looks fearfully.*
  *In the end auspicious.*

  b) *Treading on the tiger's tail,*
  *one should be extremely cautious.*
  *Ultimately good fortune.*

*Commentary*

*One should be extremely cautious*: in this way one's intentions will be realised. Good fortune in the end.

- ***Fifth line, 9***  38

  a) *Treading in split-open shoes*
  *Augury: danger.*

  b) *Walking resolutely.*
  *Determination is dangerous.*

*Commentary*

Treading resolutely, with determination, in the face of danger. Although the position (of the fifth line) is correct, there may still be trouble. One should either walk delicately or refrain from action altogether.

- *Top line, 9*

   a) Watch your steps.
      Observe the omens.
      Going back is very auspicious.

   b) Watch your conduct.
      Examine the signs.
      Going back over your steps will bring very good fortune.

*Commentary*

In this top position one has very good fortune. One should watch one's conduct and observe the signs. Retracing one's steps will bring good fortune and occasion for rejoicing.

- *Summary*

Lake below Heaven. A cloud or lake below the sky. The youngest daughter (Lake) follows the father (Heaven).

The story of this hexagram is about someone 'stepping on the tiger's tail' meaning how to act cautiously (treading) in a dangerous situation, or how to act in relation to the leader or superior. This will bring success.

Hexagram 9 was about the cultivation of virtues, and thus hexagram 10 is about conduct in society.

This hexagram is about conduct in six stages:

In the first line one treads with simplicity. If one wants to proceed alone there will be no error.

In the second line one treads with ease, and staying on the middle path one will not be confused. Persistence brings good fortune to a secluded person.

In the third line someone acts in an incompetent way, and his conduct will result in disaster.

In the fourth line, if one is extremely cautious, one's aims will be realised. Good fortune in the end.

In the fifth line one treads resolutely, but one should be cautious, because there may still be trouble.

In the sixth line one should watch one's conduct and observe the signs. In going back over one's steps there will be good fortune and occasion for rejoicing.

# 11. *Tai* / The Great, Peace

*kun* / earth, receptive, *yin*, passive, female

*qian* / heaven, creative, power, *yang*, active, male

## • Image

*Heaven below Earth.*
*Heaven and Earth act together: The Great, Peace.*
*A ruler fulfils the way of heaven and earth*
*and assists in their unfoldment,*
*thereby helping the people on all sides.*

## • Judgment

a) *The small goes, the great comes.*
   *Auspicious. Offering.*

b) *The small departs and the great arrives.*
   *Good fortune. Success.*

### Commentary

The small departs (Earth, upper or 'going' trigram), the great arrives (Heaven, lower or 'coming' trigram). Good fortune and success.
When heaven and earth interact, the myriad entities are activated; when upper and lower interact, their intentions are united.
The lower (trigram) is *yang*, the upper is *yin*; the lower is powerful, the upper compliant; the lower is a noble person, the upper a petty person.
A noble person's way will wax, a petty person's way will wane.

- **Base line, 9**  46

   a) Pulling out mao grass
      with shoot and root.
      Going on a campaign.
      Auspicious.

   b) Pull up the white grass, roots and all.
      Going out on a venture.
      Good fortune.

*Commentary*

*Pulling out white grass with shoot and root*: one will attain what one wants, and more. If one goes forth and act, there will be good fortune. One's intentions are fixed on external things and other people's welfare.

*Note. The* mao *grass is a common reed-like grass with wide spreading roots and was used for wrapping offerings, both as gifts for others and in sacrifices including state sacrifices.*

- **Second line, 9** 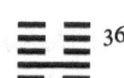 36

   a) Using a hollow gourd
      to cross the He (Yellow) River.
      He is not leaving his friends far behind,
      lest they disappear.
      He gets a reward in the middle.

   b) Bearing with the common in crossing the river.
      Not leaving one's friends in the distant,
      lest they might disappear.
      One gains esteem by practising the Middle Way.

*Commentary*

Bearing with the uncultured, not leaving his friends behind, and practising the middle way, one gains glory.

*Note. Dried, hollow gourds were girded on to be used as floats or 'life-jackets' when crossing deep waters.*

## • Third line, 9

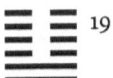

a) There is no plain without a rise.
   There is no going without a return.
   Augury of hardship.
   No misfortune.
   Don't worry: there may be a capture at the meal.
   Blessings.

b) There is no level without a slope.
   No going that does not involve a return.
   Determination in the face of difficulty.
   There will be no misfortune.
   Do not be anxious: confidence will be rewarded.
   There will be a blessing.

*Commentary*

There is no going forward without a return. This third line is at the boundary between Heaven and Earth. This suggests a setback, but because the line is extremely strong (a whole line in the right place), with confidence and determination there will be no misfortune. There will be unsought or unexpected benefit.

- *Fourth line, 6*  34

    a) Fluttering about.
    No riches shared by the neighbours.
    Not watchful about captives.

    b) Fluttering to and fro.
    Wealth is not shared by the neighbours.
    Not paying attention to sincerity.

*Commentary*

Going back and forth. Wealth is not shared by his neighbours, but he keeps his faithfulness. He is not concerned about their sincerity.

*Note. Birds are favourite sources of omens, and a fluttering bird seems to bring a message of a doubtful nature.*

- *Fifth line, 6*  5

    a) Diyi gives his youngest sister
    or daughter in marriage.
    Happiness follows.
    Most auspicious.

    b) King Diyi marries off his youngest sister (daughter).
    Blessings and great good fortune.

*Commentary*

The marriage of the king's sister (daughter) symbolises the culmination of the union of the trigrams Heaven (male) and Earth (female). Happiness. One's wishes are fulfilled. Great good fortune.

*Note. Diyi was a ruler of the Shang dynasty (c. 1600-1040 BCE.).*

- *Top line, 6*

  a) *A city wall crumbling into its moat.
  Do not use the army.
  From the city a decree is proclaimed.
  Augury: distress.*

  b) *A town wall collapses into the ditch.
  Do not use the army.
  From the town orders are issued.
  Determination brings distress.*

  *Commentary*

  *A town wall collapses into the ditch:* do not put up a fight. Orders are issued to warn the people. In this last line the way of Heaven and Earth is crumbling down, and will bring disorder and distress.

- *Summary*

Heaven below Earth. Because of the movements of the trigrams (Heaven moves up and Earth moves down), they unite, and create peace and harmony. Good fortune and success.

'The small departs and the great arrives' is about the lines of the top trigram (Earth), which are moving out of the hexagram, and the lines of the bottom trigram (Heaven), which are moving in. A noble person's way will wax, a petty person's way will wane.

The strong Heaven yields to the weak Earth. A leader (Heaven) who is humble and yielding (Earth) on the outside (upper trigram), but strong (Heaven) on the inside (lower trigram), completes the way of Heaven and Earth.

Hexagram 10, Treading, Conduct, which is about conduct in society, is followed by hexagram 11, The Great, Peace, because in this hexagram a leader manifests the way of Heaven and Earth.

The story of hexagram 11 is about a noble person fulfilling the way of Heaven and Earth in different stages:

In the first line one will attain what one wants, and more. If one ventures forth or takes some risky action, there will be good fortune. One's attention is fixed upon external things or other people's welfare.

In the second line, going on a journey, he does not leave his friends behind. Practising the middle path, he gains glory.

In the third line there is no going without a return. When one is confident and determined in the face of difficulties, there will be a blessing in the form of some unexpected benefit.

In the fourth line wealth is not shared by his neighbours, but the person keeps his faithfulness in them, whether they are sincere or not.

In the fifth line the noble person's way of heaven and earth comes to fulfilment. One's wishes are fulfilled. A marriage will be very beneficial. Great good fortune.

In the sixth line nobility and reputation are crumbling down, and bring disorder and distress. Do not put up a fight, but maintain the usual order.

# 12. *Pi* / The Small, The Petty

qian / heaven, creative, power, *yang*, active, male

kun / earth, receptive, *yin*, passive, female

- ## *Image*

    Heaven above Earth.
    Heaven and Earth do not act together: *The Small, The Petty*.
    A noble person restrains himself with virtue
    and avoids trouble.
    He does not allow himself to be honoured by rank or gifts.

- ## *Judgment*

    a) Petty men.
    Augury not favourable for the noble person.
    The great goes, the small comes.

    b) Unworthy people.
    Determination is not beneficial for the noble person.
    The great departs and the small arrives.

*Commentary*

The great departs (Heaven, upper or 'going' trigram), the small arrives (Earth, lower or 'coming' trigram). Presence of unworthy men. Determination is not beneficial for noble persons.

When heaven and earth do not interact, the myriad things are not activated. When upper and lower do not interact, under heaven there is no good government.

The lower (trigram) is *yin*, the upper is *yang*; the lower is broken, the upper is whole; the lower a petty person, the upper a noble person.
A petty person's way will wax, a noble person's way will wane.

### • *Base line, 6*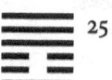

a) *Pulling out* mao *grass with shoot and root.
Augury: auspicious.*

b) *Pull up the white grass, roots and all.
Perseverance brings good fortune.*

#### *Commentary*

*Pulling out white grass with shoot and root:* one will attain what one wants and more. Perseverance brings good fortune. The noble person is steadfast in his support of the ruler who is surrounded by petty men.

*Note. For the white grass, see the note at the base line of hexagram 11.*

### • *Second line, 6*

a) *Wrap steamed meat.
For a petty person: auspicious.
Bad for a noble person.
Offering.*

b) *By offering gifts the petty person prospers.
Offering gifts will not be suitable for the noble person.*

#### *Commentary*

The noble person does not use flattery or offers gifts. One will have success. He does not involve himself with petty associations.

Note. *The meat is either food prepared and wrapped in palm leaf as a present for a superior, or is a sacrificial offering for which bronze ritual vessels are used.*

## • Third line, 6

a) *Covering the offering of prepared food.*

b) *Concealing shame.*

☷☶ 33

### Commentary

The petty man conceals his shame. One's position (third *yin* line) is not appropriate.

## • Fourth line, 9

a) *There will be a decree.*
   *No trouble.*
   *A pair of orioles in the field.*
   *Happiness.*

b) *A command is issued to the petty man.*
   *No misfortune.*
   *Those of like mind will share his good fortune.*

 20

### Commentary

The petty man only follows a command. No misfortune and no error. The petty man's intentions and ambitions will be realised. His fellow men share his good fortune.

Note. *For orioles, see the note at the second line of hexagram 30.*

- *Fifth line, 9*

    a) Stopping the petty.
       For a noble person: auspicious.
       Will it flee? Will it flee?
       Tie it to a leafy mulberry tree.

    b) Desisting the petty.
       Good fortune for the noble person.
       Might it be lost? Might it be lost?
       Then tie it to a flourishing mulberry tree.

### Commentary

The period of the petty is coming to an end, but the situation is not secure enough, and the noble person must therefore strengthen himself.
There will be good fortune for the noble person because one's position (fifth *yang* line) is correct and appropriate.

Note. In ancient times it was a custom to plant mulberry trees next to one's house for protection against wind and rain, because the roots were deep and the trees were shady and growing fast.

- *Top line, 9*

    Ending the petty.
    First bad, later joy.

### Commentary

Pettiness is ultimately overcome. How can it last long?

## • *Summary*

Heaven above Earth. Because the trigrams move away from each other they do not act together.

The great is departing (Heaven leaves the upper part of the hexagram) and the petty is arriving (Earth is moving in from below). A petty person's way will wax, a noble person's way will wane. Determination is not beneficial for the noble person. The noble person has to be steadfast in dealing with the petty.

Something strong (Heaven) on top of something weak (Earth) will easily collapse. Someone is strong (Heaven) on the outside, and weak (Earth) and petty within.

The structure of this hexagram is totally opposite, reversed, and inverted to hexagram 11. Therefore all the qualities of this hexagram are opposite.

Hexagram 11 is followed by hexagram 12 because, according to the law of extremes in the *Yi Jing*, if something comes to an extreme, high or low, it will always change into its opposite (the hexagrams are opposites).

This hexagram is about the values and attitudes of petty men in six stages:

In the first line one will attain what one wants, or more. The noble person steadfastly supports the leader who is surrounded by petty men. Perseverance brings good fortune.

In the second line the petty man offers his gifts to attain favours. The noble person refrains from such actions.

In the third line the petty man conceals his shame, after having received favours and gifts.

In the fourth line the petty man, acting according to a higher command, will have no misfortune and no error. His ambitions will be realised. His fellow men share his good fortune.

In the fifth line the values and attitudes of the petty are coming to an end but the situation is not secure enough, and must therefore be strengthened. Good fortune for the noble person.

In the last line pettiness and negativity is ultimately overcome; it cannot last.

# 13. *Tong Ren* / Assembling People

*qian* / heaven, creative, power, *yang*, active, male

*li* / fire, light, brightness, clinging

### • Image

Fire below Heaven.
Fire rises up to heaven: Assembling People.
A noble person distinguishes among things
and organises his people.

### • Judgment

a) Assembling people in the open field.
Offering.
Favourable to cross the great river.
Augury favourable for the noble person.

b) Assembling people in the countryside.
Success.
Beneficial to go on a journey.
Determination is beneficial for the noble person.

*Commentary*

Heaven above and Fire below associate with one another. The power (Heaven) is strong and the pattern is bright (Fire).
*Assembling people in the countryside:* only a noble person (leader) can gather people together to accomplish great things. Success.

*Favourable to cross the great river:* it is beneficial to go on a journey. Determination is beneficial for the noble person.

## • Base line, 9

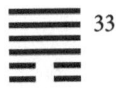

*Assembling people at the gate.
No misfortune.*

#### Commentary

*Assembling people at the gate:* there should be action in public, not in secrecy. Where is the misfortune?

Note. People were summoned to the town gate to hear proclamations.

## • Second line, 6

*Assembling people at the ancestral hall.
Distress.*

#### Commentary

*Assembling people at the ancestral hall:* in this situation, a gathering of people of the *same* clan can bring up tension and quarrels, leading to distress.

Note. The ancestral hall was the scene of ceremonial banquets, as well as sacrifices.

## • Third line, 9

*War chariots lying in ambush
in the tall weeds.
Climb the high hill
and for three years the people will not rise up.*

*Commentary*

War chariots hiding in the bushes. The enemy is strong. For three years the people will not rise up. How could they move forward?

## • *Fourth line, 9*

 37

*Mounting the wall.*
*The people will not be able to attack.*
*Auspicious.*

*Commentary*

*Mounting the wall:* the gathered people are unable to attack. In times of difficulty one does not advance. Good fortune.

## • *Fifth line, 9*

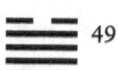 30

*Assembling the people.*
*First they weep and wail, later on they laugh.*
*The great armies are able to meet.*

*Commentary*

The great armies are able to meet and confront one another. This time the gathered people gain victory.

## • *Top line, 9*

49

*a) Assembling people at the suburban altar.*
*No regret.*

*b) Assembllng people at the outskirts.
No regret.*

*Commentary*

*Assembling people in the outskirts:* Intentions are not attained. No regret.

Note. Sacrifices were offered to the Lord on High at the suburban altar outside the city, at the solstices, and also for martial victories. Compare hexagram 5, base line and note.

## • Summary

Fire below Heaven. Fire goes up to heaven, suggesting man's tendency to associate with others.
It shows a person who is strong, decisive (Heaven) on the outside, and warm, clear minded (Fire) on the inside.
This hexagram is about a group of people cooperating together.
The story of this hexagram is about a noble person (leader) gathering people together to protect a town under siege by a strong enemy. Success. Determination is beneficial for the noble person. It is advisable to go on a journey.
Hexagram 12, the Small, the Petty, is followed by hexagram 13, Assembling People, because out of a situation where petty people dominate (hexagram 12), could emerge a movement led by a noble person to counter this negative influence.
This hexagram is about assembling people in six stages:
In the first line the people are assembled at the gate. One should act openly, not in secrecy. No misfortune.
In the second line the assembled people, being of the same clan, give rise to tension, which could lead to distress.
In the third line, because the enemy is strong, the people refrain from action for three years. One should not advance.
In the fourth line, although one does not advance (attack), the action is correct. Good fortune.

In the fifth line the enemy is confronted. First the people weep and wail but later they laugh, because they gained victory.

In the sixth line the people are assembled on the outside, but their aim is not really attained. No regret.

# 14. *Da You* / Great Possession

*li* / fire, light, brightness, clinging

*qian* / heaven, creative, power, *yang*, active, male

- ## *Image*

    Fire above Heaven.
    The sun shining in the sky: Great Possession.
    A noble person, obeying Heaven's decrees,
    suppresses evil and exalts the good.

- ## *Judgment*

    a) Great possession.
    Great offering.

    b) Possession in great measure.
    Sublime success.

*Commentary*

Fire above and Heaven below correspond with one another. The pattern is bright (Fire) and the power is strong (Heaven). A noble person answers to Heaven as occasions develop. Supreme success.

- ## *Base line, 9*

    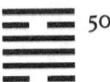 50

    a) Crosswise movement foreboding harm.
    No trouble.
    If in hardship: no misfortune.

b) *There may be an encounter with evil.*
*No trouble.*
*Even if in difficulty, there will be no misfortune.*

*Commentary*

Even when one encounters evil, there will be no trouble and no misfortune.

*Note. 'Crosswise' probably refers to the flight of birds, but may also refer to other animals. This is observed as a source of omens worldwide. Even today people in East Asia are sensitive to omens of people or animals crossing in front of them, especially in the early morning. People in the West read similar omens in the flight of crows, ravens and magpies, and in rodents and black cats crossing one's path. See also line 5, and hexagram 17, base line.*

- **Second line, 9**

    *A large cart used for transport.*
    *There will be some place to go.*
    *No misfortune.*

 30

*Commentary*

A big wagon for loading means, whatever possessions one has accumulated, they will not be lost. If one sets forth to undertake something, there will be no misfortune.

- **Third line, 9**

    a) *The duke makes an offering*
       *to the Son of Heaven (emperor).*
       *The small person is not capable of it.*

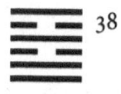 38

b) *The noble person pays a tribute to the ruler.*
*The petty person cannot do that.*

*Commentary*

The noble person makes offerings to his leader. The petty person will only come to harm if he attempts to do the same.

• *Fourth line, 9*

a) *No* peng *sacrifice at the side*
*of the ancestral temple gate.*
*No misfortune.*

b) *Not showing off.*
*No trouble.*

*Commentary*

One shies away from displaying power, influence or possessions. This is a clear and wise decision. No misfortune.

Note. The peng *sacrifice is a ritual whereby a cripple, an emaciated person or a shaman is exposed to the sun in order to make rain come during drought.*

• *Fifth line, 6*

a) *Their captives move crosswise,*
*looking terrified.*
*Auspicious.*

b) *His sincerity makes him awesome.*
*Good fortune.*

*Commentary*

Sincerity in interaction with others. His intention is trustworthy. The good fortune connected with his dignity makes him rule with ease, and allows him to make changes without warning.

Note. For 'crosswise movement', see the note at the base line.

- ***Top line, 9***

    Blessings from Heaven.
    Auspicious.
    Unfavourable for nothing.

*Commentary*

Great possession brings good fortune, because there is a blessing from Heaven. Unfavourable for nothing.

- ***Summary***

Fire above Heaven. The sun shines brightly in the sky, symbolising a man's tendency to answer to Heaven: Great Possession.

The upper and lower inner trigrams stand for gold (Heaven) and silver (Lake). Supreme success.

Hexagram 13, Gathering People, is about accomplishing great things which will often lead to hexagram 14, Great Possession.

The story of this hexagram is about great possessions of power, influence, position, and material things in six stages:

In the first line, even if one encounters difficulties, there will be no trouble and no misfortune.

In the second line one's accumulated possessions will not be lost. If one advances or undertake something, there will be no misfortune.

In the third line, only a noble person has qualities to attain a great award. The petty person should not make the attempt.

In the fourth line one is advised not to display his power or possessions. No misfortune.

In the fifth line the leader has such great respect, that he is trusted to make changes without prior preparations. Good fortune.

In the sixth line one's great possessions are a blessing from Heaven. This means that one receives help as a matter of course, *if* one remains in the *Dao* (the Way). Unfavourable for nothing.

# 15. *Qian* / Modesty, Rodent

 *kun* / earth, receptive, *yin*, passive, female

*gen* / mountain, standing still, stilling, stopping

- *Image*

    Mountain below Earth.
    A mountain hidden within the earth: Modesty.
    A noble person reduces the excessive
    and augments the deficient;
    balancing matters, he levels them out.

- *Judgment*

    a) Offering.
       Achievement for a noble person.

    b) Accomplishment.
       The noble person carries things through to the end.

*Commentary*

Wealth (Mountain) and humbleness (Earth): Modesty. Success.
The way of Heaven sends down blessings and light; the way of Earth is humble and modest.
Heaven's way decreases haughtiness and increases modesty; Earth's way transforms haughtiness and supports modesty.
The way of spirits and gods attacks haughtiness and feeds modesty; man's way rejects haughtiness and favours modesty.

In high rank modesty shines, in low rank it does not overdo. This is the achievement of a noble person.

Note. The rodent may be the great grey hamster. A rodent is related to the trigram Mountain. That is why, in this hexagram, there are six activities of the rodent.

- **Base line, 6**

 36

   a) Crunching rodent.
      A noble person crosses the great river.
      Auspicious.

   b) Very modest.
      If the noble person goes on a journey,
      it will bring good fortune.

*Commentary*

The noble person is humble through self-control. If he goes on a journey it will bring good fortune.

- **Second line, 6**

 46

   a) Grunting rodent.
      Auspicious augury.

   b) Expressing modesty.
      Perseverance brings good fortune.

*Commentary*

Modesty comes to expression. Perseverance brings good fortune because modesty comes from one's heart.

- **Third line, 9**

    a) Toiling rodent.
       For the noble person ultimately auspicious.

    b) A noble person, hard-working and modest,
       carries things to conclusion
       Good fortune.

*Commentary*

Out of respect for the hard-working, yet modest noble person, the people are willing to submit. Good fortune in the end.

- **Fourth line, 6**

    a) Tearing rodent.
       There is nothing which is unfavourable.

    b) Practising modesty.
       There is nothing not beneficial.

*Commentary*

Nothing is unfavourable for one who cultivates modesty. Such a one does not act against the (social) rules.

- **Fifth line, 6**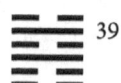

    [Rolling rodent.]
    Not wealthy because of the neighbours.
    Favourable when used to invade and attack.
    There is nothing which is unfavourable.

*Commentary*

Not wealthy on account of his neighbours, the noble person is modest about his wealth.
It is favourable to attack those who do not submit. There is nothing which is unfavourable.

- *Top line, 6* 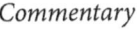 52

   a) Squealing rodent.
      Favourable for moving the troops
      to attack a town or state.

   b) Known for one's modesty.
      Beneficial to mobilise the army
      to campaign against a city or state.

*Commentary*

Modesty is expressed and advantageous, even when waging a military campaign, for it shows that the campaign is just, and has been resorted to only with reluctance, and because of much provocation.

- *Summary*

Mountain below the Earth. A mountain (wealth) hidden within the earth (humbleness) symbolises modesty. Someone who is diligent without boasting, and who has merit without displaying it.

A noble person who is wealthy and recognised, is humble and polite. This modest person decreases what is too much, and increases what is too little. Success. The noble person carries things through to the end.

Out of hexagram 14, Great Possession, hexagram 15, Modesty follows because as one's ability grows greater (hexagram 14), one becomes more humble and modest.

Modesty is seen by gods and men as a great virtue.

The rodent is related to the trigram Mountain. It has some characteristics referring to humbleness and modesty.

This hexagram is about humbleness and modesty, expressed in actions of a rodent, in six stages:

In the first line modesty is cultivated through discipline. Going on a journey will bring good fortune.

In the second line modesty comes to expression from the depths of the heart. Perseverance bring good fortune.

In the third line things are brought to fruition with modesty. Good fortune in the end.

In the fourth line, by cultivating modesty, one does not act against social convention. There is nothing not beneficial.

In the fifth line the noble person is modest about his wealth. It is favourable to take action against those who do not obey. There is nothing which is unfavourable.

In the sixth line, well-known for his modesty, it will be beneficial for the noble person to take action against those who challenge him.

# 16. *Yu* / Enthusiasm, Elephant

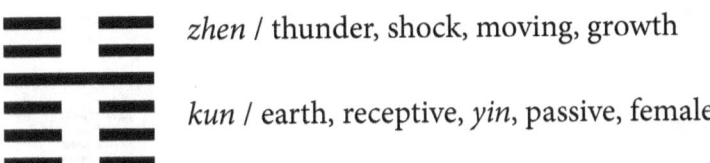

zhen / thunder, shock, moving, growth

kun / earth, receptive, *yin*, passive, female

- *Image*

    Thunder above Earth.
    Thunder rolls over the earth: Enthusiasm.
    Kings made music, honoured virtue,
    solemnly worshipped the Lord of Heaven
    and revered the ancestors.

- *Judgment*

    a) Favourable to establish a lord and move the army.

    b) Beneficial to establish order and mobilise one's forces.

*Commentary*

Compliant (Earth) and moving (Thunder). The firm (Thunder) meets with response (Earth), and there is an intention to act: Enthusiasm. It is beneficial to establish order and mobilise one's forces.

The sun and moon do not get out of their course, and the four seasons do not deviate. By such movement (Thunder) and compliance (Earth) the sages ordained just punishments, and the people submitted. The timely occurrence of enthusiasm is of great importance.

*Note. Enthusiasm is expressed in the story of an elephant's actions. Remains of Asian elephants have been found at Shang sites (c. 1560 BCE). Some of them were buried sacrificially.*

- **Base line, 6**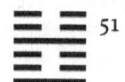

    a) Trumpeting elephant.
    Ominous.

    b) Expressing enthusiasm.
    Misfortune.

*Commentary*

Expressing enthusiasm means that one's aspirations are expressed too soon. Misfortune.

- **Second line, 6**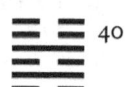

    Bound by rocks.
    Not lasting till the end of the day.
    Perseverance is auspicious.

*Commentary*

Enthusiasm is tempered. This will not last long. Perseverance brings good fortune. This is because of one's rectitude, and one's staying on the middle way.

- **Third line, 6**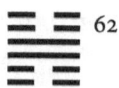

    a) Staring elephant.
    It walks slowly. There will be trouble.

b) *To gaze reposefully brings regret.*
   *If one hesitates too long, it will bring remorse.*

*Commentary*

Hesitation and tardiness brings regret.

### • Fourth line, 9

a) *Wary elephant.*
   *There will be a great catch.*
   *Do not doubt.*
   *Why not string the cowries?*

b) *Enthusiasm will bring great gain.*
   *Do not be doubtful.*
   *Friends will gather around you like a string of cowry shells.*

*Commentary*

*Enthusiasm will bring great gain*: with enough confidence and with the help of friends, one's ambitions will be realised in great measure.

Note. Tortoise-shells and cowries would be gifts from the king. These were objects of great value.

### • Fifth line, 6

a) *Augury of illness.*
   *Perform the* heng *ritual*
   *and there will be no death.*

b) *Suffering from a stubborn illness.*
   *By being steadfast one will not die.*

*Commentary*

A sign of prolonged illness, but by persevering and not abandoning the middle way, one will not die.

Note. For the heng *ceremony, a perpetuation rite, see also the note at the base line of hexagram 5.*

- **Top line, 6**

    a) *Elephant in darkness.*
       *There will be a collapse in the wall.*
       *No misfortune.*

    b) *Enthusiasm is at its height.*
       *If one changes one's way:*
       *no misfortune.*

35

*Commentary*

Enthusiasm at its height. This should not last long.

- **Summary**

Thunder above the Earth, meaning thunder rolling over the earth, indicating a time of new undertakings and great enthusiasm. It will be beneficial to establish order and mobilise one's forces. The timely occurrence of enthusiasm is of great importance.

Out of the combination of Great Possessions (hexagram 14) and Modesty (hexagram 15), one may say that Enthusiasm (hexagram 16), or a strong interest to undertake new things, can emerge.

This hexagram is about enthusiasm expressed in the story of an elephant's actions in different stages:

In the first line enthusiasm is expressed too soon. Misfortune.

In the second line enthusiasm is tempered, but this will last only for a short period. Staying on the middle path and perseverance will bring good fortune.

In the third line hesitation and tardy action will lead to regret.

In the fourth line, with enough confidence (enthusiasm) and help from friends, one will attain great gain.

In the fifth line an almost hopeless situation (prolonged illness) can be overcome by strong perseverance, and keeping to the middle path.

In the sixth line enthusiasm is at its height. Only by changing one's way will there be no misfortune.

# 17. *Sui* / Following, Pursuit

*dui* / lake, still water, cloud, joy, pleasing

*zhen* / thunder, shock, moving, growth

- ***Image***

    *Thunder below Cloud.*
    *Thunder follows the cloud: Following, Pursuit.*
    *A noble person, when evening comes,*
    *goes inside to rest and relax.*

- ***Judgment***

    a) *Great offering.*
    *Favourable augury.*
    *No misfortune.*

    b) *Sublime accomplishment.*
    *Perseverance is beneficial.*
    *No misfortune.*

### Commentary

Moving (Thunder) and pleasing (Lake, Cloud): Following. Sublime accomplishment. Perseverance is beneficial. No misfortune.

For everything under heaven, the principle of following, or doing things in accord with the pulse of time, is great indeed. The noble person, when evening comes, goes inside to rest.

• **Base line, 9**

a) *A neglected building.*
*Augury auspicious.*
*In going outdoors, if there is a crossing,*
*one will have success.*

b) *Values and norms are changing for the worse.*
*Perseverance brings good fortune.*
*Going out of the door to associate with people*
*will have results.*

*Commentary*

Values and norms are changing for the worse. Pursuing what is right and perseverance will bring good fortune. Leaving home and associating with others brings success.

Note. The building is either an old establishment or guest house. The crosswise passing is probably a reference to people or animals crossing one's path, which is often recognised as an omen. See note at the base line of hexagram 14.

• **Second line, 6**

a) *Binding the youngster*
*but losing the grown man.*

b) *Clinging to the boy*
*but losing the mature man.*

*Commentary*

*Clinging to the boy*: she cannot be with both at the same time. By choosing for the boy she loses the man.

- **Third line, 6**   49

    a) Binding the man, but losing the youngster.
    In pursuit one gets what is sought.
    Favourable augury for a dwelling.

    b) Clinging to the man, but losing the boy.
    By pursuing one obtains what one seeks.
    Beneficial to persevere in a dwelling.

    *Commentary*

*Clinging to the man:* her intention is such that she abandons the boy. In following the man (husband), she gets what she wants. It is beneficial to persevere in staying where we are.

- **Fourth line, 9**  3

    a) In pursuit there will be a catch.
    Augury: ominous.
    There will be a capture on the way.
    If it is used to make an agreement,
    what misfortune will there be?

    b) One's pursuit has hidden motives.
    An omen of disaster.
    If being sincere on the way, leads to clarity,
    what misfortune could there be?

    *Commentary*

One's pursuit brings success, but if one's motives are in violation with the way of virtue, there will be disaster. With sincerity and clarity, what misfortune could there be?

*Note. The agreement or covenant may have been a sacrificial matter, involving the captives referred to in line 5 and the top line. They were instruments of diplomacy and war, essentially what now are called pacts.*

- **Fifth line, 9**

    a) Captives at the celebration.
    Auspicious.

    b) Sincerity is praiseworthy.
    Good fortune.

*Commentary*

Sincerity is praiseworthy. Good fortune: his rectitude manifests itself in good works, and inspires others to follow him, bringing good fortune.

- **Top line, 6**

    a) They grabbed and bound them,
    then loosely tied them.
    The king sacrifices them
    at Mount Qi (West Mountain).

    b) Seize and bind them,
    then so tied up, make them follow.
    Thus the king's achievement
    extends to the western mountains.

*Commentary*

A firm allegiance (or pact) is made with force successfully. The way of Following has come to an end.

## • *Summary*

Thunder below Cloud means that thunder follows the clouds.

Both trigrams also indicate a strong young man (eldest son, Thunder) pursuing a beautiful young girl (youngest daughter, Lake). The principle of following is about doing things at the right time or following the natural patterns of change (the *Dao*). When evening comes, the noble person goes inside and rest, because that is the natural thing to do. Sublime accomplishment. Perseverance is beneficial.

This hexagram is basically about following and pursuit in relation to certain values and norms.

When beginning new undertakings with great enthusiasm (hexagram 16), one has to be aware of making the right choices (following what is right) in hexagram 17.

The hexagram is about following and pursuing what is right, expressed in six stages:

In the first line values and norms are crumbling. Pursuing what is right and perseverance will bring good fortune. Going out and meeting others brings success.

In the second line the woman follows the boy (the lesser choice), and loses the man (her husband). By choosing for the immature person or idea one loses the good and beneficent.

In the third line the woman follows the man (husband, the better choice) and gains what she seeks. Here she pursues material well-being. Persevering to stay where we are is beneficial.

In the fourth line something is pursued without correct motives. With sincerity and clarity misfortune can be avoided.

In the fifth line Following reaches its peak when people follow a person who manifests good works and inspires others. Good fortune.

The sixth line is about a leader who has brought all subjects together with an agreement to follow him. Here Following is coming to an end, because the followers are forced to follow.

# 18. *Gu* / Decay, Deterioration, Mildew

*gen* / mountain, standing still, stilling, stopping

*xun* / wind, gentle, penetrating

## • *Image*

Wind below the Mountain.
Wind blowing strongly at the foot of the mountain:
Decay, Deterioration.
A noble person stimulates the people to cultivate virtue.

## • *Judgment*

a) Great offering.
Favourable to cross the great river
three days before a jia day and three days after a jia day.

b) Great success.
Beneficial to go on a journey,
before the beginning three days
and after the beginning three days.

*Commentary*

The strong above (Mountain, standing still) and the weak below (Wind, gentle), symbolise decay, deterioration, corruption.
*Great success:* things will become well-ordered again.
*Favourable to cross the great river:* it is beneficial to go on a journey.

*Before the beginning three days and after the beginning three days:* every end is followed by a new beginning. This is heaven's way. The beginning or change mentioned here is about an event or circumstance, occurring at the third day after this consultation of the *Yi Jing*.

Note. Mildew is appearing either on the wooden tablets that represented the ancestors in the clan temple, or on the sacrificial food set before them. Such mildew would be regarded as ominous.
Jia is the first day in the ancient Chinese ten-day 'week'.

- **Base line, 6**

 26

a) Mildew for a deceased male ancestor.
If there is a son,
the deceased father will be without misfortune.
Danger, but in the end auspicious.

b) Rectifying the father's moral corruption.
If there is a son,
the deceased father will be without blame.
Danger, but ultimately good fortune.

*Commentary*

Correcting the corruption of moral values caused by the deceased father. One carries on with his father's duties.

- **Second line, 9**

 52

a) Mildew for a deceased female ancestor.
Augury is possible.

b) Rectifying the mother's moral deterioration
One must not be too determined in this.

*Commentary*

Correcting the corruption of moral values caused by the deceased mother. One practices the middle way.

## • Third line, 9

a) Mildew for a deceased male ancestor.
   There will be a little trouble
   but no great misfortune.

b) Rectifying the fathers corruption of virtues.
   There will be a little regret, but no great blame.

*Commentary*

Correcting the corruption of moral values caused by the deceased father. There will be some trouble, but no great misfortune.

## • Fourth line, 6

a) Mildew for the bathed forefather.
   If one continues, one sees distress.

b) Tolerating the father's abundant corruption.
   By continuing this, one will meet with humiliation.

*Commentary*

Tolerating the abundant corruption caused by the deceased father. Proceeding with this will bring much trouble.

Note. The oracle may refer to a high ancestor of the Shang dynasty.

- *Fifth line, 6*  57

  a) *Mildew for a deceased male ancestor.
  Use a* yu *incantation-sacrifice.*

  b) *Rectifying the father's corruption.
  One meets with praise.*

### Commentary

Correcting the corruption of moral values caused by the deceased father. One thereby meets with praise. This is an undertaking in accord with the way of virtue.

*Note.* Yu *means speech. The sacrifice includes an incantation expressing praise.*

- *Top line, 9*  46

  a) *Serving neither king or lord,
  but preferring one's own work.*

  b) *Not serving king or lord,
  one sets oneself higher goals.*

### Commentary

One does not serve king or lord. The intention is right and proper. Instead of serving worldly goals, one chooses for higher, spiritual goals. One's aspiration serves as a model for others.

## • *Summary*

Wind below the Mountain, means wind blowing strongly at the foot of the mountain, which may lead to erosion, indicating a situation of decay.

In this hexagram decay is represented as mildew in an offering pot to the ancestors, meaning a deterioration of moral values of those who are deceased.

This hexagram is about moral deterioration of values of the mother or father. The descendants have to assume responsibility for their actions and correct them. Great success. It is beneficial to go on a journey.

Every situation of decay may again change into some new beginning. In this case, three days before a new beginning or change, and three days after that beginning or change (occurring at the fourth day after this consultation of the *Yi Jing*), are regarded as auspicious. (See also hexagram 57, line 5.)

Hexagram 18, Decay, Mildew, is about the mistakes of the past, and it follows hexagram 17, Following, Pursuit, because it is about the result of choices made in hexagram 17.

The process of decay and deterioration is described in different stages:

In the first line the presence of a son who will correct the mistakes of the father will bring good fortune.

In the second line, in correcting the mistakes of the mother, one should not be too determined, but follow a middle path.

In the third line, taking responsibility for the mistakes of the father will involve some regret, but no great blame.

In the fourth line, tolerating the mistakes of the father will bring distress and humiliation.

In the fifth line, correcting the mistakes of the father will bring us praise.

In the sixth line one does not serve authority, but chooses to go one's own way. One chooses to aspire for higher (spiritual) goals instead of worldly goals.

# 19. *Lin* / Approaching, Wailing

*kun* / earth, receptive, *yin*, passive, female

*dui* / lake, still water, pool, marsh, joy, pleasing

- *Image*

    Lake below Earth.
    A lake under the earth: Approaching.
    A noble person, [approaching the people,]
    teaches and cares
    and generously supports the people without end.

- *Judgment*

    a) Great offering.
    Favourable augury.
    When the eighth month arrives, misfortune.

    b) Sublime accomplishment.
    Benefit in perseverance
    but in the eighth month there will be misfortune.

*Commentary*

Joyous (Lake) and compliant (Earth): Approaching. The firm enters and grows strong (the two whole lines).
Sublime accomplishment is achieved by being upright. This is the way of Heaven. Perseverance is beneficial. But by the eighth moon there will be misfortune. Decline is not slow in coming.

*Note.* The name of the hexagram is Wailing, in the sense of ceremonial or funeral wailing. In China this kind of wailing has always been dramatically noisy.

In China the first month begins on the day of the new moon (New Year's day) which occurs between 21 January and 20 February, so the eighth new moon will fall in the month of August or September.

The statement about misfortune coming by the eighth moon has to do with the trigram Lake or the season of fall (autumn) when everything in nature starts to decline.

- ***Base line, 9***

    a) *Tears of wailing.*
       *Augury auspicious.*

    b) *Approaching together.*
       *Determination brings good fortune.*

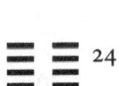

*Commentary*

One approaches with a companion (second line).
*Determination brings good fortune:* one's goal is pursued with rectitude.

- ***Second line, 9***

    a) *Salty tears of wailing.*
       *Auspicious.*
       *Unfavourable for nothing.*

    b) *Approaching together.*
       *Good fortune.*
       *There is nothing not beneficial.*

*Commentary*

One approaches with a companion (base line). Good fortune.
There is nothing not beneficial, but there is still some disobedience, because one is not compliant with orders from above.

- ***Third line, 6***

    a) *Sweet tears of wailing.*
       *Favourable for nothing.*
       *Being grieved: no misfortune.*

    b) *A pleasing approach.*
       *There will be nothing beneficial.*
       *But if one is concerned, there will be no trouble.*

*Commentary*

*A pleasing approach:* there will be nothing beneficial. But being concerned there will not be much trouble.

- ***Fourth line, 6***

    a) *Excessive wailing.*
       *No misfortune.*

    b) *A perfect approach.*
       *No trouble.*

*Commentary*

A perfect way of approaching. One's position is appropriate. No misfortune.

- *Fifth line, 6*  60

 a) Restrained wailing.
 A great ruler's yi sacrifice
 to the spirit of the soil.
 Auspicious.

 b) A wise approach, such as befits a great lord.
 Good fortune.

*Commentary*

Approaching wisely is appropriate for a great ruler. This means that he practices the middle way. Good fortune.

Note. The yi sacrifice was made to the spirit of the soil. It was possibly done when an army went on a campaign, and the drums were smeared with sacrificial blood.

- *Top line, 6*  41

 a) Unrestrained wailing.
 Auspicious.
 No misfortune.

 b) A generous approach.
 Good fortune.
 No trouble.

*Commentary*

A great-hearted approach has good fortune. One's intention to approach people is directed from within. No trouble.

## • *Summary*

Lake below Earth. Lake under the earth, means the earth moves down into the lake, symbolising approach. Sublime accomplishment. Perseverance will be beneficial, but when the eighth month comes, there will be misfortune.

The story of this hexagram is about wailing at a funeral ceremony in which the process of approaching (someone or something) is expressed. Often funeral ceremonies are occasions of meeting and approaching one another.

Wailing at a funeral ceremony (hexagram 19), and approaching each other, is directly related to hexagram 18, Decay (about corruption of the virtues of the ancestors), because at the funeral people may discuss the past of the deceased. After a situation of decay, wailing follows.

This hexagram is about approaching someone or something in six stages:

In the first line approaching with a companion is done in a correct way. Determination brings good fortune.

In the second line, one is approaching with a companion. Good fortune. There is nothing not beneficial. There will still be some disobedience.

In the third line, although the approach is pleasing, it is not correct. Nothing beneficial. But if one is concerned about it, there will not be much trouble.

In the fourth line the approach is perfect. No misfortune.

In the fifth line there is a wise approach, in accordance with the middle way. Good fortune.

In the sixth line there is a great-hearted and spontaneous approach. Good fortune. No trouble.

# 20. *Guan* / Observing, Contemplation

*xun* / wind, gentle, penetrating

*kun* / earth, receptive, *yin*, passive, female

- *Image*

    Wind above Earth.
    Wind blows over the earth: Observation.
    Kings inspected the regions,
    observed the people, and gave instructions.

- *Judgment*

    a) Ceremonial pouring is done, but not the offering.
    There will be captives with heads held high.

    b) The ceremonial washing has been made
    but not the offering.
    There is sincerity evoking respect.

*Commentary*

Receptivity (Earth) and gentleness (Wind). Great observation resides above showing compliance (Earth) and gentleness (Wind). Central and correct, viewing the whole world.
The ablution has been made, but not yet the offering. Those below are observing the ritual and are transformed.

Observing Heaven's way (*Dao*), the four seasons never vary. By contemplating the Way (*Dao*) the sages establish their teachings, and all under heaven submit.

Note. Guan *means 'pouring of a liquid' during an offering.*

- ***Base line, 6***

    A child's view.
    For petty men: no misfortune.
    For the noble person: distress.

*Commentary*

'A child's view' means having a childish view. This is the way of petty men not worthy of a noble person. Distress.

- ***Second line, 6***

    a) Peeping.
    Favourable augury for a maiden.

    b) Observing secretly.
    Beneficial for a maiden's perseverance.

*Commentary*

This secret watching can be beneficial for a persevering young woman.

Note. *'Peeping' may be a reference to brief sighting through a narrow opening of a future spouse during marriage arrangements.*

- **Third line, 6**

    a) *Observing our victims
    advance or withdraw.*

    b) *Contemplating one's own life
    whether to advance or retreat.*

    *Commentary*

Observing one's own life, one can choose to advance or retreat, in order not to lose the Way.

- **Fourth line, 6**

    *Observing the glory of the state.
    It will be favourable to be the king's guest.*

    *Commentary*

One's view is extended to the nation's splendour.
One decides to become the ruler's guest after having found the ruler worthy to be instructed.

- **Fifth line, 9**

    a) *Observing their victims.
    No misfortune for a noble person.*

    b) *Observing other people's lives.
    No blame for a noble person.*

*Commentary*

The ruler observes the lives of the people for he is the master of (moral) transformation.
If the people commit crimes, the fault for them shall reside with this ruler himself. Thus he observes the customs of the people in order to find how well they are practising the Way (*Dao*). No blame.

- ***Top line, 9***

    a) *Observing our victims.*
       *No misfortune for a noble person.*

    b) *Contemplating one's own life.*
       *No blame for a noble person.*

*Commentary*

Contemplating his own life, he does not slacken his intentions, because his aspiration has not yet been realised.

- ***Summary***

Wind above Earth. The wind blows over the earth or a bird flies over the land symbolising observing, viewing, overlooking, contemplation. Preparation has been done, but not the actual work (sacrifice, offering). Sincerity will bring respect.

The story of the hexagram is about kings making tours of inspection, and establishing their instructions in conformity with their observation of the people.

In hexagram 19 the main idea was of approaching others – according to the old story – during a funeral ceremony gathering. In approaching other people one generally looks, observes, views (hexagram 20) how they act, and thus may find out how to instruct them.

This hexagram is about observing, watching, looking over, and contemplation in six stages:

The first line tells about a childish view that is not worthy of a noble person. Distress.

In the second line a secret watch may be beneficial for a persevering young woman, but it will still involve some shame.

In the third line one contemplates one's own life to decide whether to advance or retreat, in order not to lose the Way.

In the fourth line one observes someone's life or actions to decide whether it is worthwhile to instruct him.

In the fifth line one observes, watches over other people's lives to inspire and transform them. No blame.

In the sixth line one contemplates one's own life in order to continue the practice of the Way (*Dao*), because one has not realised it yet. No blame.

Hexagram 20 is also about a method of meditation (observation of whatever appears in consciousness) related to the Daoist and Buddhist tradition.

# 21. *Shi Ke* / Biting and Chewing, The Law

*li* / fire, lightning, brightness, clinging

*zhen* / thunder, shock, moving, growth

## • Image

*Thunder below Fire.*
*Thunder and lightning: Biting and Chewing, The Law.*
*Kings proclaimed laws and executed punishments.*

## • Judgment

*a) Offering.*
*Favourable to call upon the law.*

*b) Success.*
*Beneficial for legal matters.*

### Commentary

Movement (Thunder) and brightness (Fire, lightning) unite in one pattern. Strong and weak are equally divided (whole and broken lines).
The hexagram is shaped like an open mouth. Something between the jaws symbolises biting (through) and chewing. Biting through means success. This hexagram is favourable for legal matters.

- *Base line, 9* 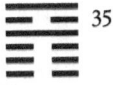 35

   *Wearing foot shackles
   and cutting off the toes.
   No misfortune.*

   *Commentary*

Wearing stocks on the feet and thereby mutilating the toes. This means that one cannot go further. One is prevented from transgressing the law.

- *Second line, 6*  38

   *Biting into the flesh
   and cutting off the nose.
   No misfortune.*

   *Commentary*

Biting through the flesh and thereby mutilating the nose. This means that one executes punishment by relying on strength and harsh measures in order to restrain criminals. No misfortune.

- *Third line, 6* 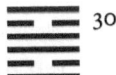 30

   *Biting into dried meat and finding poison.
   Little distress.
   No misfortune.*

   *Commentary*

One's position is not appropriate (a weak line in a strong place). Here the law falls short of what justice demands, but it does not have great consequences. No misfortune.

- **Fourth line, 9**                                   ䷚ 27

   a) *Biting dried meat to the bone*
      *and finding a metal arrowhead in it.*
      *Favourable in hardship.*
      *Augury auspicious.*

   b) *Biting into dried bony meat*
      *and finding a metal arrowpoint in it.*
      *Advantageous in the face of difficulties.*
      *Determination brings good fortune.*

*Commentary*

One will benefit from determination when encountering hardship (in establishing laws). This will bring good fortune, but it is not manifesting yet.

- **Fifth line, 6**

   a) *Biting dried meat*
      *and finding yellow metal in it.*
      *Augury: danger.*
      *No misfortune.*

   b) *Biting into dried meat*
      *and finding a piece of yellow metal in it.*
      *Determination is dangerous,*
      *but there will be no trouble.*

*Commentary*

Determination is dangerous (a weak line in a strong place), but there will be no misfortune. Even if there are hindrances (in establishing the law), there will be no trouble.

- *Top line, 9*

    Shouldering a cangue
    and cutting off the ears.
    Disaster.

*Commentary*

Bearing a cangue on the shoulders and thereby mutilating one's ears. This means that one is not hearing clearly and attentively. This portrays someone who pays no heed to the evil he has done. This behaviour requires severe punishment.

*Note. The cangue was a heavy plank of wood with a hole through which the neck of a criminal stuck. He could walk only if he could bear the weight of the plank with his hands.*

- *Summary*

Thunder below Fire. Thunder and lightning (both movement) symbolise biting through and chewing.
  The hexagram is shaped like an open mouth (the *yang* lines are the lips and the *yin* lines the teeth) with an obstacle in it (a piece of wood, the *yang* line in the fourth position). The obstacle is difficult to move (lower inner trigram, Mountain). One must chew forcefully to get nourishment. Success. This hexagram is favourable for legal matters.
  After keeping watch (hexagram 20, Observing) over the people in the different regions, the kings set up rules and established laws (hexagram 21 The Law).
  The story of this hexagram is about establishing the law or legal matters in six stages:
  In the first line one is prevented from transgressing the law. No misfortune.
  In the second line the law is established with force and harsh measures. No misfortune.

In the third line the law is failing, but this does not have much consequence. No misfortune.

In the fourth line, remaining determined in spite of obstructions (in establishing the law) will bring good fortune, but it is not manifesting yet.

In the fifth line, dealing with obstructions (while establishing the law) is dangerous, but it will bring no trouble.

In the sixth line, someone who does not heed the warnings (not hearing clearly and not paying attention), will be punished severely.

## 22. *Bi* / Beautifying, Adornment

*gen* / mountain, standing still, stilling, stopping

*li* / fire, light, brightness, clinging

- *Image*

    Fire below Mountain.
    Fire at the foot of the mountain: Adornment.
    A noble person clearly understands
    the different aspects of governance,
    and does not lightly pass criminal judgments.

- *Judgment*

    a) *Offering.*
    Somewhat favourable in having somewhere to go.

    b) *Success.*
    Moderately beneficial to undertake something.

*Commentary*

Brightness (Fire) and stopping (Mountain) are the patterns of noble men. Generally the strong and the weak (lines) alternate, and form a pattern. This is the pattern of heaven. By observing the patterns of heaven the course of time is calculated. By observing the patterns of man society can be transformed. Some advantage can be gained from going somewhere or undertaking something. But if there is some difficulty, then it is *not* advantageous to seek that destination or goal.

- *Base line, 9*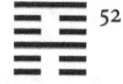

  Adorned are his feet.
  He discards the carriage and walks.

### Commentary

*He discards the carriage and walks*: one casts aside an unrighteous opportunity in pursuit of one's goal.

- *Second line, 6*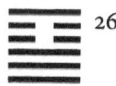

  He adorns his beard.

### Commentary

*He adorns his beard*: a superficial beautification to adjust either to one's superior or to society.

- *Third line, 9*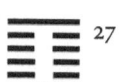

  Appearing clad
  with adornments and lustre.
  Long-term augury: auspicious.

### Commentary

The third line, being a strong line in the right place, makes adornment appropriate. A long-term perseverance brings good fortune.

- **Fourth line, 6** 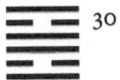 30

    Appearing clad with adornments,
    looking fair on white plumed horses.
    Not bandits, but fetching a bride.

    *Commentary*

Their appearance is elegant, but leaves doubt.
*Not bandits, but fetching a bride*: what causes delay and hesitation is not an obstacle, but a matter of betrothal. Ultimately there will be no blame.

- **Fifth line, 6**  37

    Adorned [one strolls] in the hill garden.
    The roll of silk is small and slight.
    Distress, but in the end auspicious.

    *Commentary*

The gift or offering is inadequate. This gives rise to disgrace.
Although this is a weak position (a *yin* line in a strong place), there will be good fortune in the end.

*Note. Chinese gardens were symbols of adornment, usually found in higher social classes.*

- **Top line, 9** 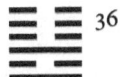 36

    Adorned in white.
    No misfortune.

*Commentary*

Adorned with simplicity. No misfortune. This represents one who has fulfilled his intentions or goals.

## • *Summary*

Fire below Mountain means fire at the foot of the mountain, symbolising beautification, adornment, decoration, elegance, and gracefulness. The sun (Fire) is shining at the foot of the mountain, beautifying the scenery, but it is twilight and evening is near. Adornment – which is, generally, superficial beautification – is not about essential things.

Success. It is somewhat favourable to go somewhere or undertake something. Advantage can be gained from having a particular goal or destination, but if some difficulty is encountered in its pursuit, it will *not* be advantageous to seek that goal or destination.

After proclaiming laws and executing punishments (hexagram 21), the noble person, desiring to ensure the good functioning of the state, tries to bring society to perfection through adornment and beautification (hexagram 22).

In this hexagram adornment or beautification is described in six aspects:

In the first line one refuses to take an unrighteous opportunity in pursuit of one's goal.

In the second line beautification or adornment is done to conform to others.

In the third line adornment is appropriate. Prolonged persistence will bring good fortune

In the fourth line adornment gives rise to some doubt or suspicion but ultimately there is no blame. A matter of betrothal causes delay or hesitation.

In the fifth line adornment and beautification are not adequate enough. Here one encounters a setback or disgrace, due to one's own fault. Distress is ultimately followed by good fortune.

In the sixth line simple adornment indicates fulfilment of one's goal. No misfortune.

## 23. *Bo* / Stripping Away, Flaying

 gen / mountain, standing still, stilling, stopping

kun / earth, receptive, *yin*, passive, female

- **Image**

    Mountain above Earth.
    A mountain standing on the earth: Stripping Away.
    A noble person maintains peace in the state
    by generosity to those below.

- **Judgment**

    a) Not favourable in having somewhere to go.

    b) Not beneficial to undertake something.

*Commentary*

Compliant (Earth) and stopping (Mountain), means watching the omens involving one's position.
The weak are trying to change the strong (top line). It is not beneficial to go somewhere or undertake something: petty men are increasing.
One treats those below with generosity to avoid having one's position being 'stripped away'.
The noble person observes the ebbing and flowing, waxing and waning of things, for this is the course of Heaven.

- **Base line, 6**  27

    a) Flaying a ewe, starting at the legs.
       Augury for casting out: ominous.

    b) Stripping the bed of its legs.
       Expelling with determination brings disaster.

               *Commentary*

Flaying a ewe (sheep), starting at the legs: those below are removed. Determination brings disaster.

- **Second line, 6**  4

    a) Flaying a ewe, starting at the knees.
       Augury for casting out: ominous.

    b) Stripping the bed of its frame.
       Expelling with determination brings disaster.

               *Commentary*

Flaying a ewe (sheep), starting at the knees: losing one's associates (friends). Determination brings disaster.

- **Third line, 6**  52

    Flaying [the shanks].
    No misfortune.

               *Commentary*

Flaying [the shanks]: losing contact with those above and below. No misfortune.

- **Fourth line, 6**

    a) *Flaying a ewe, starting with the skin.*
    *Ominous.*

    b) *Stripping the bed to the mattress.*
    *Disaster.*

    *Commentary*

Flaying a ewe (sheep), starting with the skin: disaster is impending. One is close to a terrible misfortune, which may not manifest *if* one takes the proper precautions.

- **Fifth line, 6**

    *Like a string of fish,*
    *palace concubines are favoured.*
    *Unfavourable for nothing.*

    *Commentary*

Palace concubines are favoured: giving favours to those below will not threaten one's position. Unfavourable for nothing.

Note. Dried fish were strung together, symbolising the palace women who were called to the king in prescribed order.

- **Top line, 9**

    *A large [ripe] fruit not eaten.*
    *A noble person gets a carriage.*
    *The petty man loses a hut.*

*Commentary*

*A large [ripe] fruit not eaten:* given favours are not accepted, or opportunities are not taken.
*The noble person gets a carriage:* he is supported by the people.
*The petty man loses a hut:* he ends up as useless.

## • *Summary*

Mountain above Earth. A mountain standing alone on the earth can be worn down by erosion and earthquakes and therefore symbolises flaying, skinning, stripping away or peeling off.

It is not beneficial to go somewhere or undertake something: petty men are increasing.

The story of this hexagram is about the flaying of a ewe (female sheep) or stripping a bed, symbolising the removal of hindrances or hinderers who are severely criticising and threatening one's position.

Here is someone who is sitting on a bed (seat, position) surrounded by petty men, who he removes one after the other.

After adornment and beautification of the government by the kings or rulers (hexagram 22) follows stripping away (hexagram 23), because when the position of the leader is threatened by petty men, he removes them one after the other.

In this hexagram stripping away is done in different stages:

In the first line one starts to remove one's subordinates. Expelling them with determination brings disaster.

In the second line one loses associates or friends. Expelling them with determination brings disaster.

In the third line one loses contact with those above and below. No misfortune.

In the fourth line a terrible misfortune comes very close, but will not manifest *if* one takes the proper precautions.

In the fifth line one allows favours to women ('of the palace') in order to secure one's position. There is nothing for which this (giving favours) is not favourable.

In the sixth line an opportunity is not taken. If one is a noble person, one attains the support of others. If one is a petty man, one is found useless for anything.

## 24. *Fu* / Return, The Turning Point

*kun* / earth, receptive, *yin*, passive, female

*zhen* / thunder, shock, moving, growth

### • *Image*

*Thunder below Earth.*
*Thunder rumbles within the earth: Return.*
*Kings closed the border passes at the winter solstice,*
*merchants and strangers did not travel,*
*lords did not visit (inspect) their territories.*

Note. The solstices were times for sacrifices. The winter solstice has been celebrated as the resting time of the year. In China it has been the practice for people to return to their homes for celebration of the great yearly festivals. Return in this sense is highly auspicious.

### • *Judgment*

*Offering.*
*In going out and coming in there will be no harm.*
*A friend (or friends) will come.*
*No misfortune.*
*He will turn around and go back on his way.*
*He will return in seven days.*
*Favourable for having somewhere to go.*

*Commentary*

Success. Moving (Thunder) and compliant (Earth). The strong (*yang* line) returns at the bottom of the hexagram. The strong is increasing. The waxing cycle of *yang* is symbolised by the dynamic course of heaven. In this action the heavenly *yang* principle brings about the renewal of life on earth.
In going out and coming in there will be no misfortune. A friend (or friends) will arrive without misfortune.
Going back to the way and returning in seven days. 'Return' also means a return to the Way (*Dao*). It will be beneficial to go somewhere or undertake something.

*Note.* 'Seven days' is a general expression of a period that does not last too long. In the Yi Jing *is also mentioned a period of 'three days', which can be considered short, and a period of 'ten days', which can be considered long.*

- ***Base line, 9***

    *Returning from not far away.*
    *No harm or trouble.*
    *Very auspicious.*

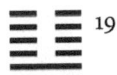

*Commentary*

One returns before having gone (too) far. This is a means for cultivating self-discipline. There will be no harm or trouble. Very good fortune.

- ***Second line, 6***

    *An easy return.*
    *Auspicious.*

*Commentary*

The good fortune of an easy return is the result of one's benevolence (acting helpful or friendly). Good fortune.

## • *Third line, 6*

a) *Returning along the riverbank.*
   *Danger.*
   *No misfortune.*

b) *Turning back frequently.*
   *There will be danger.*
   *No trouble.*

*Commentary*

Making repeated returns is dangerous, but as one does not get confused there will be no misfortune (trouble).

## • *Fourth line, 6*

a) *Returning alone in the middle of the way.*

b) *Walking a middle course, returning alone.*

*Commentary*

Travelling with others, one walks the middle path and returns alone. This means one follows the Way (*Dao*), and this sometimes implies that one has to leave companions behind who are leading one astray.

- *Fifth line, 6*

    *Returning for a purpose.*
    *No trouble.*

    #### Commentary

    A purposeful return brings no trouble. One uses self-examination to reflect on one's deeds in relation to the Way.

- *Top line, 6*

    *Returning and losing the way: ominous.*
    *There will be disaster and calamity.*
    *If the army is set in motion,*
    *in the end there will be a great defeat.*
    *For the ruler of the state: ominous.*
    *For ten years it is not possible to put things right.*

    #### Commentary

    Returning and losing the way: disaster and calamity. If the army is set in motion, there will be a great defeat. Disaster is about to overtake the ruler and for ten years it will not be possible to put things right. This is because the way of the noble person, or the *Dao*, is violated.

- *Summary*

Thunder below Earth. Thunder rumbles in the earth, symbolising Return. What seems cold outside (Earth), is strong and energetic (Thunder) inside.

The first (*yang*) line is moving into a mainly *yin* hexagram (five lines). The *yang* principle brings about the renewal of life on earth. In going out and coming back there will be no misfortune. Friend(s) arrive without misfortune. Someone will turn around and come back in seven days.

When going somewhere or undertaking something, it will be beneficial to have a goal or destination in view.

The story of this hexagram is about the return of people to their homes to celebrate yearly festivals. It is also about the return to the Way (*Dao*).

Hexagram 23, Flaying, is followed by hexagram 24, Return, because in hexagram 23 the position of the leader was attacked, and thus in hexagram 24 the leader closed the border passes and abstained from visiting territories to prevent his position being undermined.

In this hexagram returning is expressed in six stages:

In the first line returning to the Way begins with self-discipline. Very good fortune.

In the second line return to the Way is expressed as friendly and helpful behaviour. Good fortune.

In the third line returning to the Way is affected by confusion. Frequent returns. No trouble.

In the fourth line we leave companions behind because they lead us astray from the Way.

In the fifth line return to the Way is attained through self-examination. Someone may return for a good reason. No trouble.

In the sixth line there is a deviation from the Way which will result in disaster and calamity. Disaster for a leader, and for ten years it will not be possible to put things right. If the people are mobilised, there will be a great defeat.

# 25. *Wu Wang* / The Unexpected

*qian* / heaven, creative, power, *yang*, active, male

*zhen* / thunder, shock, moving, growth

- ## *Image*

    Thunder below Heaven.
    Thunder roars in the sky: The Unexpected.
    Kings brought about prosperity,
    stimulating the growth of all things
    in accordance with the seasons [time].

- ## *Judgment*

    a) Great offering.
    Favourable augury.
    If it is not correct, there will be calamity.
    Not favourable for having somewhere to go.

    b) Sublime accomplishment.
    Benefit in perseverance.
    If one is not upright, there will be disaster.
    Not beneficial to undertake something.

### Commentary

Movement (Thunder) and strength (Heaven) are joined. Strength comes from outside (upper trigram) and effects a shock within (lower trigram) causing something unexpected.

Being upright (integrity), is in accordance with heaven's decrees. Sublime accomplishment. Perseverance is beneficial.
*If one is not upright, there will be disaster:* how can one go forward without heaven's blessing? Then it will not be beneficial to go somewhere or undertake something.

## • *Base line, 9*

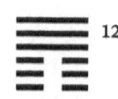

*Going unexpectedly.*
*Auspicious.*

#### Commentary

*Going unexpectedly:* one's aims are realised. Good fortune.

## • *Second line, 6*

*Not ploughing, yet reaping a harvest.*
*Not breaking the ground,*
*yet tilling ripe fields.*
*Favourable for having somewhere to go.*

#### Commentary

*Not ploughing, yet reaping a harvest:* doing something without expectation or anticipation.
It will be beneficial to go somewhere or undertake something, because one either has good results for little effort, or success because of good luck.

## • *Third line, 6*

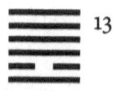

*An unexpected disaster.*
*Someone tied up an ox.*

*It is the traveller's gain,
but the townsman's disaster.*

#### Commentary

The traveller takes the ox, and therefore it is an unexpected disaster for the townsman. Someone gains something at the cost of others.

- ***Fourth line, 9***

   a) *Augury is possible
   No misfortune.*

   b) *One can be persisting.
   No trouble.*

#### Commentary

If one keeps firm (fourth *yang* line as part of the upper trigram Heaven) and persists, there will be no trouble.

- ***Fifth line, 9***

   *An unexpected illness.
   Don't treat with medicine.
   Then there will be joy.*

#### Commentary

For this illness medicine should not be given.
Do not do anything against the unexpected; this will bring happiness.

- *Top line, 9*  17

    An unexpected journey.
    There will be a calamity.
    There is nothing for which this is favourable.

    *Commentary*

If one were to undertake an unexpected journey, one meets with calamity caused by exhaustion.

- *Summary*

Thunder below Heaven. Thunder roars in the sky, symbolising the unexpected. Movement (Thunder) and power (Heaven) are joined. Sublime accomplishment. Perseverance is beneficial.

Integrity, being upright, is in accordance with heaven's decrees. *If* one is not upright, there will be disaster. Then it will not be beneficial to go somewhere or undertake something.

The story of this hexagram is about things and events happening unexpectedly.

In hexagram 24 the ruler closed the border passes to prevent his position being undermined. In hexagram 25 the ruler brings prosperity to the people to prevent losing the mandate from heaven. In ancient China the idea was that the emperors only could remain in power with the mandate from heaven. If they did not govern correctly, they may lose this mandate and their position.

In this hexagram the unexpected manifests in different kinds of events:

In the first line, going somewhere or doing something unexpectedly, will fulfil one's aims. Good fortune.

In the second line, doing something without anticipation – and thus without expectation – will bring good fortune. It will be beneficial to go somewhere or undertake something, because one has either good results with little effort, or success due to good luck. But one should not expect to become rich soon.

In the third line someone gains something unexpectedly at the cost of others. An unexpected disaster.

In the fourth line the unexpected can be dealt with if one keeps firm and persists. Then there will be no trouble.

In the fifth line nothing should be done against the unexpected. Then there will be happiness.

In the sixth line an unexpected journey will lead to exhaustion. Nothing is favourable.

# 26. *Da Chu* / Great Cultivation

*gen* / mountain, standing still, stilling, stopping

*qian* / heaven, creative, power, *yang*, active, male

- ## *Image*

    Heaven below Mountain.
    Heaven's power within a mountain: Great Cultivation.
    A noble person acquires knowledge
    of what has been said and done by sages of the past
    in order to cultivate his virtue.

- ## *Judgment*

    a) Favourable augury.
       Auspicious for not eating at home.
       Favourable to cross the great river.

    b) Determination will be beneficial.
       Not having meals at home brings good fortune.
       Beneficial to go on a journey.

### Commentary

Firm (Mountain) and strong (Heaven), sincere and true, the noble person gloriously renews his virtue with each new day. By restraint (Mountain) in the use of power (Heaven), one is able to cultivate oneself. Determination will be beneficial.

*Not having meals at home brings good fortune:* being strong at the top (the top line, a sage), one nurtures those worthy of his knowledge. It is beneficial to go on a journey, because one is in resonance with heaven.

### • *Base line, 9*

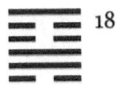

*Danger.*
*It will be favourable to stop.*

Commentary

There is danger. It is beneficial to stop. One should desist because advancing will bring misfortune.

### • *Second line, 9*

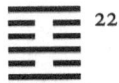

*A carriage loses its axle.*

Commentary

The carriage loses its axle (a whole line in an incorrect position). If one abides in the Mean while facing difficulties, there will be no blame.

### • *Third line, 9*

a) *A fine horse is following.*
  *Favourable augury in hardship.*
  *Forming a barricade of carts for protection.*
  *Favourable for having somewhere to go.*

b) *Good horses are chasing each other.*
  *Beneficial to be determined in the face of difficulty.*

*Practise chariot driving for defence.*
*Beneficial to undertake something.*

*Commentary*

Though there is danger and difficulty, with determination and defensive measures, there will be no harm. It is beneficial to go somewhere or undertake something.

### • Fourth line, 6

*A horn-protecting board for a calf.*
*Very auspicious.*

*Commentary*

Because danger and disaster have been prevented (a 'horn-protecting board'), there will be happiness. If someone has not yet attained his full strength (a calf), it is better to restrain oneself. Very good fortune.

Note. A horn-protecting board was bound across a calf's budding horns to show that it was meant as a sacrificial animal, and also to protect the horns from causing injury.

### • Fifth line, 6

*Tusks of a castrated boar.*
*Auspicious.*

*Commentary*

Tusks of a castrated boar means that there will be blessings. The good fortune that is associated with this line indicates great joy.

- *Top line, 9*

  a) Receiving heaven's blessing.
  Offering.

  b) Blessed by heaven.
  Success.

*Commentary*

*Blessed by heaven*: one moves forward along the way of the *Dao*.

- *Summary*

Heaven below Mountain, means heaven's power within the mountain symbolising the storing of great internal strength and knowledge for a vast undertaking. This implies a successful future. Determination will be beneficial. Nurturing the worthy will bring good fortune.

Heaven below Mountain also indicates the sky amidst mountain peaks pointing to something far off. It is beneficial to go on a journey.

This hexagram is about a noble person or sage, cultivating his virtue. Going on a journey, he is trying to share his knowledge with others.

Hexagram 9 is about the cultivation of virtues: how to deal with others to have a harmonious relationship in society. Hexagram 26 is about the cultivation of higher virtues, based on the knowledge and actions of the wise men of the past.

In hexagram 25 the leader brings prosperity to the people in order to secure his mandate from heaven. In hexagram 26 the leader nourishes his virtue with the words and conduct of the wise men of the past, and attempts to bring the cultivation of higher virtues to the people.

In the first line a danger is threatening. Advance will bring misfortune.

In the second line there is trouble, but if the noble person stays with the Mean while facing difficulties, there will be no blame.

In the third line, the noble person, being in difficulties, will not encounter harm if he stays determined, and defends himself. When going somewhere or undertaking something, it is beneficial to have a goal or destination in view.

In the fourth line there is happiness, because danger and disaster have been prevented. Very good fortune.

In the fifth line there is unsought or unexpected good fortune (blessings). This will bring great joy.

In the sixth line, the noble person, free of obstructions, moves forward on the way of the *Dao*. 'Heaven's blessings' means that he receives help as a matter of course, *if* he remains in the *Dao*.

# 27. Yi / Nourishing, Jaws

 gen / mountain, standing still, stilling, stopping

zhen / thunder, shock, moving, growth

- *Image*

    Thunder below Mountain.
    Thunder rumbles at the foot of the mountain: Nourishing.
    The noble person is careful with his speech
    and moderate in eating and drinking.

- *Judgment*

    a) Augury: auspicious.
       Observe the jaws.
       Seek something to fill your own mouth.

    b) Perseverance brings good fortune.
       Consider the mouth.
       Look for your own proper nourishment.

*Commentary*

Movement (Thunder) and stillness (Mountain) are combined in Jaws (the hexagram portrays an open mouth): Nourishment.
As heaven and earth nurture the ten thousand beings, so the sages nurture the worthy, and through them all the people are nourished.

Considering right nourishment, and persevering herein, brings good fortune. Observe the nourishing of others, and observe how you nourish yourself. The timely occurrence of nourishment is of great importance.

• ***Base line, 9***

   a) *Abandoning your sacred turtle
   and watching with drooping jaws.
   Ominous.*

   b) *Losing your spiritual tortoise
   and observing with open jaws.
   Disaster.*

*Commentary*

The sacred tortoise was considered to be possessed of supernatural powers living on air and not needing earthly nourishment.
Here it symbolises someone abandoning his spirituality (spiritual duty) out of greed or desire. Being envious of how and what another provides for his nourishment, he leaves his freedom and independency. This behaviour (greed, envy) is a deviation from the right path (*Dao*), and will therefore result in disaster.

• ***Second line, 6***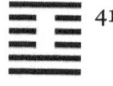

   a) *Filling the jaws,
   he scrapes his shanks on the hill.
   Ominous for an attack.*

   b) *Seeking nourishment,
   he is hurt on the path up the hill.
   Advancing brings disaster.*

*Commentary*

*He scrapes his shanks on the hill*: someone who seeks (spiritual) nourishment and thereby leaving others, is hurt in his attempt, because he lacks any genuine desire for (spiritual) knowledge. To continue to do so brings misfortune (disaster).

- *Third line, 6*

    a) Scraping the jaws.
       Augury: ominous.
       Do not act for ten years.
       There is nothing for which this is favourable.

    b) Disregarding nourishment.
       Perseverance brings disaster.
       Do not take action for ten years.
       There is nothing for which this is beneficial.

*Commentary*

One does not take action for a long period, because one has disregarded one's (spiritual) nourishment in such a manner, that thereby the right way (*Dao*) is violated. Persevering herein brings disaster.

- *Fourth line, 6*

    a) Filling the jaws.
       Auspicious.
       The tiger is staring fiercely with great desire.
       No misfortune.

    b) Seeking nourishment.
       Good fortune.

*Gazing intently like a tiger with a strong appetite.
There will be no misfortune.*

#### Commentary

Here the person is qualified and eager for (spiritual) nourishment, and attains the fruit of his endeavour. Good fortune. There will be no misfortune.

### • Fifth line, 6

a) *He scrapes his shanks.
Auspicious augury for a dwelling
One cannot cross the great river.*

b) *He is hurt.
Persisting to abide in a dwelling brings good fortune
One should not go on a journey.*

#### Commentary

*Auspicious augury for a dwelling:* someone who seeks (spiritual) nourishment should stay where he is, and follow the one above (his superior) willingly.

### • Top line, 9

a) *Drawing out the jaws.
Danger.
Auspicious.
Favourable to cross the great river.*

b) *Depending on nourishment.
Danger is threatening, but there will be good fortune.
Beneficial to go on a journey.*

*Commentary*

Dependent on (spiritual) nourishment, one is aware of the dangers of the (spiritual) path. There will still be good fortune. This good fortune may come in the form of blessings.
*Favourable to cross the great river:* usually it is advisable to go on a journey but in this line it is specifically about the attainment of a (spiritual) goal.

## • *Summary*

Thunder below Mountain means thunder rumbles at the foot of the mountain. This symbolises nourishment, because it will soon rain and nourish the earth.

The hexagram also portrays an open mouth (jaws) with the broken lines as the teeth. The upper jaw (Mountain) is still, and the lower jaw (Thunder) is moving.

It also symbolises speech. The noble person is careful with his speech, and moderate in eating and drinking. Perseverance brings good fortune.

This hexagram Jaws is about nourishment of oneself (eating and drinking) and of others (speech).

In hexagram 26 the noble person (the ruler) is trying to teach higher virtues of the wise men of the past to the people. In hexagram 27 the noble person encounters persons seeking spiritual nourishment of different qualities.

This hexagram is about seeking spiritual nourishment in various stages, and points to certain qualities such as interest, worthiness, readiness, obedience and awareness.

In the first line, the person seeking spiritual nourishment is not really worthy of it, because he chooses the material above the spiritual. This will lead to disaster.

In the second line, the person seeking spiritual nourishment is not yet ready. To continue brings misfortune (disaster).

In the third line, the person turns away from spiritual nourishment for a long time ('ten years'). Perseverance brings disaster.

In the fourth line, the person seeking spiritual nourishment is ready and eager, and attains the fruit of his endeavour. Good fortune. There will be no misfortune

In the fifth line, the person seeking spiritual nourishment should stay where he is and follow his superior (teacher). Good fortune.

In the sixth line, the spiritual seeker, being aware of the dangers of the (spiritual) path, will attain his goal in the form of blessings. It is advisable to go on a (spiritual) journey.

# 28. *Da Guo* / Great Excess

*dui* / lake, still water, pool, marsh, joy, pleasing

*xun* / wood, gentle, penetrating

- *Image*

    Lake above Wood.
    Trees submerged in water: Great Excess.
    The noble person stands alone unafraid
    and withdraws from the world without regret.

- *Judgment*

    a) The ridge pole sags.
    Favourable to have somewhere to go.
    Offering.

    b) The roof beam is bending.
    Beneficial to undertake something.
    Success.

*Commentary*

With joy (Lake) and gentleness (Wind, Wood) combined, it is beneficial to go somewhere or undertake something.
*The ridge pole sags*: there is something surpassingly strong (four whole lines in the centre of the hexagram), with two weak ends (first and last broken lines).
The timely occurrence of excess is of great importance.

- *Base line, 6*  43

   For an offering mat use white grass.
   No misfortune.

#### Commentary

*For an offering mat use white grass:* being in a low position one should handle things with care and gentleness, then there will be no mistake.

*Note. Mats were used in ceremonies and sacrifices to wrap offerings. Ordinary people sometimes laid their offerings to the spirits or ancestors on white grass. Mats of white* cogon *or* mao *grass symbolise simplicity and closeness to the earth. (See also the note for the base line of hexagram 11.)*

- *Second line, 9*  31

   A withered willow tree grows new shoots.
   An old man takes a young wife.
   There is nothing for which this is unfavourable.

#### Commentary

Although an old man marrying a young wife is something out of the ordinary it is not unfavourable.

- *Third line, 9*  47

   The ridge pole sags.
   Ominous.

#### Commentary

The disaster of the sagging ridge pole is due to being without adequate support. The ridge pole sags or subsides under pressure.

• *Fourth line, 9*  48

> The ridge pole is upheld.
> Auspicious.
> Otherwise there will be regret.

*Commentary*

*The ridge pole is upheld:* it does not sag downward or fall. Auspicious in the sense that the unexpected misfortune will not manifest. Good fortune. No regret.

• *Fifth line, 9*  32

> A withered willow tree grows flowers.
> An old woman takes a young husband.
> There will be no blame, no praise.

*Commentary*

*A withered willow tree grows flowers:* how can this last long?
*An old woman takes a young husband:* there will be neither approval nor disapproval.

• *Top line, 6*  44

> Exceeding oneself in crossing the river.
> He gets his head under water: ominous.
> No blame.

*Commentary*

Undertaking action which is beyond one's capability can be disastrous. But there will be no blame.

## • *Summary*

Lake above Wood means a forest submerged in water, symbolising something excessive like a flood.

This hexagram also portrays a ridge pole, the highest beam supporting the roof of a house, with two weak ends (the top and bottom line) unable to bear the weight.

The noble person withdraws from the world without regret, because he regards the world full of excessive situations. When going somewhere or undertaking something, it is beneficial to have a goal or destination in view. Success.

In hexagram 27 the noble person tried to teach the old values to spiritual seekers of different qualities. In hexagram 28, having done his work, he withdraws from the world without regret.

This hexagram is about excessive situations manifesting in six lines:

The first line is about the beginning of an excessive situation where one is advised to be careful and gentle in order to avoid mistakes.

In the second line (which is not in the right position), the situation is excessive (an old man with a young wife), but it is not unfavourable.

In the third line, an excessive situation collapses. Disaster.

In the fourth line the misfortune, due to a situation of excess, does not manifest. Good fortune. No regret.

In the fifth line an excessive situation (an old woman with a young husband), will not be approved or disapproved.

In the sixth line an excessive situation is disastrous, but there will be no blame. In some cases it could mean disaster from drowning or due to excessive drinking.

All the lines of this hexagram express situations of excess, but in line two (old man with a young wife), and in line five (old woman with a young husband) we can clearly see the influence of old values in Chinese culture.

Line two, being in a wrong position (a whole line in a *yin* position), is still considered rather favourable, while line five, being in a correct position (a whole line in a *yang* position), is considered less favourable.

According to the meaning of the trigrams, line two should be about an older woman (Wood is eldest daughter or old woman), and line five should be about a younger woman (Lake is youngest daughter or young woman).

Although the meaning of these two lines are not correct according the inner structure of the hexagram (the trigrams Wood and Lake), in the experience of working with the *Yi Jing*, the answers about relationships (old man with young woman, or old woman with young man) were always connected with the traditional positions of the lines in the book (line two and line five). (See *Appendix ii: Yi Jing Corrections*, p. 411.)

# 29. *Kan* / Water, Danger, Pitfall

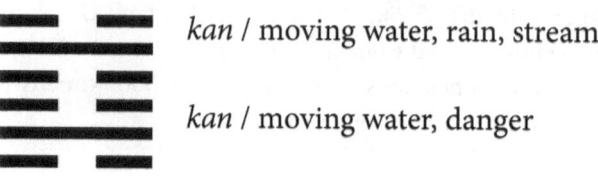

kan / moving water, rain, stream

kan / moving water, danger

- ## *Image*

    Double Water.
    Water flows on and on: Grave Danger.
    A noble person [in spite of the danger,]
    constantly practices higher virtues
    and continues his teachings to others.

- ## *Judgment*

    a) There are captives: bind them.
    Offering.
    Travelling brings reward.

    b) Having confidence in the heart and mind will bring success.
    Setting forth will have its reward.

### Commentary

Double Water signifies grave danger. Water is flowing continuously, but does not overflow.
Undertaking action is dangerous, but one does not lose confidence. This brings success because one stays firm and centred.
Going out on a journey or proceeding with something will bring results.

The perilous heights of heaven are dangerous to reach, because heaven maintains its exalted majesty.

The dangerous places of earth are mountains, rivers, and heights. Kings and dukes use these as protection for their states. Timely use of the advantages of dangerous conditions is of great importance.

- *Base line, 6*

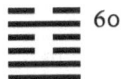 60

> Dangerous pitfall.
> Falling into it.
> Ominous.

### Commentary

*Dangerous pitfall. Falling into it:* there is a danger of losing one's way (the *Dao*). Disaster.

- *Second line, 9*

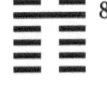 8

> a) In the dangerous pitfall.
>    Getting little relief.
>
> b) In a pitfall with a steep drop.
>    Seeking a small gain.

### Commentary

In a dangerous situation one can only strive for small attainments. The danger is still present.

- *Third line, 6* 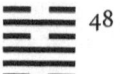 48

   The pitfall is steep and deep.
   Falling into it.
   Do not use this.

*Commentary*

Being in a gravely dangerous situation, any effort is useless. There is nothing we can do to help ourselves. Do not act. This presages our failure to accomplish anything.

- *Fourth line, 6*  47

   A flask of wine and a bowl of food
   in plain earthenware.
   Hand them through the hole.
   In the end there will be no misfortune.

*Commentary*

*A flask of wine and a bowl of food. Hand them through the hole*: someone is passing food and drink, thereby relieving one's difficult situation. No misfortune.

- *Fifth line, 9*  7

   a) The pit is not full.
      The earth spirit is already calmed.
      No harm.

   b) The pit is not overflowing, but only filled to the brim.
      No misfortune.

*Commentary*

*The pit is not full:* the precarious condition of being in a pitfall is not so grave. There will be no trouble.

Note. The earth spirit is a spirit that has to be pleased to prevent danger (pitfall).

- **Top line, 6**

    Bound with a rope of three strands
    and a black cord of two strands.
    Put in a thick and thorny bush.
    For three years there will be no relief.
    Ominous.

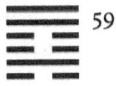 59

*Commentary*

Someone is restricted in his movements (imprisoned). There will be misfortune for three years. One has lost the way (deviated from the *Dao*). Disaster.

Note. Omens are seen in strands of a rope. Prisons in ancient China are said to have been surrounded by thorny bushes and trees. Pits are sometimes used as prisons.

- **Summary**

Water doubled means water flowing increasingly into the depths, symbolising grave danger. Water is flowing continuously, but does not overflow.

Undertaking action is dangerous, but one should not lose confidence. Going on a journey or proceeding with something will bring results.

Hexagram 28, Great Excess, represents excessive situations that will usually lead to dangerous situations (hexagram 29, Grave Danger).

This hexagram is about dangerous situations or conditions symbolised by the pitfall.

In the first line someone enters a dangerous situation (falls into the pit) and may lose his way. Disaster.

In the second line, being in a dangerous situation (the pit), one can only seek small attainments.

In the third line, being in a dangerous situation (a pit), there is nothing one can do to help oneself. It presages a failure to accomplish anything. It is best not to act.

In the fourth line the dangerous situation (of being in a pit) is relieved by help from outside. No misfortune.

In the fifth line a precarious situation is not so grave or bad (the pit is not overflowing). No misfortune.

In the sixth line, being in a dangerous situation (a pit), and restricted in one's movements (bound by ropes), one is incapacitated for three years, and has lost one's way. Disaster.

# 30. *Li* / Fire, Light, Oriole

*li* / fire, light, brightness,

*li* / fire, clinging

- *Image*

    Double Fire.
    Fire rising in two flames: Light, Brightness, Clinging.
    A great person shines his light
    to the four quarters of the earth.

- *Judgment*

    a) Favourable augury.
    Offering.
    Auspicious for raising cows.

    b) Determination is beneficial.
    Success.
    Rearing cows brings good fortune.

*Commentary*

Double Fire indicates something unusually auspicious. It corrects, transforms, and perfects all under heaven. Too much fire may, on the other hand, cause disaster.
Sun and moon are clinging to heaven. The myriad grains, plants and trees are clinging to the earth. Determination is beneficial. Success.
The cow is a metaphor for the farmer's wealth. Raising cows will therefore bring prosperity. Good fortune.

- **Base line, 9**  56

    *Treading crosswise.*
    *Respect them.*
    *No misfortune.*

*Commentary*

*Treading crosswise:* not approaching bluntly, but with respect and reverence. In this way one avoids trouble. No blame.

- **Second line, 6** 14

    a) *A yellow oriole (lia bird).*
       *Very auspicious.*

    b) *Yellow light.*
       *Very good fortune.*

*Commentary*

Yellow light indicates brightness. Very good fortune (the yielding line is central and correct).

Note. The lia bird or black-necked oriole (oriolus chinensis), has beautiful golden yellow feathers. The bird is seen as an omen, and depending on the context (here as line 2 or 3), it can be good or bad.

- **Third line, 9**  21

    a) *An oriole (lia bird) at sunset.*
       *Not beating the earthen drum and singing,*
       *the old people sigh piteously.*
       *Ominous.*

b) *The (yellow) light of the setting sun.*
   *One does not beat the earthen drum and sing:*
   *the elderly people bemoan the approach of old age.*
   *Disaster.*

### Commentary

*An oriole (lia bird) at sunset:* how can the sunset beauty last long? The *lia* bird and the setting sun together were seen as a sad omen. The beating of drums and singing was usually done to scare away the darkness, which is related to the sadness, sorrow, and tragedy of old age. Our present happiness or success will not endure (the sun is setting). We must prepare for a setback.

• **Fourth line, 9**

*Sudden is its coming:*
*as if it burns, dies, and is abandoned.*

### Commentary

So sudden is the appearance of the light (flame), that it finds no acceptance. Something will suddenly appear, but because of lack of support, it will be discarded.

• **Fifth line, 6**

*Tears are flowing.*
*They sigh piteously.*
*Auspicious.*

### Commentary

Although a broken (*yin*) fifth line is in an incorrect position, it denotes good fortune, like line two. Both are in the middle of the trigram of Fire but line 2 is in a correct position, and line 5 not. Therefore the sighing, but good fortune in the end.

## • Top line, 9

*The king goes out on a campaign.
There is a celebration
with the chopping of heads [of the leaders]
but their followers are not captured.
No misfortune.*

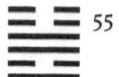

### Commentary

The king goes forth to remove the leaders, but their followers are spared. He does this to correct the order of the state. No misfortune.

## • Summary

Fire doubled means fire rising in two flames, symbolising light, brightness but also clinging. A flame is not stable, always in motion, indicating external conditions which are constantly changing, and internally a restless mind.

Too much fire may cause disaster. It can mean anger and hate, but also enlightenment. Determination is beneficial. Taking care of others brings good fortune. Success.

Hexagram 29 is about a noble person who constantly practices higher virtues and continues his teaching to others. In hexagram 30 a great person shines his light (higher virtues) to the four corners of the earth.
This hexagram is about different expressions of light:

In the first line one is advised to approach something or someone (as a 'beacon' or 'light') with respect and reverence to avoid trouble.
No blame.

In the second line the light manifests itself clearly. In a spiritual sense it may indicate Enlightenment. Very good fortune.

In the third line the disappearance of the light (sunset) is bewailed. Our present happiness or success will not endure. We must prepare for a setback. Disaster.

In the fourth line something (the light) appears suddenly, and because of lack of support, it will be abandoned. It does not last.

In the fifth line there is great light, accompanied by tears, sighing, and sadness, but there will be good fortune in the end.

In the sixth line the leader reestablishes the order of things by taking away the evil-doers but not their followers. No misfortune.

Hexagram 30 is also about the different stages of Enlightenment.

# 31. *Xian* / Feeling, Sensation, Attraction

*dui* / lake, still water, pool, joy, pleasing

*gen* / mountain, standing still, stilling, stopping

- ## *Image*

    Lake above Mountain.
    A lake on top of the mountain: Feeling, Attraction.
    The noble person stimulates the people
    and receives them without selfishness.

- ## *Judgment*

    Offering.
    Favourable augury for taking a maiden as wife.
    Auspicious.

*Commentary*

A yielding trigram (Lake, youngest daughter) above a strong trigram (Mountain, youngest son). These two respond to and stimulate each other. Success. This means it is a *favourable augury for taking a maiden as wife*. Good fortune.

By the mutual stimulation of heaven and earth the myriad things are created. The sage influences men's mind and all is peaceful under heaven. Observe how things are stimulated and the nature of all things can be known.

- **Base line, 6**

    Sensation in the big toe.

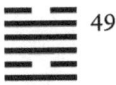
49

### Commentary

*Sensation in the big toe*: one's intention (will) is directed outward.

- **Second line, 6**

    Sensation in the calf.
    Ominous.
    Auspicious for a dwelling.

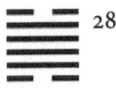
28

### Commentary

*Sensation in the calf*: a tendency to act or move. Disaster.
To abide in a dwelling (staying in one place) brings good fortune. Not acting rashly, but staying still and being compliant, one will come to no harm.

- **Third line, 9**

    Sensation in the thigh.
    Holding on to those following.
    Continuing like this will be distressing.

45

### Commentary

*Sensation in the thigh*: one feels restless.
Following, clinging to those below (first and second *yin* lines, women).
To continue like this will bring humiliation and distress.

- **Fourth line, 9** 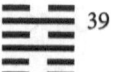 39

    [Sensation in the heart.]
    Augury auspicious.
    Troubles will go away.
    Feeling indecisive, one is moving to and fro.
    Only a friend is following your thought.

    *Commentary*

Determination brings good fortune. Troubles will disappear. Hesitation. Only friend(s) will follow your thoughts. There is no glory yet.

- **Fifth line, 9**  62

    Sensation in the spine (upper back).
    No trouble, no regret.

    *Commentary*

*Sensation in the spine*: tension and anxiety, a foreboding of something negative. One's will and influence are limited. This line is central and correct therefore there is no trouble and no regret.

- **Top line, 6**  33

    Sensation in the cheeks, jaws and tongue.

    *Commentary*

One's words are those of a babbler (empty talk).

## • *Summary*

Lake above Mountain means a lake on top of the mountain, symbolising feeling, sensation, attraction, stimulation, affection.

A joyous woman (Lake, youngest daughter), and a strong young man (Mountain, youngest son) are strongly attracted to each other. Success. It is beneficial to be determined and take the maiden as wife. Good fortune.

This hexagram is about courtship and betrothal, and hexagram 32 is about an enduring marriage.

Hexagram 30 is followed by hexagram 31, because in hexagram 30 the noble person's character and virtues illumine the four corners of the world and in hexagram 31 his character and virtues influence and stimulate others.

This hexagram pictures sensation or stimulation in different parts of the body. These sensations in the body are considered as omens. For example sensation in the upper part of the spine means tension and anxiety, as a foreboding of something negative (see the fifth line).

In the first line sensation in the toe indicates that the intention (will) is directed to external matters.

In the second line sensation in the calves indicates that a tendency to move or act rashly should be stopped. If one stays in one place, there will be good fortune.

In the third line sensation in the thighs indicates a situation of clinging (attachment) to something or someone (a woman), which will lead to humiliation and distress.

In the fourth line sensation has reached the heart (for the Chinese it is also the seat of the mind and the will), and indicates restlessness, hesitation and indecisiveness. Being determined brings good fortune.

In the fifth line sensation in the upper back of the spine indicates tension and anxiety as a foreboding of something negative. One's influence (will) is limited. No trouble, no regret.

In the sixth line sensation in the cheeks, jaws and tongue indicates that one talks too much or one's words have not much content.

## 32. *Heng* / Lasting, Enduring, Constancy

zhen / thunder, shock, moving, growth

xun / wind, gentle, penetrating

- ***Image***

    Thunder above Wind.
    Thunder followed by wind: Lasting, Enduring.
    The noble person stands firm and continues on his way.

- ***Judgment***

    a) Offering.
    No misfortune.
    Favourable augury.
    Favourable to have somewhere to go.

    b) Success.
    No misfortune.
    Perseverance is beneficial.
    Beneficial to undertake something.

*Commentary*

Thunder (moving, strong) and Wind (gentle, yielding) are working together. Success. No misfortune. Favourable augury. It is beneficial to go somewhere or undertake something.

Enduring means lasting. Enduring, like the way of heaven and earth, never stops. Sun and moon, placed in heaven, shine forever. The four seasons are changing one into the other, and thus go on forever.

The sage is steadfast in the Way (*Dao*), so that all things under heaven are brought to completion. Observe what is enduring, and the nature of heaven and earth, and the ten thousand things can be known.

*Note. The title of the hexagram symbolises the* heng *perpetuation rite, which is an offering made with the purpose of fixing or prolonging ('enduring') a specific condition or situation, such as fate or fortune. (See also hexagram 5, line 1, hexagram 16, line 5, and hexagram 42, line 6.)*

- ***Base line, 6*** 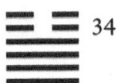 34

    *Seeking endurance.*
    *Determination: ominous.*
    *There is nothing for which this is favourable.*

    *Commentary*

    Seeking constancy at the start brings misfortune. Favourable for nothing.

- ***Second line, 9*** 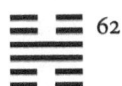 62

    *Troubles will go away.*
    *Regret disappears.*

    *Commentary*

    Regret disappears because one is able to keep to the middle path, avoiding extreme actions.

- **Third line, 9**

    *His virtue is not constant
    and he may encounter disgrace.
    Persistence brings distress.*

 40

*Commentary*

If he does not maintain his virtue, no one will tolerate him.

- **Fourth line, 9**

    *In the hunt there will be no game.*

 46

*Commentary*

Being in a wrong place (a *yang* line in a *yin* position) for long, how can one achieve anything?

- **Fifth line, 6**

    *Constancy of virtue
    is auspicious for a wife
    but ominous for a husband.*

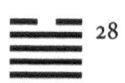 28

*Commentary*

Here the virtue is about the qualities of a woman (wife), namely following her husband, and being obedient. If the husband would behave like an obedient woman, it would mean misfortune, for a man should take charge and make decisions.

- **Top line, 6**       50

  *Prolonged and determined activity brings misfortune.*

*Commentary*

Prolonged determination will lead to great failure, without any result.

- **Summary**

Thunder and Wind. Thunder is always followed by wind, symbolising lastingness, duration and constancy.

The eldest son (Thunder) and the eldest daughter (Wind) represent a husband and wife in an enduring marriage. Success. No misfortune.

Perseverance is beneficial. When going somewhere or undertaking something, it is advisable to have a goal or destination in view.

A noble person stands firm and continues on his way. He keeps to his principles without compromising.

Hexagram 32, Lasting, Enduring, follows hexagram 31, Feeling, Sensation because in hexagram 31 a young man (Mountain) and a young woman (Lake) were very attracted to each other. In hexagram 32 they have become an older man (Thunder) and an older woman (Wind) in an enduring and lasting marriage.

This hexagram is about endurance and constancy in different stages:

In the first line one seeks endurance too soon. This will bring misfortune.

In the second line troubles will disappear because one stays to the middle path, avoiding extreme actions. No regret.

In the third line one is not constant in his virtue, and if one continues in this way, it will lead to disgrace and distress.

In the fourth line, persevering in the wrong place for long will bring no gain.

In the fifth line the constancy of the female virtue of following and obedience will bring good fortune to the wife, but not to the husband. A husband has to lead and make decisions.

In the sixth line continuous determination will be without any worthwhile result. Misfortune.

# 33. *Dun* / Withdrawal, Retreat, Pig

qian / heaven, creative, power, *yang*, active, male

gen / mountain, standing still, stilling, stopping

- **Image**

    Mountain below Heaven.
    *A mountain beneath the sky: Withdrawal, Retreat.*
    *A noble person distances himself from petty men*
    *not with resentment, but with dignity.*

- **Judgment**

    Offering.
    Somewhat favourable augury.

*Commentary*

An old man (trigram Heaven) retreats in the mountain (trigram Mountain). The petty men (the two *yin* lines of the lower trigram) are gradually advancing, and growing in strength.
In withdrawal lies success: acting at the right time and the right manner. In small matters perseverance is beneficial. The timely occurrence of withdrawal is of great importance.

*Note.* The Chinese character dun, *meaning 'to withdraw', has a resemblance with* tun, *meaning a 'young pig' (the pig is related to the trigram Heaven).*

- **Base line, 6**

    a) *Tail of a young pig.
    Danger.
    Do not use this in having somewhere to go.*

    b) *Into retreat.
    Threatening.
    Do not use this line as an encouragement
    to undertake something.*

    *Commentary*

Being in an unsuitable position (a *yin* line in a wrong place), one is beset by unfavourable circumstances. This is the time for withdrawal. It would be best to refrain from further action.

- **Second line, 6**

    *Binding with yellow oxhide.
    It [the young pig] cannot get loose.*

    *Commentary*

One is firm in his intention to withdraw.

- **Third line, 9**

    a) *A tied up young pig.
    There will be a sickness.
    Danger.
    Auspicious for keeping male and female servants.*

b) *A confined retreat.*
   *There will be fatigue and illness.*
   *Threatening.*
   *Keeping servants (helpers) will bring good fortune.*

### Commentary

Restricted in his retreat one suffers from fatigue and illness. This can be dangerous. Having reliable helpers will bring good fortune.

## • Fourth line, 9

a) *A fine young pig.*
   *Auspicious for the noble man*
   *bad for the petty man.*

b) *A correct withdrawal.*
   *For the noble person good fortune*
   *but bad for the petty man.*

### Commentary

The noble person correctly withdraws himself. Good fortune. If the petty man does so, it will mean trouble.

## • Fifth line, 9

a) *A young pig at a celebration.*
   *Augury auspicious.*

b) *An admirable withdrawal.*
   *Determination brings good fortune.*

*Commentary*

A praiseworthy withdrawal. Continuing in the rightful way will bring good fortune.

- **Top line, 9**

  a) *A fat young pig.*
  *Unfavourable for nothing.*

  b) *A smooth retreat.*
  *There is nothing for which this is unfavourable.*

*Commentary*

*A smooth retreat*: there is no hesitation or doubt about the right choice of withdrawal. Nothing unfavourable.

- **Summary**

Mountain below Heaven means a mountain beneath the sky, symbolising withdrawal, retreat. An old man (Heaven) in retreat or seclusion in the mountain.

Withdrawal at the right time brings success. Perseverance in small matters will be beneficial.

Hexagram 32, Lasting, Enduring, is followed by hexagram 33, Withdrawal, Retreat, because according to the law of change, something may last long (endure), but it can never last forever. Therefore, when duration comes to an extreme (the law of extremes), things will be withdrawn (retreat). Life is mainly directed outwardly. When it endures for long, and one becomes old, life starts to withdraw. As an example, when someone grows old (life endures for long), the old man (Heaven) retreats in the mountain (hexagram 33).

This hexagram is about withdrawal or retreat in six stages:

In the first line, the beginning of withdrawal, one should be aware of danger, not go anywhere, and refrain from further action.

In the second line there is a strong determination for withdrawal.

In the third line a restricted withdrawal (retreat) may lead to fatigue and illness. Danger. Help from others ('servants' or 'concubines') will relieve some suffering. Good fortune.

In the fourth line a correct (right) withdrawal means good fortune for the noble person, but trouble for the petty person.

In the fifth line withdrawal is admirable because it stems from rectitude. Persistence will bring good fortune.

In the sixth line there is no doubt about the correct choice of withdrawal. There is nothing for which this is unfavourable.

## 34. *Da Zhuang* / Great Strength, Ram

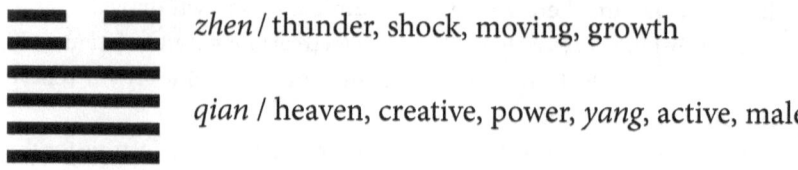

*zhen* / thunder, shock, moving, growth

*qian* / heaven, creative, power, *yang*, active, male

- *Image*

    Thunder above Heaven.
    Thunder in the sky: Great Strength, Power.
    The powerful noble person does not speak a word
    or take a step opposing the rules.

- *Judgment*

    a) Favourable augury.

    b) Determination is beneficial.

### Commentary

Strength (Heaven) and movement (Thunder): this is Great Strength. The great are powerful.
What is great is correct. This means that the great behaves with rectitude. Being correct and great, the inner nature of heaven and earth can be known.
It is beneficial to be determined.

- **Base line, 9**

    a) Strength in the feet.
    Going on a campaign: ominous.
    There will be captives.

    b) Strength in the feet.
    Going out on a venture brings disaster.
    Have confidence.

    *Commentary*

*Strength in the feet*: there is not enough power to go forth and act. If something is undertaken, it will bring disaster (injury). However, confidence remains.

- **Second line, 9**

    a) Augury auspicious.

    b) Determination will bring good fortune.

    *Commentary*

Although the second line is a *yang* line in a wrong position, determination will bring good fortune.

- **Third line, 9**

    a) If the petty man uses his strength
    he will be injured.
    If the noble person uses it, he will not.
    Augury: danger.
    A ram butts a fence and gets his horns entangled.

b) *The petty man uses his power*
   *but the noble person refrains from doing so.*
   *Determination is dangerous.*
   *A ram gets his horns entangled in a fence.*

### Commentary

If someone uses his strength, he will be injured. The noble person, knowing this, refrains from using power. Determination will lead to stagnation. Danger. Great strength can be very useful, but it must be applied at the right time.

- *Fourth line, 9*

a) *Augury auspicious.*
   *Troubles go away.*
   *The fence breaks, the ram is free.*
   *Great strength of a cart axle.*

b) *Determination brings good fortune.*
   *Troubles disappear.*
   *The fence opens. No more entanglement.*
   *Great strength.*

### Commentary

Although the fourth line is a *yang* line in a wrong position, determination brings good fortune, because it is supported by the trigram Heaven (strength). With great strength the entanglement disappears, and one can go forward.

- *Fifth line, 6*

   a) *Losing sheep at* Yi.
      *No regret.*

   b) *Losing a sheep in the field without regret.*

   #### Commentary

Losing a sheep unexpectedly (Thunder), there is no regret, and he does not waste time bemoaning his loss, but concentrates on rebuilding the herd. This line is a *yin* line in a wrong position, therefore there is a loss, but no regret.

*Note.* Yi *refers to another state in ancient China where the herdsmen took their cattle.*

- *Top line, 6*

   *A ram butts a fence.*
   *He is not able to withdraw*
   *nor to push through.*
   *There is nothing for which this is favourable.*
   *Difficulty, but then good fortune.*

   #### Commentary

Not being able to withdraw or push through indicates that there is nothing which is beneficial. But it will not last long. First there will be difficulty, and later good fortune (a *yin* line in a correct position).

## • *Summary*

Thunder above Heaven means thunder in the sky, symbolising great strength. Strength (Heaven) in movement (Thunder) means great power.

A young man (Thunder, eldest son) on a horse (Heaven) signifies movement and strength. Determination is beneficial.

Hexagram 33, Withdrawal, Retreat, is followed by hexagram 34, Great Strength, Power, because it is in situations of retreat that great power can be collected.

This hexagram is about great strength and power in different situations:

The first line indicates the beginning of great strength, but not enough to undertake something. If action is undertaken anyway, there will be disaster. Still, one should remain confident.

In the second line strong determination brings good fortune.

In the third line the petty man uses his power, but the noble person refrains from doing so, because determination (strength) leads to stagnation or entanglement. Danger.

In the fourth line entanglement or stagnation will disappear, and one can go forward. Determination will bring good fortune.

In the fifth line something is lost, but one should not regret it, and stay determined to continue.

In the sixth line great strength comes to an end. There is nothing which will be beneficial, but it will not last long. First there is difficulty, but later there will be good fortune.

# 35. *Jin* / Advancing, Progress

*li* / fire, light, brightness, clinging

*kun* / earth, receptive, *yin*, passive, female

- ## *Image*

    Fire above Earth.
    The sun rising over the earth: Advancing, Progress.
    A noble person's character shines with virtues.

- ## *Judgment*

    [Augury: auspicious.]
    The lord of Kang *was presented with numerous horses.*
    *He was granted audience [by the king]*
    *three times in one day.*

### Commentary

Brightness (the sun) appears above the earth. Advancing means progress. Here the progress is indicated by the lord who was presented with horses and granted audience three times.

- *Base line, 6*

   a) A striking advance.
   Augury: auspicious.
   Troubles go away.
   The capture will be abundant.
   No misfortune.

   b) A decisive advance.
   Determination brings good fortune.
   Troubles will disappear.
   There is enough confidence.
   No misfortune.

   *Commentary*

Having enough confidence, one advances decisively. By taking the liberty to act on one's own to do what is right, troubles will disappear, and there will be no misfortune.

- *Second line, 6*

   a) Advance with sorrow.
   Augury: auspicious.
   He receives great blessings from the king's mother.

   b) Advancing with sadness.
   Perseverance will bring good fortune.
   He receives blessings from the queen mother.

   *Commentary*

Advancing with sadness, but perseverance will bring good fortune. One receives blessings from a woman in authority (fifth *yin* line).

- **Third line, 6**  56

  For the common people troubles go away.

  *Commentary*

When ordinary people are loyal (a quality of the bottom Earth trigram) they 'move upward' (advance). Troubles will disappear.

- **Fourth line, 9** 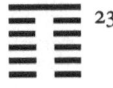 23

  Advance like a rodent.
  Augury: danger.

  *Commentary*

*Advance like a rodent*: advancing too quickly. Determination will bring danger.

- **Fifth line, 6**  12

  Troubles go away.
  Care not for loss or gain.
  Auspicious for going somewhere.
  Nothing unfavourable.

  *Commentary*

Do not worry about loss or gain. Trouble will disappear. Going somewhere or undertaking something will bring good fortune. There is nothing for which this is unfavourable.

### • Top line, 9

*Advancing with horns to attack a town.*
*Danger.*
*Auspicious. No misfortune.*
*Augury: distress.*

*Commentary*

Advancing with force ('horns') to move forward. Although there is danger it will still be auspicious (the bright trigram Fire) to advance. No misfortune. But determination will lead to distress.

### • Summary

Fire above Earth means the sun rising over the earth, symbolising advance and progress. The sun (Fire) advances through the sky over the earth.

Progress is indicated by a leader who is presented with gifts, and granted audience three times in one day. Advancing will bring good fortune.

Hexagram 35, Advancing, Progress, follows hexagram 34, Great Strength, Power, because only with power and strength can progress be made.

This hexagram is about advancing and progress in different stages:

In the first line, in the beginning of advancement or progress, one has enough confidence, and takes the liberty to do what is right. There will be no misfortune, and troubles will disappear.

In the second line advance is made with sadness, but perseverance will bring good fortune. There will be help or good fortune coming from a woman in authority.

In the third line the ordinary, loyal people move upward (advance). Trouble will disappear.

In the fourth line progress is made too quickly, and will have serious consequences. Danger.

In the fifth line one should not worry about loss or gain. When going somewhere or undertaking something, it will bring good fortune. There is nothing which is unfavourable.

In the sixth line progress is in its last stage. Advancing with force will be dangerous. Determination will lead to distress. But it will still be auspicious to move forward. No misfortune.

# 36. *Ming Yi* / Darkening Light, Pheasant

 *kun* / earth, receptive, *yin*, compliant, female

*li* / fire, light, brightness, clinging

- *Image*

    Fire below Earth.
    The sun is sinking under the earth: Darkening of the Light.
    In approaching people the noble person conceals his light but nevertheless shines with virtue.

- *Judgment*

    a) Favourable augury in hardship.
    b) Determination is beneficial in the face of difficulties.

*Commentary*

The light (Fire, sun) has gone under the earth. Brightness is obscured.
Inside, all light (Fire, bottom trigram) and virtue; outside, yielding and compliant (Earth, upper trigram). This is how one should be when confronted by hardship, like king *Wen*.
In the face of difficulties determination will be beneficial, *if* one conceals one's brilliance (of mind and character). In the midst of hardship one is able to keep his will fixed on what is right, like prince *Ji*.

Note. King *Wen was imprisoned by the last, wicked,* Shang *king. Prince* Ji *was a minister of this king, against whom he protested with no avail. He withdrew from court.*

- **Base line, 9**

  a) A crying pheasant
  flies with drooping wings.
  A noble person on travel does not eat for three days.
  If there is somewhere to go, there will be talk.

  b) As the light darkens,
  one acts like a flying bird, lowering its wings.
  The noble person, during his travel,
  goes without food for three days.
  When undertaking something
  those in charge will grumble.

*Commentary*

During his travel the noble person goes without food for three days in a row when duties requires this of him. If one has somewhere to go or undertake something, one's superiors have something to say about his attitude.

- **Second line, 6**

  a) The crying pheasant
  is wounded in the left thigh.
  Use a gelded horse: health.
  Auspicious.

  b) As the light darkens, one is wounded in the left thigh.
  One is saved by using a strong horse.
  Good fortune.

*Commentary*

This good fortune comes from compliance (a *yin* line) with the dangerous situation (bottom inner trigram Water).

A strong horse symbolises a strong ally to help someone, or a strong effort to pull oneself out of the situation.

- **Third line, 9**  24

    a) *A crying pheasant*
    *shot at a hunt in the south.*
    *Catching the great chief.*
    *A hasty augury is not possible.*

    b) *As the light darkens*
    *one is wounded on a campaign in the south*
    *but captures the leader.*
    *There should not be a hurried determination.*

*Commentary*

The campaign in the south symbolises determination to accomplish a great task. Although one is wounded on the campaign, the rebel leader is captured. It is not possible to accomplish things in a hurry (the bottom trigram Fire stands for speed, quickness, etc.)

Note. Originally the central kingdom of ancient China was in the north. The south was considered wild and rebellious.

- **Fourth line, 6**  55

    a) *Entering the left side of the belly*
    *hitting the crying pheasant's heart.*
    *Going out of the gate and courtyard.*

b) Entering the left side of the belly,
   perceiving the darkened heart.
   Leaving the courtyard.

*Commentary*

Approaching the ruler (leader) from the left side (dark, *yin*), one perceives what is in his heart and mind (darkness).
Perceiving danger (bottom inner trigram Water) the minister (fourth line) goes out of the door and leaves the court. (See also commentary line five and note Judgment.)

- **Fifth line, 6**

   a) Prince Ji's *crying pheasant.*
      *Augury: favourable.*

   b) Prince Ji *suffers injury.*
      *Determination is favourable.*

*Commentary*

Because of perceiving the darkened heart and mind of the ruler, prince *Ji* suffers injury. His determination or persistence is such that his light cannot be extinguished. (See also commentary line four, and note Judgment.)

- **Top line, 6**

   a) Not light but darkness.
      First he ascends to heaven,
      and later descends into the earth.

*b) No light in the darkness.*
   *It first rises in the sky, and later enters into the earth.*

*Commentary*

*It first rises into the sky, and later enters into the earth:* one's light ascends and illumines the four directions, but later one's light descends into the earth (darkness), because one has not followed the right way (*Dao*).

## • *Summary*

Fire below Earth means the sun is sinking under the earth, symbolising darkening of the light. It is night and darkness everywhere.

When confronted with hardship, one should conceal one's light (Fire) and be yielding and compliant (Earth). In the face of difficulties it will be beneficial to stay determined.

Hexagram 35, Advancing, Progress, is followed by hexagram 36, Darkening Light, because progress will often meet with resistance and hindrances. This will lead to the 'darkening of the light', injury or damage.

The story of the hexagram refers to the hunting of a pheasant.

This hexagram is about darkening of the light in six stages:

In the first line someone performs his duty in times of difficulty, and is determined to do it at all costs. But his superiors will have something to say about neglecting his own well-being.

In the second line someone is injured and is helped by a strong person, or one's own effort. Good fortune.

In the third line one is determined to accomplish a great task. Although injured, one attains what one wants, but one should not do things in a hurry.

In the fourth line, approaching someone (a superior), one perceives the darkness in his heart. Perceiving danger, it is advisable to leave the situation.

In the fifth line, having suffered injury, one's determination is such that one's light (spirit) cannot be broken.

In the sixth line someone's light (personality, status) rises and illumines his surroundings or other people, but later his light is darkened because he did not follow the right way (*Dao*).

# 37. Jia Ren / The Family

 *xun* / wind, wood, gentle, penetrating

*li* / fire, light, brightness, clinging

- **Image**

    Wind above Fire.
    Wind rising from fire: The Family.
    The noble person ensures that her words have substance and her deeds endure.

- **Judgment**

    a) Augury favourable for a woman.

    b) Perseverance and steadfastness is beneficial for a woman.

*Commentary*

Hot air rises from fire and makes wind. In accord with the great principle of heaven and earth, man and woman keep to their proper place.
Woman's proper place is inside (*yin*), man's proper place is outside (*yang*).
The family has strict rules. When father and mother, sons and daughters, all act in accordance with their various positions within the family; when husband and wife play their proper role: then the way of the family will be bright. When the family is in order, the world will be set right.

- **Base line, 9**  53

    a) *The family within an enclosure.
    Troubles go away.*

    b) *Keeping the family secure.
    Troubles will disappear.*

*Commentary*

*Keeping the family secure:* the family's intentions and goals are secured.

- **Second line, 6**  9

    a) *Nothing can be done.
    Making food in the middle.
    Augury auspicious.*

    b) *Nothing can be achieved.
    Preparing food within the family.
    Perseverance brings good fortune.*

*Commentary*

*Nothing can be achieved:* one should not follow whims and desires. Women stay inside preparing the food. Perseverance brings good fortune due to constancy and compliance to the rules of the family.

- **Third line, 9**  42

    *The family is run by strict rules.
    There is sighing.
    Trouble threatens.
    Auspicious.*

> When women and children are giggling and tittering
> there will be distress in the end.

*Commentary*

The family members are strictly ruled. Although trouble may occur, there will be good fortune. But if women and children behave in an unserious way it will ultimately lead to disorder within the family.

### • *Fourth line, 6*

 13

> A wealthy family.
> Most auspicious.

*Commentary*

The wealth of the family is due to the woman's perseverance. As this line is a *yin* line in the right place, there will be great good fortune.

### • *Fifth line, 9*

 22

> The king proceeds to his home and family.
> Do not worry.
> Auspicious.

*Commentary*

The king (head of the family) draws near to his family and has a good influence on them. There is no need for anxiety. There will be good fortune.

- **Top line, 9**

  a) *There are captives, looking terrified.
  In the end auspicious.*

  b) *There is sincerity and awe.
  Good fortune in the end.*

  *Commentary*

  The king's sincerity gives him respect. There will be good fortune in the end because he subjects himself to critical self-reflection.

- **Summary**

Wind above Fire means wind rising from fire, symbolising the family. The family consists of the eldest daughter (Wind, upper trigram), and two middle daughters (Fire, lower trigram and upper inner trigram), indicating the importance of women in the family. Women keep the fire of the household burning (wind rising from fire). A woman's steadfastness and perseverance will be beneficial.

Hexagram 36, Darkening Light, is followed by hexagram 37, The Family because if someone is injured in the world (on the outside), he or she draws back to the family (a save place) to recover.

This hexagram is about the order of the family in different stages:

In the first line the intentions and goals of the family are secured.

In the second line nothing great can be achieved. One should not follow one's desires or whims. A woman's perseverance will bring good fortune in matters concerning the family.

In the third line, if things are dealt with in an unserious or childish way, in the end there will be disorder and distress within the family (or group).

In the fourth line the wealth of the family is increased by the steadfastness and perseverance of the woman (wife). Great good fortune.

In the fifth line the head of the family (leader) maintains the order in his household (nation) with affection (love). Good fortune.

In the sixth line the leader commands respect from the family (group) because he is sincere and subjects himself to critical self-examination. Good fortune in the end.

# 38. *Kui* / Opposition

*li* / fire, light, brightness, clinging

*dui* / lake, still water, pool, marsh, joy, pleasing

- *Image*

    Fire above Lake.
    Fire above a marshy lake: Opposition.
    The noble person recognises the differences among things but remains sensitive to their similarities.

- *Judgment*

    a) Auspicious for small matters.

    b) In small matters good fortune.

*Commentary*

Fire moves upward and water (Lake) moves downward.
The two daughters (Lake and Fire) may live together, but their intentions (nature of the trigrams) are not the same (opposition).
Heaven and earth are opposites, but they have united goals. Man and woman are opposites, but they strive for union.
The myriad things may be contrary to each other, but as functioning entities they all strive for order. Opposites attract each other.
Opposition seems to be the natural prerequisite for union, therefore *in small matters good fortune*. This means that, although the hexagram indicates opposition, there still is some good fortune. The timely occurrence of opposition is of great importance.

- **Base line, 9**

   *Troubles go away.*
   *Losing a horse, do not go after it.*
   *It will return by itself.*
   *Seeing an evil man.*
   *No misfortune.*

   ### Commentary

   When losing a horse, one should not pursue it, because it will return by itself. Even when seeing an evil man, there will be no misfortune.

- **Second line, 9**

   *Meeting the master in a narrow lane.*
   *No misfortune.*

   ### Commentary

   When meeting a superior in an awkward situation ('a narrow lane') unexpectedly, there is no error, because one is not at fault.

- **Third line, 6**

   *Seeing a cart dragging an ox*
   *with one horn up and one horn down.*
   *A person branded on the forehead and his nose cut off.*
   *No good beginning.*
   *There will be an end.*

*Commentary*

The third line is a *yin* line in a wrong place, therefore all the images are indicating opposition: a peculiar ox behind the cart, and a man with a branded forehead and cut-off nose (a criminal).
A poor beginning, but there will be an end to this (humiliating) situation.

*Note. The images of the cart and ox are related to the old Chinese astronomical signs of which the cart was also seen as the 'Heavenly Punisher'. The images of branded forehead and cut-off nose were old Chinese customs of marking and punishing criminals.*

## • *Fourth line, 9*

a) *Setting sight on a fox.*
   *She meets her husband.*
   *Captives tied up crosswise.*
   *Danger.*
   *No misfortune.*

b) *Estranged and alone in opposition*
   *one meets a like-minded person.*
   *There is confidence.*
   *Although there is danger, there will be no error.*

*Commentary*

Someone who is isolated due to opposition ('setting sight on a fox'), meets a like-minded person ('husband'). Associating in good faith, they can realise their goals. Although the situation is dangerous, it will be no mistake.

- *Fifth line, 6*

    Troubles go away.
    He bites through the skin
    in the ancestral hall.
    What misfortune will there be in going?

10

#### Commentary

Trouble disappears. Biting through the flesh or meat means proceeding with determination, which will result in blessings. If one advances, what misfortune will there be?

*Note. Most of the food for the offering to the ancestors was eaten afterwards by the people who made the offerings.*

- *Top line, 9*

    Setting sight on a fox.
    He saw pigs with mud on their backs
    and a cart carrying ghosts.
    He first drew his bow and later loosened it.
    They are not bandits, but fetching a bride.
    If in going one meets with rain, it is auspicious.

54

#### Commentary

Estranged and alone ('setting sight on a fox').
He saw a bad omen ('pigs covered with mud and a cart full of ghosts').
First he wanted to take action ('drew his bow'), but later he refrained from it ('loosened his bow').
*Not bandits, but fetching a bride:* it is not an obstacle, but a matter of betrothal which causes delay and hesitation.
If rain falls on the way, then there will be good fortune. This implies the dispersal of all doubts and suspicion.

Note. In general, rainfall is regarded as a good omen (in hexagram 9, Judgment and line 6; hexagram 38, line 6; hexagram 50, line 3; hexagram 62, line 5). Only in hexagram 43, line 3, it is seen as an annoyance.

## • Summary

Fire above Lake means a fire above a marshy lake (water), symbolising opposition in nature.

Fire evaporates water, and water extinguishes fire. They oppose each other and cannot be together.

Two women (Fire, the middle daughter, and Lake, the youngest daughter) whose natures are opposite, living under one roof, have different intentions.

Although opposites generally oppose each other, they also can attract one another. Opposition seems to be the natural prerequisite for union.

There will be some good fortune or good fortune in small matters.

Hexagram 37, Family, is followed by hexagram 38, Opposition, because the women in the family have opposite characters, and their wishes do not accord, they become totally opposed to each other in hexagram 38.

This hexagram is about the condition of opposition in different situations:

In the first line one may lose something, but should not pursue it, for it will return by itself. Even if one encounters evil (persons, adversity), there will be no misfortune.

In the second line we unexpectedly find ourselves in an awkward situation but it is not our fault. No misfortune.

In the third line, although one is in a very bad (humiliating) situation, there will be an end to it.

In the fourth line, someone who is estranged and lonely due to opposition, meets a like-minded person. Although the situation is dangerous, it is possible to attain one's goal. No misfortune.

In the fifth line, proceeding with one's plans in a determined way, will result in blessing (unexpected good fortune or benefit).

In the sixth line, someone estranged and alone, sees bad omens ('dirty pigs and ghosts'). It is not an obstacle, but a matter of betrothal which causes delay. If rain falls (a good omen) while conducting one's affairs, there will be good fortune. The rain (as a good omen) should take away all our doubts as to the successful outcome of our plans.

# 39. *Jian* / Trouble, Obstruction

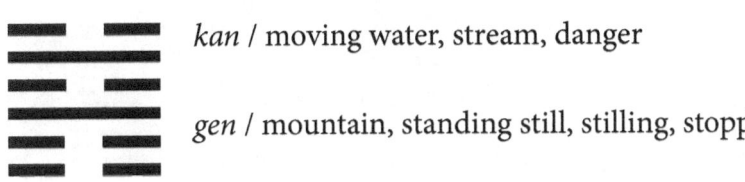

*kan* / moving water, stream, danger

*gen* / mountain, standing still, stilling, stopping

- ## *Image*

    Water above Mountain.
    Water running down the mountain: Trouble, Obstruction.
    The noble person [in times of trouble]
    reflects on himself to cultivate his character.

- ## *Judgment*

    Favourable to the west and south
    unfavourable to the east and north.
    Favourable to see a great man.
    Augury: auspicious.

*Commentary*

This hexagram is about trouble, obstructions, and difficulties.
Danger (Water) lies ahead (upper trigram). Seeing danger (Water), and being able to stop it (Mountain), or avert it, is wisdom.
Going to the west and south (Fire) is beneficial because we shall be able to steer a middle course. The east and north (Mountain, northeast) are not favourable because the way is running out.
It is beneficial to visit a person of wisdom because this will bring good results.
Perseverance will bring good fortune, because through it things can be put right, and the community (state or country) will be well ordered.

The timely occurrence of trouble and obstruction is of importance. Time of trouble and difficulty may offer opportunities.

- **Base line, 6**

    *Going brings trouble*
    *coming back wins praise.*

*Commentary*

If one sets forth one will meet with trouble, but if one returns one will win praise.
It is appropriate to wait.

- **Second line, 6**

    *The king's servant*
    *meets with trouble upon trouble.*
    *It is not his own cause.*

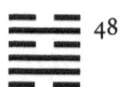

*Commentary*

The king's servant (second line) comes to the aid of the ruler (fifth line) who is in danger (upper trigram Water), and on his way he meets with trouble upon trouble (obstructions, lower trigram Mountain, stopping), but it is not his fault (a *yin* line in a correct position).

- **Third line, 9**

    *Going brings trouble, therefore turn back.*

*Commentary*

If one sets forth one will meet with trouble, but staying within (lower trigram Mountain, stilling) leads to happiness.

- *Fourth line, 6*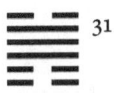

    *Going brings trouble.*
    *Coming back one finds an ally.*

*Commentary*

If one sets forth one will meet with trouble, but if one returns one will find support from a friend.

- *Fifth line, 9*

    *Severe trouble.*
    *Friends come.*

*Commentary*

In the midst of severe trouble (Water, danger) friends arrive.

- *Top line, 6*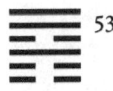

    *Going brings trouble.*
    *Coming back in greatness.*
    *Auspicious.*
    *Favourable to see a great man.*

*Commentary*

If one sets forth one will meet with trouble, but if one returns one will have great success and good fortune.
One's attention should be directed inwardly. It is beneficial to visit a person of wisdom.

## • *Summary*

Water above Mountain means a strong river running down the mountain symbolising trouble, obstructions, and difficulties. Seeing danger (Water) and being able to stop it (Mountain), or avert it, is wisdom.

The west and south directions are favourable because we shall be able to keep to the middle path. The east and north directions are not favourable because both the Way (of the *Dao*), and the way towards those directions are running out.

It is beneficial to see a person of wisdom. Perseverance brings good fortune.

Hexagram 38, Opposition, is followed by hexagram 39, Trouble, Obstruction, because situations of opposition (trigrams Fire and Water of hexagram 38, and inner trigrams Fire and Water of hexagram 39) will generally lead to obstruction and trouble.

This hexagram is about trouble, obstructions, and difficulties in six stages:

In the first line proceeding leads to trouble, while returning will win praise. It is advisable to wait.
In the second line someone will meet with difficulty upon difficulty, but it is not his fault.

In the third line, to proceed will lead to trouble, therefore turn back. Staying within (indoors and directing the attention inward) will lead to happiness.

In the fourth line proceeding leads to trouble, but if one returns one will be supported by friends.

In the fifth line friends arrive in the midst of severe trouble.

In the sixth line, to proceed leads to trouble, while returning will bring great success and good fortune. It is advisable to direct the will inwards. It is beneficial to see a person of wisdom, and to follow his advice.

# 40. *Jie* / Release, Liberation

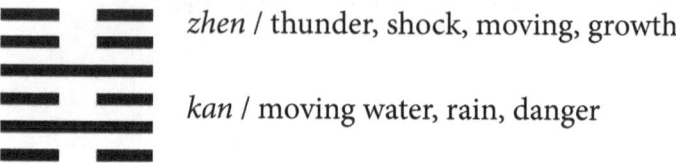

zhen / thunder, shock, moving, growth

kan / moving water, rain, danger

- ## *Image*

    *Thunder above Water.*
    *Thunder and rain: Release, Liberation.*
    *The noble person forgives wrongdoings*
    *and pardons misdeeds.*

- ## *Judgment*

    *Favourable to the west and south.*
    *Having nowhere to go: auspicious for coming back.*
    *Having somewhere to go: auspicious for going early.*

*Commentary*

When there is danger (Water) one should move (Thunder). This will bring release.

Heaven and earth bring forth thunder and rain, which will make the seeds of fruits, plants, and trees burst open and grow.

The west and south are favourite directions to go, because there one may obtain support from others.

If there is no place where one has to go, returning ('coming back') to one's former position will mean good fortune.

If there is some place where one has to go, hastening will bring good results.

The timely occurrence of release and liberation is of great importance.

- **Base line, 6**   54

    No error.

#### Commentary

A *yin* line at the bottom of the hexagram indicates a weak person in a low place, who is not in a position to bring about release on his own. Only by working with a stronger partner will release begin. Therefore there will be no error and no misfortune.

- **Second line, 9**   16

    In the hunt three foxes are caught
    with one yellow arrow.
    Augury: auspicious.

#### Commentary

*In the hunt three foxes are caught with one yellow arrow:* one is released from three kinds of negative influences. Persistence will bring good fortune, which is due to successful action ('yellow arrow').

Note. Foxes are considered as cunning, tricky, secretive, and undesirable animals. They were often shot for their tails. The three foxes stand for petty men, or the three negative influences: greed, ignorance, and fear, or lust, ignorance, and hate.

- **Third line, 6**  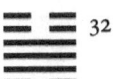 32

    Carrying things on the back while riding
    will attract bandits.
    Perseverance brings distress.

*Commentary*

*Carrying things on the back while riding will attract bandits:* if someone shows off his wealth and attracts robbers, who will be to blame? Perseverance will bring distress.

## • *Fourth line, 9*

Untying the big toe.
Friends come to the captive.

*Commentary*

'Untying the big toe' (upper trigram Thunder), means release from entanglement. Friends (allies) arrive and they can be trusted.

## • *Fifth line, 6*

a) A noble person's rope is untied.
Auspicious.
There will be a capture among small men.

b) A noble person is released.
Good fortune.
There will be sincerity towards petty men.

*Commentary*

The *yin* lines in this hexagram, except for this fifth line (ruler or leader) generally stand for negative influences symbolised by petty men.
The fifth line is about a leader who is released from entanglement. Good fortune.
The noble person puts his trust in the petty men, but when he offers them release, they withdraw.

- *Top line, 6*

    *The duke shoots a hawk on a high wall
    and hits it.
    There is nothing for which this is unfavourable.*

    *Commentary*

The hawk stands for a high official close to the ruler. By hitting the hawk the ruler releases himself from a petty person in a high position ('high wall') who does not follow his orders.
Nothing unfavourable.

- *Summary*

Thunder above Water means that with thunder comes rain, symbolising release, liberation. When thunder brings rain, new life can begin.
  The west and south are favourable directions to go.
  If one has no goal or destination, turning back will bring good fortune.
  If one has a goal or destination, hurrying will bring good results.
  Hexagram 39, Trouble, Obstruction, is followed by hexagram 40, Release, Liberation, because in this hexagram the troubles and difficulties (of hexagram 39) are dissolved.
  This hexagram is about release and liberation from difficulties and obstructions in different stages:
  The first line is the beginning of release, which still needs some support. No error.
  In the second line someone is liberated from three negative influences (greed/lust, ignorance, and fear/hate, or petty men), by taking successful action. Persistence will bring good fortune.
  In the third line someone attracts negative influences due to his (ostentatious) behaviour. Persevering will bring distress.
  In the fourth line someone is released from entanglements. Friends who arrive can be trusted.

In the fifth line a superior person is released from entanglements. Good fortune. He has confidence in petty men, but when he offers them release, they withdraw.

In the sixth line a leader liberates himself from a petty man in a high position, who disobeys him. Nothing unfavourable.

Hexagram 40 is also about the different stages of Liberation after the attainment of Enlightenment.

# 41. *Sun* / Loss, Decrease

*gen* / mountain, standing still, stilling, stopping

*dui* / lake, still water, marsh, joy, pleasing

## • *Image*

Lake below Mountain.
A marshy lake at the foot of the mountain: Loss, Decrease.
The noble person keeps his desires
and pleasures under control.

## • *Judgment*

a) There will be a capture.
   Very auspicious.
   No misfortune.
   Augury is possible.
   Favourable for having somewhere to go.
   What is to be used?
   Two bowls can be used for the offering.

b) There will be confidence.
   Very good fortune.
   There will be no misfortune.
   One can be persistent.
   It will be beneficial to undertake something.
   What is to be used?
   Two bowls can be used for the sacrificial offering.

*Commentary*

Stilling (Mountain) that what is pleasing (Lake): Decrease.
The hexagram indicates that loss or decrease accompanied with confidence will lead to good fortune. There will be no error. It will be advisable to stay persistent. It will be beneficial to go somewhere or undertake something.
A small offering ('two bowls of food') can be used at the proper time.
All things decrease (loss) and increase (gain) in turn, and occur in accordance with the time. The timely occurrence of loss and decrease is of importance.

- ***Base line, 9***

    *A sacrificial service.*
    *Going quickly: no error.*
    *A libation: loss.*

*Commentary*

If one goes quickly after a sacrifice (large offering), there will be no error.
If one does so after a libation (small offering), there will be loss.
After having performed one's duties, going away quickly will be no mistake. Still, one should consider how much decrease this action will cause.

- ***Second line, 9***

    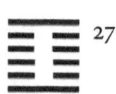

    a) *Favourable augury.*
       *Ominous for an attack.*
       *Not loss, but gain.*

    b) *Determination is beneficial.*
       *Moving forward brings disaster.*
       *Not decreasing, but increasing.*

*Commentary*

It is beneficial to be determined as a means to fulfil one's aims. Advancing will be disastrous. This is not a time for decreasing, but for increasing.

## • Third line, 6

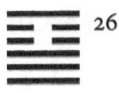 26

*When three people travel together,
one will be lost [on the way].
One who travels alone, finds a friend.*

*Commentary*

One should travel alone, for three persons may cause disagreement or give rise to suspicion.

## • Fourth line, 6

 38

*One decreases one's illness.
Acting quickly: there will be joy.
No misfortune.*

*Commentary*

Diminishing the illness. If one acts quickly, there will be joy. No error.

## • Fifth line, 6

 61

*Someone is enriched with a turtle
worth ten pairs of cowrie shells.
He cannot oppose it.
Auspicious.*

*Commentary*

Someone is enriched with a small fortune ('worth ten pairs of cowrie shells'). He cannot refuse it. Good fortune. These blessings come from above.

### • *Top line, 9*

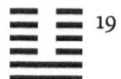

*No loss, but gain.*
*No misfortune.*
*Determination auspicious.*
*Favourable to have somewhere to go.*
*One will get a servant, but not a family.*

*Commentary*

There is no decrease, but increase. There will be no misfortune. Determination will bring good fortune. It is beneficial to go somewhere or undertake something.
One will get a servant (follower), but not a family (home). One's intention or aim will be fulfilled.

### • *Summary*

Lake below Mountain means a marshy lake at the foot of the mountain symbolising loss, decrease.

The mountain slowly crumbles into the lake, indicating loss, decrease or reduction. All things decrease (loss) and increase (gain) in turn, and occur in accordance with the time. Loss accompanied with confidence will bring good fortune. If done at the proper time, a small offering (gift) can be used to lessen the decrease.

When going somewhere or undertaking something, it will be beneficial to have a goal or destination in view.

Hexagram 40, Release, Liberation, is followed by hexagram 41, Loss, Decrease, because after the thunder and rain of hexagram 40, the lake will be overflown, and the mountain crumbles into it.

The release (hexagram 40) of troubles and difficulties will be decreased in hexagram 41.

This hexagram is about loss, decrease, and diminishing in different stages:

In the first line someone sets forth quickly after having performed his duties. This will be no mistake, but one should consider how much loss this hasty departure will cause.

In the second line it is good to be determined, but to advance will lead to disaster. This is no time for decrease, but for increase. Determination will fulfil one's aim.

In the third line one is advised to travel alone, for travelling with three persons will lead to discord or give rise to suspicions.

In the fourth line one decreases one's illness. If one acts quickly there will be joy and no mistake.

In the fifth line one is enriched with a small fortune, which cannot be refused. There will be unexpected or unsought good fortune coming from above.

In the sixth line there is no decrease, but increase. Determination will bring good fortune. When going somewhere or undertaking something, it is advantageous to have a goal or destination in view.

One will get supporters, but not a family or home. One's intention or goals will be fulfilled.

# 42. *Yi* / Gain, Increase

xun / wind, wood, gentle, penetrating

zhen / thunder, shock, moving, growth

- *Image*

    Wind above Thunder.
    A forest of blooming trees in spring: Gain, Increase.
    A noble person, seeing the good, follows it
    and corrects his errors.

- *Judgment*

    a) Favourable to have somewhere to go.
    Favourable to cross the great river.
    b) It will be beneficial to undertake something.
    Beneficial to go on a journey.

*Commentary*

Increase moves (Thunder) gentle and mild (Wind) in daily progress without limit.
To decrease what is above is to increase what is below: the gladness of the people is boundless. That which proceeds from above to what is below, is a way (*Dao*) that is good and glorious. Heaven bestows and earth receives, thereby things increase infinitely.
It will be beneficial to go somewhere or to undertake something. If one finds the right means (Wood, boat), to go on a journey will be beneficial.
The way of increase proceeds in harmony with the time. The timely occurrence of increase is of importance.

- *Base line, 9* 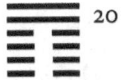 20

    *Favourable to undertake something great.*
    *Very auspicious.*
    *No error.*

                    Commentary

    The time is favourable to undertake something great. Good fortune. No error. But those who occupy lowly positions (base line), or are at the beginning of their career, should not engage themselves in important undertakings.

- *Second line, 6*  61

    *Someone is enriched with a turtle,*
    *worth ten pairs of cowrie shells.*
    *He cannot oppose it.*
    *Long-term augury: auspicious.*
    *The king used this turtle for a sacrifice*
    *to the Lord of Heaven (Di).*
    *Auspicious.*

                    Commentary

    Someone is enriched with a small fortune ('worth ten pairs of cowrie shells').
    He cannot refuse it. The one who enriches him comes from elsewhere.
    A long-term perseverance brings good fortune.
    The fortune may be dedicated to the service (offering) of the country.
    Good fortune.

    Note. Di *was the supreme god of the* Shang *dynasty, who was also worshipped by the* Zhou *people.*

- **Third line, 6**     ☰ 37

    a) Gain through unfortunate affairs.
       No blame.
       There is a capture.
       They reported in the middle of the road.
       The duke used a jade gui.

    b) Increasing through unfortunate events.
       No error.
       There is sincerity and confidence.
       They reported in the middle of the journey.
       The duke used his jade emblem of rank.

*Commentary*

Someone gains through unfortunate means or circumstances. No blame. If he reports with sincerity, and keeps to the middle way, he can carry his emblem of authority.

*Note.* A *gui* is an elongated, pointed jade scepter-tablet held by ancient rulers (sometimes by envoys) on ceremonial occasions.

- **Fourth line, 6**      25

    a) Reporting in the middle of the road.
       The duke followed.
       Favourable to move the state of the Yin people.

    b) Reporting in the middle of the journey.
       The duke agreed.
       It is beneficial to move the capital.

*Commentary*

If he reports and agrees to act without extremes (keeps to the middle way) it is beneficial to give him a great task.

*Note. The task probably refers to removing the capital because of floods.*

- **Fifth line, 9**

    a) There will be captives: let it be the heart.
    Don't ask.
    Very auspicious.
    There will be captives: let it be us who get them.

    b) There is sincerity in a kind heart.
    Don't ask questions.
    Very good fortune.
    There is sincerity and confidence:
    we will get what we want.

*Commentary*

If there is sincerity and confidence, and we do not ask questions, we will receive very good fortune and attain our goal.

- **Top line, 9**

    He enriches no one.
    Someone strikes him.
    Setting up the hearts.
    Do not perform the *heng* rite.
    Ominous.

*Commentary*

He brings no increase to others. There are those who strike at him. There is no consistency in his heart and mind. Do not continue with this. A disaster threatens from outside.

Note. About the heng *perpetuation rite, see note hexagram 5, base line.*

## • *Summary*

Thunder above Wind, symbolising a forest of blooming trees in spring, indicates a time of increase.

Increase moves (Thunder) gentle and mild (Wind) in a daily progress.
All things increase (gain) and decrease (loss) in turn, and occur in accordance with the time.

When going somewhere or undertaking something, it will be beneficial to have a goal or destination in view. If one finds the right means (Wood, boat), it will be beneficial to go on a journey.

Hexagram 41, Loss, Decrease, is followed by hexagram 42, Gain, Increase because – according to the law of extremes – when something (decrease) reaches an extreme, it will change into its opposite (increase).

This hexagram is about gain or increase in different stages:

In the first line it is favourable to undertake something great. Good fortune. No error. But those in lowly positions should not engage in important undertakings.

In the second line someone is enriched by a small fortune, and cannot refuse it. The one who enriched him comes from elsewhere. In some cases it may come from a woman (trigram Wind, eldest daughter). This good fortune may be dedicated to the service of others.
A long-term perseverance brings good fortune.

In the third line someone gains through unfortunate means or circumstances. No blame. If *not* done with sincerity, and in the middle way, then there will be misfortune.

In the fourth line someone agrees to act without extremes (in a middle way), and it it will be beneficial to give him a great task.

In the fifth line, if we are sincere and confident, and refrain from asking questions, we will get what we want. Very good fortune.

In the sixth line someone does not benefit others, and if he has no constancy of heart, he gets injured by someone from outside.
Do not continue with this. Disaster threatens.

# 43. *Guai* / Decisiveness, Resolution

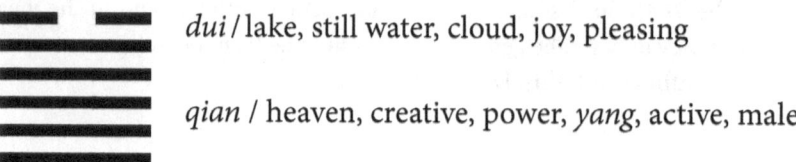

*dui* / lake, still water, cloud, joy, pleasing

*qian* / heaven, creative, power, *yang*, active, male

- **Image**

    Lake above Heaven.
    A cloud (with rain) in the sky: Decisiveness, Resolution.
    The noble person bestows his wealth upon those below without hesitation.

- **Judgment**

    a) Displayed at the court of the king.
    The captives cry out.
    Danger.
    Report from a town: not favourable for taking up arms.
    Favourable for having somewhere to go.

    b) Shown at the royal court.
    Sincerity is outspoken: danger.
    It is reported from a town:
    unfavourable for taking up arms.
    It will be beneficial to undertake something.

*Commentary*

Strength (Heaven) is combined with joy (Lake), decisiveness (Heaven) with peacefulness (Lake). Resolution (determination) means taking decisive actions.
The strong (five *yang* lines) determine the affairs of the weak (one *yin* line).
A proclamation is made at the king's court. If sincerity is outspoken, it will be dangerous.
There is a report from town: it is unfavourable to resort to violence.
It will be beneficial to go somewhere or undertake something.

### • *Base line, 9*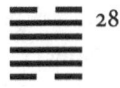

*Too much strength in the feet.*
*Going forward, but unable to attain.*
*Injury.*
*Mistake.*

*Commentary*

To set forth with too much decisiveness leads to failure (injury). This may bring shame.

### • *Second line, 9*

*He is wary and cries out.*
*In the evening and night there is violence.*
*No fear.*

*Commentary*

Being on the alert, he cries out for alarm. There is fighting in the night.
If one remains on the middle path (middle line of bottom trigram), there is no need for worry.

- **Third line, 9**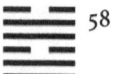

    *Strength in the cheekbones.*
    *Misfortune.*
    *A noble person walks alone and meets with rain.*
    *If he gets wet he will be displeased.*
    *No error.*

    *Commentary*

*Strength in the cheekbones:* displaying too much strength will bring misfortune.

A noble person is travelling alone and firmly determined. If he encounters disagreeable situations (rain, getting wet), he will have resentment, but no need for shame.

- **Fourth line, 9**

    *No skin on the thighs (haunches).*
    *He walks falteringly.*
    *If led like a sheep, trouble will go away.*
    *Hearing the words, not believing.*

    *Commentary*

If one goes forward by oneself, it is difficult to proceed. If one allows oneself to be led (by others) regret vanishes. He might hear what is said, but does not trust it.

Note. 'No skin on the thighs (haunches)' in this line is due to hard labour. This is the reason he walks falteringly. In hexagram 44, line 3, 'no skin on the buttocks (haunches)' is due to sexual activity, because hexagram 44 has many indications of sexual symbolism.

- *Fifth line, 9*  34

    *A mountain goat hopping
    in the middle of the road.
    There will be no misfortune.*

    *Commentary*

A wild goat (trigram Lake) is jumping in the middle of a herd (sheep). Firm resolution is necessary to remove him. Treading the middle path, one avoids blame. But the result will not be great.

- *Top line, 6* 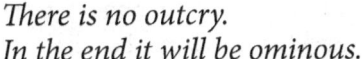 1

    *There is no outcry.
    In the end it will be ominous.*

    *Commentary*

In the end misfortune (disaster) will come without warning. This is because one fails to persist to the end.

- *Summary*

Lake above Heaven means a cloud heavy with rain in the sky. It symbolises water which has risen too high, and which can overflow and break through its barriers.

Strength (Heaven) is combined with joy (Lake) means decisiveness.
The strong (five *yang* lines) determine the affairs of the weak (one *yin* line).

Speaking out sincerely about the true state of affairs will be dangerous. It is unfavourable to resort to violence. When going somewhere or undertaking something, it will be beneficial to have a goal or destination.

Hexagram 42, Gain, Increase, is followed by hexagram 43, Decisiveness, Resolution, because the thunder and wind of hexagram 42 is always accompanied with clouds heavy with rain in the sky (hexagram 43). If increase (hexagram 42) continues, it may become too much, and burst or break through (hexagram 43).

This hexagram is about decisiveness and resolution in different stages:

In the first line one advances with too much strength (decisiveness). This may lead to failure and shame.

In the second line someone is alert and cries out for alarm. There is violence in dark times. If one keeps to the middle path, and stays even-minded, there is no need for anxiety.

In the third line someone is firmly determined to travel alone. If he meets with hindrances (rain and getting wet), he will be irritated, but there is no need for shame. No error.

In the fourth line, if one goes forward by oneself, it is difficult to proceed. If one allows oneself to be led by others, regret vanishes. One may hear what is said, but does not follow it.

In the fifth line firm resolution is necessary to remove something disturbing. Taking the middle course will avoid blame, but the result will not be great.

In the sixth line misfortune (disaster) will come without warning, because one fails to persist to the end.

# 44. *Gou* / Meeting, Contact, Encounter

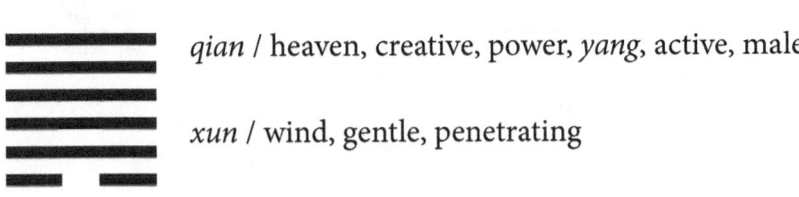

qian / heaven, creative, power, *yang*, active, male

xun / wind, gentle, penetrating

## • *Image*

Wind below Heaven.
Wind blowing beneath the sky:
Meeting, Contact, Encounter.
The ruler issues orders and makes them known
to the four quarters of his kingdom.

## • *Judgment*

A healthy and strong maiden.
Do not take the maiden as wife.

*Commentary*

The soft and gentle (Wind) meets the hard and strong (Heaven). There is a woman (one *yin* line) with many men (five *yang* lines).
*Do not take the maiden as wife*: the woman is strong (Heaven) and her behaviour is fickle (Wind). A relationship will not last.
When heaven and earth meet (mate), all things will manifest. The timely occurrence of meeting (mating) is of great importance.

### • Base line, 6

a) *Tied to a metal brake.*
   *A captive lean pig jumps about.*
   *Augury: auspicious.*
   *Having somewhere to go: ominous.*

b) *Bound by a metal brake.*
   *A captured weak pig is jumping about.*
   *Perseverance brings good fortune.*
   *When undertaking something, one encounters disaster.*

#### Commentary

The way of the weak (*yin* line) is to be led and brought under control ('tied to a metal brake'), but this will lead to disagreement ('a captive lean pig jumps about').

Perseverance will bring good fortune. If someone goes somewhere or undertakes something, it will bring disaster.


### • Second line, 9

a) *There is fish in the basket.*
   *No fault.*
   *Not favourable for the guest.*

b) *There is fish in the kitchen.*
   *No mistake.*
   *Not beneficial for the guests.*

#### Commentary

There is something in store. No error. But this is of no advantage to the guests.

- **Third line, 9**  6

    No skin on the buttocks (haunches).
    He walks falteringly.
    Danger.
    No great misfortune.

### Commentary

If one goes forward it is difficult to proceed. Threatening, but no great harm.

*Note.* 'No skin on the buttocks (haunches)' is due to sexual activity, because hexagram 44 has many indications of sexual symbolism.

- **Fourth line, 9**  57

    a) There is no fish in the basket.
       Ominous to act.

    b) There is no fish in the kitchen.
       Acting brings disaster.

### Commentary

Nothing of value is available. The disaster comes from keeping oneself away from the people.

- **Fifth line, 9** 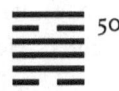 50

    a) The melon is wrapped in
       purple willow leaves.
       Hold a jade talisman in the mouth.
       Something falls from heaven.

b) *Great qualities are hidden.*
   *Concealment of talent or beauty.*
   *Some blessing falls from heaven.*

### Commentary

Out of humility (the melon is a fruit in a low place) someone is hiding his great qualities ('willow leaves'), and concealing his talents or beauty ('holding a jade talisman in the mouth').
The image is about a worthy person who remains out of people's attention and leads an insignificant life.
*Something falls from heaven,* because one's intention is in consonance with heaven's decrees, and what is willed will be manifested.

## • *Top line,* 9

*They lock their horns.*
*Distress.*
*No misfortune.*

### Commentary

Stuck in an encounter ('they lock their horns'). Distress, but there will be no misfortune.

## • *Summary*

Wind under Heaven means the wind blows beneath the sky. It symbolises a strong man (Heaven) who encounters a mature woman (Wind, eldest daughter). However, a relationship is not favoured.

Five *yang* lines and one *yin* line indicate a woman who has many men.
The wind blowing under heaven is fickle, and moves everywhere. One should *not* marry this woman.

This hexagram is also about sexual contact or intercourse. (See the sexual symbolism of line 2 and 4 'fish in the basket', and line 5, 'a melon wrapped in willow leaves', and a little bit more obvious in line 3, 'no skin on the buttocks'.)

Hexagram 43, Decisiveness, Resolution, is followed by hexagram 44, Meeting, Contact, because the heavy clouds in the sky (Lake, hexagram 43) may be accompanied by strong winds (hexagram 44).

With enough resolution (hexagram 43) one is sure to encounter (hexagram 44) opportunity.

This hexagram is about meeting, encounter, (sexual) contact in different stages:

In the first line the weak (*yin*) have to be led and brought under control. This will lead to disagreement, but perseverance will bring good fortune. Going somewhere or undertaking something will bring disaster.

In the second line something of value is available, but it is of no advantage to the guests. No error.

In the third line, if one goes forward it is difficult to proceed. The situation is dangerous, but there will be no great misfortune.

In the fourth line nothing of value is available. This gives rise to misfortune. The disaster comes from keeping oneself away from the people.

In the fifth line someone is hiding his great qualities (talent and beauty) out of humbleness. There will be some unsought or unexpected good fortune. What is willed will be manifested.

In the sixth line a close contact will lead to distress, but there will be no misfortune.

# 45. Cui / Coming Together, Gathering

*dui* /lake, still water, joy, pleasing

*kun* / earth, receptive, *yin*, compliant, female

- **Image**

    Lake above Earth.
    A lake where streams come together: Gathering.
    A noble person gathers his weapons
    to guard against the unexpected.

- **Judgment**

    a) Offering.
    The king arrives at his temple.
    Favourable augury.
    Favourable to see a great man.
    Use a big sacrificial victim.
    Auspicious.
    Favourable to have somewhere to go.

    b) Success.
    The king arrives at his temple.
    Perseverance will be beneficial.
    It will be beneficial to see a great person.
    Good fortune to use a big sacrificial animal.
    It will be beneficial to undertake something.

*Commentary*

Compliance (Earth) and joy (Lake).
The king arrives at his temple to fulfil his ancestral duties in order to maintain public prosperity. Perseverance will be beneficial.
It will be beneficial to see a person of wisdom. Gathering together is done for putting things right. To perform great offerings will bring good fortune. It will be beneficial to go somewhere or to undertake something.
Observing how things gather together one can understand the inner nature of all things in heaven and earth.

- ***Base line, 6***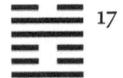

    a) *There will be a captive.*
    *If not tied at the end,*
    *there will be disorder, not gathering.*
    *First a cry, then a laugh.*
    *Do not worry.*
    *Going, no misfortune.*

    b) *If confidence is not kept to the end,*
    *there will be disorder instead of gathering.*
    *First there is a cry, and later a laugh.*
    *Do not worry.*
    *Going forward, there will be no error.*

*Commentary*

Only with confidence there will be a coming together. First there is a warning but later reassurance. There is no cause for anxiety. In advancing there will be no mistake.

- *Second line, 6*   47

    a) Drawn together: auspicious.
    No misfortune.
    There are captives.
    It is favourable to use the yue sacrifice.

    b) Being drawn together: good fortune.
    There will be no error.
    With sincerity it will be beneficial
    to perform a yue sacrifice.

                *Commentary*

Being drawn together, one has good fortune, and is without mistake. With sincerity, even a small spring offering will be beneficial.

*Note.* The yue *sacrifice is normally translated as a 'summer sacrifice', but considering the place of the hexagram in the Chinese seasonal calendar, hexagram 45 is a spring sacrifice, whereas hexagram 46 is a winter sacrifice, hexagram 50 a summer sacrifice, and hexagram 63 an autumn sacrifice.*
*See also hexagram 46, line 2, hexagram 50, Image and Judgment, and hexagram 63, line 5.*

- *Third line, 6*   31

    Gathering together with sighs.
    There is nothing for which this is favourable.
    In going forward there will be no misfortune.
    There will be some distress.

                *Commentary*

A gathering with sighs and distress. There is nothing for which this is favourable, yet in advancing there will be no error.

- *Fourth line, 9*

   Most auspicious.
   No misfortune.

   *Commentary*

Gathering the people together for the ruler and the country. His plans will reap great good fortune and are without error.

- *Fifth line, 9*

   a) Gathering those holding rank.
   No misfortune.
   Very auspicious.
   No capture.
   Prolonged determination.
   Trouble goes away.

   b) Assemble those holding rank.
   There will be no misfortune.
   Very good fortune.
   Without sincerity:
   with a long-term persistence trouble will disappear.

   *Commentary*

In gathering together those holding a position, there will be no misfortune. Very good fortune.
If there is no sincerity or confidence, only with a long-term determination will trouble disappear.

### • Top line, 6

*Sighing and sobbing.*
*Sniffing and tears.*
*No misfortune.*

*Commentary*

Although there is sighing and lamentation, the person will be without blame.

### • Summary

Lake above Earth means a lake where streams come together. It symbolises gathering. If the lake becomes too full, it may overflow. Therefore the noble person gathers his weapons to guard against the unexpected. Gathering together is done to put things right. Perseverance will be beneficial.

It will be beneficial to see a person of wisdom. To make great offerings will bring good fortune. When going somewhere or undertaking something it will be beneficial to have a goal or destination in view.

Hexagram 44, Meeting, Encounter, is followed by hexagram 45, Gathering because, when strong winds blow below the sky (hexagram 44) clouds gather above the earth (hexagram 45). The upper trigram Lake is a body of water, and could also mean a cloud.

When people meet each other (hexagram 44), a larger gathering may result (hexagram 45).

Hexagram 45 is about coming together, gathering, expressed in different stages:

In the first line, if confidence or sincerity does not remain to the end there will be disorder instead of gathering. There is a warning, but later confidence is restored. There is no reason for anxiety. In advancing there will be no error.

In the second line, being drawn together will bring good fortune and no error. With sincerity, even a small offering (action) will be beneficial.

In the third line there are difficult gatherings accompanied with sighs and distress. There is nothing for which this is favourable, yet to advance will be without error.

In the fourth line someone gathers people together for an important cause. This will lead to great good fortune and no error.

In the fifth line those holding positions are gathered together. Very good fortune. If they have no sincerity or confidence, only with long persistence will trouble disappear.

In the sixth line, at the end of gathering together there is distress, but the person is not to blame.

# 46. Sheng / Climbing, Rising

kun / earth, receptive, *yin*, passive, female

xun / wind, wood, gentle, penetrating

## • Image

> Earth above Wood.
> Trees growing upwards from the Earth: Climbing, Rising.
> The noble person acts in accordance with his virtues
> and accumulates the small
> in order to achieve something high and great.

## • Judgment

a) Great offering.
   Favourable for seeing a great man.
   Do not worry.
   Auspicious in going to the south.

b) Great success.
   Beneficial to see a great person.
   Do not worry.
   Going to the south will bring good fortune.

*Commentary*

Gentleness (Wood) and acceptance (Earth) are joined together. The gentle (Wood) rises at the proper time. Great success. It is beneficial to see a man of wisdom. There is no cause for anxiety. Proceeding to the south will bring good fortune. What is willed will be realised.

- **Base line, 6**

    He surely climbs upward.
    Most auspicious.

*Commentary*

He certainly moves upward. Great good fortune. His will accords with those above.

- **Second line, 9**

    a) There are captives.
    It is favourable to use the yue *sacrifice*.

    b) With sincerity it will be beneficial to perform a yue *sacrifice*.

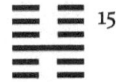

*Commentary*

If the small offering (of a *yue* sacrifice) is performed with sincerity, it will lead to happiness or joy.

*Note. The sacrifice in this line is generally mentioned as a summer sacrifice, but in the Chinese calendar it should be a winter sacrifice. (See also note hexagram 45, line 2.)*

- **Third line, 9**

    One climbs up to an empty town.

*Commentary*

*One climbs up to an empty town:* one has no doubt, and no one opposes it ('empty town'). It also means that the arising or ascending is meaningless ('empty').

- ***Fourth line, 6***

    *The king makes a sacrifice
    on Mount Qi (West Mountain).
    Auspicious.
    No misfortune.*

*Commentary*

*The king makes an offering on Mount Qi:* he does this in compliance with tradition, duty and responsibility. Good fortune. There will be no misfortune.

Note. The capital of the Zhou dynasty was located near Mount Qi. Offerings were meant to bring good order and prosperity to one's family, city or state.

- ***Fifth line, 6***

    *Augury: auspicious.
    Climbing up the stairs.*

*Commentary*

Perseverance brings good fortune. The ascent must be made step by step. One's intention or aim is fulfilled.

Note. 'Climbing up the stairs' could mean that people were climbing the stairs of a mountain shrine.

- *Top line, 6*

    *Climbing in darkness.*
    *Augury favourable for not resting.*

### Commentary

Going up in the darkness. Perseverance. It is beneficial to continue, and not to rest.

- *Summary*

Earth above Wood means trees growing upward from their roots under the earth, and spreading their branches and leaves towards the sky. This symbolises climbing, rising, ascending.

Sublime success. It is advisable to see a person of wisdom. There is no cause for anxiety. Moving to the south will bring good fortune. One will attain what one wants.

Hexagram 45, Coming Together, Gathering, is followed by hexagram 46, Climbing, Rising, because the small streams gathering at the lake (hexagram 45) result in much water, which moisten the roots of the trees growing rapidly from the earth (hexagram 46).

In certain circumstances of gathering (hexagram 45) there are always possibilities to raise (hexagram 46) one's position.

Hexagram 46 is about rising, climbing, and ascending in different stages:

In the first line one is certainly moving upwards. Great good fortune. One's ascending is in accordance with those above.

In the second line a small offering (action) done with sincerity will lead to happiness.

In the third line one moves upwards without doubts because there is no one who opposes. But this promotion is without meaning.

In the fourth line, to attain good fortune, an offering (action) is made in accordance with tradition, duty or circumstance. There will be no misfortune.

In the fifth line perseverance will bring good fortune, if the ascent is made step by step. This will lead to fulfilment of what is willed.

In the sixth line there is some blind progress. It is beneficial to persevere in one's ascending and not to rest.

# 47. *Kun* / Adversity, Exhaustion

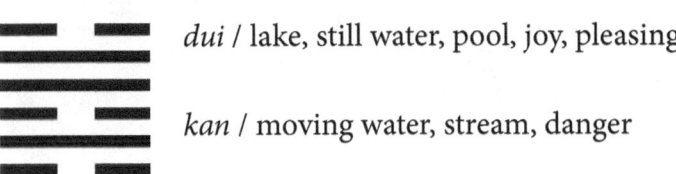

*dui* / lake, still water, pool, joy, pleasing

*kan* / moving water, stream, danger

- ### *Image*

    Water below Lake.
    A lake drained by a stream: Adversity, Exhaustion.
    The noble person risks his life to achieve his goal.

- ### *Judgment*

    a) Offering.
    Augury auspicious for the great man.
    No misfortune.
    There are words not believed.

    b) Success.
    Determination brings good fortune for the great person.
    There will be no misfortune.
    Though words be spoken, they are not believed.

    *Commentary*

Danger (Water) and joy (Lake) meet. When the great person meets with adversity, he remains cheerful (Lake) despite all the dangers (Water). Only a great person's determination will bring good fortune and success. Since what is spoken is not believed, it would be better to stop talking.

- **Base line, 6**

    He sits exhausted on a tree trunk.
    He enters a dark valley
    and is not seen for three years.

    *Commentary*

    Because of difficult circumstances ('dark valley'), he encounters no one for three years.

- **Second line, 9**

    Difficulties amidst food and drink.
    Men with vermilion garments
    from the Fang state arrive.
    Favourable for offering sacrifice.
    No misfortune.
    Ominous for an attack.

    *Commentary*

    *Difficulties amidst food and drink*: men of high rank ('vermilion garments') from the border state arrive. It will be beneficial to offer sacrifice. There will be no error. Advancing will bring disaster.

- **Third line, 6**

    Bothered by rocks
    and holding on to thorns and thistles.
    Entering his house he does not see his wife.
    Ominous.

#### Commentary

Bothered by extreme difficulties, and nothing to hold on to, he enters his house, but cannot find his wife. Disaster.

- ***Fourth line, 9***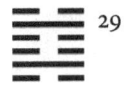

    *Coming very slowly.*
    *Trouble with a metal-clad carriage.*
    *Distress.*
    *There will be an end.*

#### Commentary

Coming very slowly because of troubles with one's position (minister, 'metal-clad carriage', fourth line). There will be distress, but it will end.

- ***Fifth line, 9***

    *Nose and feet are cut off.*
    *Humiliation by men with red garments.*
    *Gradually there will be a removal.*
    *Favourable for offering sacrifice.*

#### Commentary

*Nose and feet are cut off*: one suffers humiliation because of difficulties with men of middle rank ('red garments'). Gradually the difficulties will be removed. It will be beneficial to offer sacrifice to ensure some good fortune.

*Note.* See hexagram 38, line 3, where the nose is cut off, also indicating humiliation.

- *Top line, 6*

    Bothered by creepers and vines,
    and tripped by a tree stump.
    Moving is difficult.
    There will be trouble.
    Auspicious for an attack.

*Commentary*

Bothered by extreme difficulties. One is hampered in one's movements. There will be trouble. If one has regret, advancing will bring good fortune.

- *Summary*

Water below the Lake means the water runs away from the bottom of the lake. The lake is drying up, and the fish, plants and animals are in difficulty for lack of water. This symbolises adversity and exhaustion.

This is one of the four 'danger' hexagrams of the *Yi Jing*: hexagrams 29, 39, 47, and 59.

Determination brings good fortune to the great person. Success. No misfortune. Since what is spoken is not believed, it would be better to stop speaking.

Hexagram 46, Climbing, Rising, is followed by hexagram 47, Adversity, Exhaustion, because when advancing goes on without stopping it will soon lead to exhaustion. The trees that grow from within the earth (hexagram 46), will be exhausted due to lack of water that is drained from the lake (hexagram 47).

Hexagram 47 is about adversity and difficulties in six stages:

In the first line one encounters difficult situations, and sees nobody for three years.

In the second line, amidst favourable circumstances (food and drink) difficulties appear (men of high rank). It will be advisable to offer something. No mistake. Advancing will bring disaster.

In the third line one is faced with extreme difficulties, and has no one to support him. Disaster.

In the fourth line one arrives slowly because of trouble in a rather high position. Distress, but there will be an end to this trouble.

In the fifth line there is humiliation due to difficulties with men of middle rank. What we want now will not be realised. Gradually the difficulties will go away. It will be advisable to offer something to ensure some good fortune.

In the sixth line one encounters extreme difficulties, and is hindered in one's progress. There will be much trouble. Provided regret is felt, moving forward will bring good fortune.

# 48. Jing / The Well

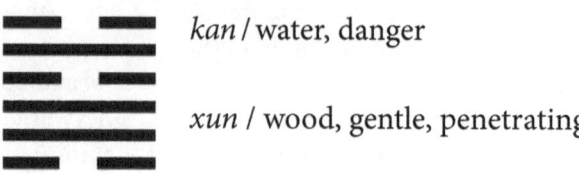

kan / water, danger

xun / wood, gentle, penetrating

- **Image**

    Water above Wood.
    Water contained by wood: The Well.
    The noble person helps the people
    with encouragement and advice.

- **Judgment**

    *A town is moved, the well is not moved.*
    *No loss, no gain.*
    *They come and go in an orderly way.*
    *When the well rope is too short to draw water*
    *or the bucket breaks: ominous.*

*Commentary*

The bucket (trigram Wood) penetrates the water (trigram Water) to bring it up. The well nourishes yet is never exhausted. The well is constant, there will be no loss or gain. A town can be moved, but not a well. If the rope is too short to draw the water, it means that one does not achieve one's aim. If the bucket breaks, it means disaster.

- ***Base line, 6***

    *A muddy well.*
    *No one drinks from it.*
    *At an old well there are no animals.*

    *Commentary*

As the well is old and soiled with mud, no one uses it. One's purpose cannot be realised.

- ***Second line, 9***

    *Shoot a silver carp in the depth of the well:*
    *the bucket is damaged and leaks.*

    *Commentary*

Shooting fish in the valley-shaped well, the bucket gets damaged and leaks. Because of inadequate means, one cannot attain one's goal.

- ***Third line, 9***

    *The well has been cleaned out*
    *but it is not drunk from:*
    *our heart is sad.*
    *It can be used for drawing water.*
    *The king's covenant: all will receive its blessings.*

    *Commentary*

The well has been cleaned out, but to our heart's sorrow no one drinks from it. If the king is wise, everyone will share his good fortune.

- *Fourth line, 6*

    The well is lined with bricks.
    No misfortune.

                    *Commentary*

The well is under repair. There will be no error.


- *Fifth line, 9*

    The well is clear.
    A cold water spring.
    One can drink from it.

                    *Commentary*

The well is a pure water spring, and can be used for nourishment.


- *Top line, 6*

    a) The well is frequently used.
        Do not cover it.
        There is a capture.
        Very auspicious.

    b) The well is frequently used.
        One should not cover it.
        There is confidence.
        Very good fortune.

*Commentary*

The well continues to supply water, and is used without hindrance. If there is confidence, it will lead to very good fortune.

## • *Summary*

Water above Wood means a well lined with wood to prevent the water to be mixed with mud. It also means a wooden bucket in which water is drawn up from a well. It symbolises a steady source one can draw from, but if conditions are difficult ('rope too short', or 'broken bucket'), one does not achieve one's aim. Disaster.

Hexagram 47, Adversity, Exhaustion, is followed by hexagram 48, The Well, because the water that is drained from the lake (hexagram 47) appears in another place as a well (hexagram 48).

Hexagram 48 is about drawing something from a source in six stages:

In the first line one cannot achieve one's aim because there are no possibilities.

In the second line we cannot attain our goal because of inadequate means. This is due to silliness or unskilfulness.

In the third line there are enough opportunities, but they are not seized. If we are wise, we should take the good fortune.

In the fourth line there is some necessary delay, but the situation is hopeful. No misfortune.

In the fifth line one can draw upon a great source of possibilities available to all.

In the sixth line there is a source well-used. With confidence it will lead to a great achievement. Very good fortune.

# 49. *Ge* / Radical Change, Revolution

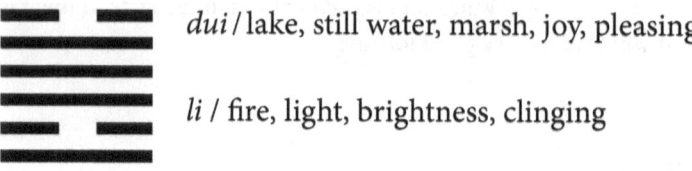

*dui* / lake, still water, marsh, joy, pleasing

*li* / fire, light, brightness, clinging

- *Image*

    Fire below Lake.
    A fire within the lake: Radical Change, Revolution.
    The noble person sets a calendar
    to order the times and seasons.

- *Judgment*

    a) If it is a sacrifice day, take captives.
    Great offering.
    Favourable augury.
    Trouble goes away.

    b) On the day of a radical change, have confidence.
    Sublime accomplishment.
    Determination is beneficial.
    Troubles disappear.

*Commentary*

Water (Lake, youngest daughter) and Fire (middle daughter) oppose each other. They live together but their wishes are in conflict. This is a reason for radical change.

On the day of radical change one should have confidence. An enlightened (Fire) attitude brings joy (Lake). Determination will bring great benefit and makes it possible to put things in order. Sublime accomplishment.

Heaven and earth bring about change and produce the progress of the four seasons. *Tang* (the founder of the *Shang* dynasty), and *Wu* (the founder of the *Zhou* dynasty) brought about political revolution because they were in compliance with the will of Heaven and the wishes of the people. The timely occurrence of Radical Change is of great importance.

*Note. Ge (radical change), and ge (hide) are written with the same Chinese character. As a verb ge means 'to skin', 'to get rid off', indicating a radical change.*

- ***Base line, 9***

    Bind them with yellow oxhide.

    *Commentary*

Binding with yellow oxhide means to strengthen one's position, but one should not take action yet.

- ***Second line, 6***

    a) If it is a sacrifice day, then change.
    Auspicious for an attack.
    No misfortune.

    b) On the day of a radical change, act.
    Taking action brings success.
    There will be no error.

*Commentary*

On the right day, make changes. When the time for radical change is there take action. This will bring success. There will be no error.

## • Third line, 9

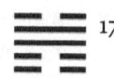 17

a) Ominous for an attack.
   Augury: danger.
   An oxhide harness with three girdles.
   There will be a capture.

b) To advance will bring disaster.
   Determination is dangerous.
   Radical change is heard three times.
   There will be confidence.

*Commentary*

Advancing will bring disaster, and determination will lead to danger. When radical change is mentioned ('heard') three times, then act with confidence.

## • Fourth line, 9

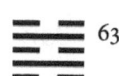 63

a) Trouble goes away.
   There will be a capture.
   Auspicious for changing command.

b) Troubles will disappear.
   There will be confidence.
   To change a mandate brings good fortune.

*Commentary*

Troubles will disappear and confidence is established. A change of order (government) brings good fortune. When change is so willed, one acts accordingly. He believes in the will of those below, and acts to carry out the mandate of the people.

- **Fifth line, 9** 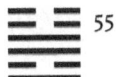 55

    a) The great person changes like a tiger.
       There will be a capture before divination.

    b) The great person makes changes
       in a brave and powerful way.
       There will be confidence even before consulting the oracle.

*Commentary*

The great person makes the radical change in a brilliantly civilised manner like a tiger, whose skin patterns shine with great brilliance. He is believed (trusted) by those below, even before the oracle is consulted.

- **Top line, 6**  13

    a) The noble person changes like a leopard.
       Small men wear masks of rawhide.
       Ominous for an attack.
       Augury for a dwelling: auspicious.

    b) The noble person makes the changes in an elegant way.
       Petty men change their faces.
       Advance brings disaster.
       Persisting to remain where we are brings good fortune.

*Commentary*

The noble person makes the radical change in a graceful manner, like a leopard, whose skin patterns shine with beauty. The petty men change their allegiance, and follow the noble person with obedience. Advance brings disaster. Persisting to remain where we are brings good fortune.

## • *Summary*

Fire below Lake means a fire within the lake. Revolution is meant in the sense of reform, renewal or radical change. Both primary and inner trigrams represent situations of conflict. The fire will dry up the lake, or the water will put out the fire. The fire and the lake also represent two women (the middle daughter and the youngest daughter), who cannot get along, and are quarrelling.

The upper inner trigram (Heaven) represents metal, and the lower inner trigram (Wind) represents wood. According to the relationships of the five elements, wood injures metal (see *Introduction* p. xxiv).

Both the inside and outside trigrams of this hexagram are calling for radical change. On the day of radical change one should be confident. Determination will be beneficial. A revolution makes it possible to put things in order. Sublime accomplishment.

Hexagram 48, The Well, is followed by hexagram 49, Radical Change, Revolution, because the water in the well, coming from the lake, is dried up and the city has to be moved. This brings revolution (hexagram 49).

Hexagram 49 is about radical change, revolution, reform, and renewal in different stages:

In the first line one should strengthen one's position (within the old structure), but should not take action yet.

In the second line, when the time for radical change comes, one should take action, but one must not advance before certain changes have been noticed. Taking action brings good fortune. It will be no mistake.

In the third line determination will be dangerous and advancing brings disaster. When radical change is mentioned or heard three times, act with confidence. But one must make sure that a rumoured change has indeed occurred before taking further actions.

In the fourth line troubles will disappear and confidence is established. A change of order or government will bring good fortune. Having confidence one acts accordingly.

In the fifth line one makes the change in a brilliantly civilised manner. He is so confident that he does not need to consult the oracle. Others believe (trust) him.

In the sixth line one makes the change in an elegant and graceful manner. Petty men change their attitude and follow the leader with obedience. Moving forward brings disaster. Persisting to remain where we are brings good fortune.

Hexagram 49 is also about the radical changes during a spiritual process of transformation.

# 50. *Ding* / The Cauldron, Transformation

*li* / fire, light, brightness, clinging

*xun* / wind, wood, gentle, penetrating

- ***Image***

    Fire above Wind.
    Wood within the fire: The Cauldron.
    The noble person establishes his position
    and follows the will of Heaven.

- ***Judgment***

    Great offering.
    Auspicious.

*Commentary*

Wood and Fire combine to cook the sacrifice. The *ding* is a symbol for sacrificial offerings and establishing the new. The sage (or king) cooked offerings for the Lord of Heaven, and nourished men of virtue and wisdom. Sublime success. Good fortune. By gentle (Wood) employment perception (Fire) is sharpened.

*Note.* A **ding** *was originally an ancient Chinese vessel with two loop handles and three or four legs. The three-legged* **ding** *is round, and the four-legged one is square. It was cast of bronze and decorated with sacred inscriptions. In the* **ding** *substances were* **transformed**. *It was used for both cooking and sacrificial offerings. The emperor used it to prepare sacrificial offerings to the Lord of Heaven, and to nourish persons of virtue and wisdom. Later on the* **ding** *was* used in the temple of ancestors at a family memorial ceremony. The ding was used at specific times of sacrifice, such as spring, summer, autumn, and winter. See also hexagram 45, line 2, Note.

## • Base line, 6

a) The cauldron's feet are turned up.
   Favourable to remove the bad meat.
   He gets a slave woman with a child.
   No misfortune.

b) The cauldron is turned upside down.
   It is favourable to remove stale residue.
   He gets a concubine for the sake of her son.
   There will be no error.

### Commentary

It is not wrong to turn the cauldron upside down for removing the stale residue.
He takes a concubine, either for the sake of her son, or to beget a son.
It is not wrong to do something out of the ordinary *if* it is done with a noble intention. No error.

## • Second line, 9

The cauldron is filled with food.
My mate has an illness,
but it can not reach me.
Auspicious.

### Commentary

The cauldron is full. One's companion has ill-will, but it cannot harm one. Good fortune.

- **Third line, 9**  64

    *The cauldron's ears are coming off.*
    *Its use is blocked.*
    *The fat meat of the pheasant is not eaten.*
    *It is about to rain.*
    *Trouble, but ultimately auspicious.*

    *Commentary*

It is difficult to move the cauldron because its ears are coming off. The good food in it cannot be eaten. One's activities are obstructed. When the rain falls, regret disappears. Good fortune in the end.

- **Fourth line, 9**  18

    *The cauldron's legs are broken*
    *spilling the duke's stew.*
    *His body is soaked.*
    *Ominous.*

    *Commentary*

The duke's stew is spilled and his body is soaked, means that he loses his trustworthiness and is punished severely. Disaster.

- **Fifth line, 6**  44

    *The cauldron*
    *has yellow (golden) carrying rings.*
    *Favourable augury.*

*Commentary*

The yellow signifies centrality, or keeping to the middle path. The golden rings signify hardness and strength. It is beneficial to be persistent.

- *Top line, 9*

    *The cauldron has jade carrying rings.*
    *Very auspicious.*
    *Unfavourable for nothing.*

*Commentary*

The jade rings signify a balance between hardness (strength) and mildness (compliance). Very good fortune. There is nothing for which this is unfavourable.

- *Summary*

Fire above Wind means the wind (air) blows into the fire. Wind is also wood, meaning there is wood within the fire. The image of the hexagram represents a cauldron. The bottom lines of the hexagram represent the legs of the cauldron. The lower inner trigram (Heaven) is the metal of which the cauldron is made. The upper inner trigram (Lake) represents the content of the cauldron. The broken fifth line represents the ears or rings of the cauldron, and the whole top line represents the carrying bar of the cauldron. Great success and good fortune.

Lightning (Fire) within the cloud (hexagram 49) is followed by lightning (Fire), accompanied by wind (hexagram 50). Hexagram 49, Radical Change, Revolution, is followed by hexagram 50 The Cauldron, Transformation because in hexagram 49 the old is abolished (revolution), and in hexagram 50 the new is established (transformation). This hexagram – cooking ingredients in a sacrificial vessel as an offering – is about the (spiritual) process of transformation.

Hexagram 50 is about transformation in six stages:

In the first line it is not wrong to perform something out of the ordinary (conventions) *if* it is done with a noble motive. There will be no error.

In the second line one's companion has ill-will, but he cannot do any harm. Good fortune.

In the third line one's activities are obstructed, and one cannot attain one's goal. When the rain falls (a good omen), regret vanishes. Good fortune in the end.

In the fourth line one's person is soiled because one has lost the confidence (trust) of others, and is punished severely. Disaster.

In the fifth line one should keep strongly to the middle path, and it will be beneficial to be steadfast.

In the sixth line one should keep a balance between strength and compliance. Very good fortune. There is nothing which is not favourable.

# 51. Zhen / Thunder, Arousing

zhen / thunder, shock, moving

zhen / thunder, growth

- *Image*

    Double Thunder.
    Rumbling thunder: Arousing, Shock.
    The noble person, in fear [from shock],
    examines and cultivates himself.

- *Judgment*

    Offering.
    Claps of thunder:
    [afterwards] there is laughing and talking.
    Thunder frightens people for a hundred li.
    He does not lose the sacrificial ladle and wine.

    *Commentary*

Double Thunder indicates success. When thunder comes people tremble with fear. Thunder startles those far away, and frightens those who are near. Fear brings caution, and being alert leads to good fortune. First there is thunder, but 'afterwards there is laughing and talking', and everything will be in order.

*He does not lose the sacrificial ladle and wine:* someone comes forward to protect the ancestral shrine and the altar of the harvest gods. This one is qualified to be the leader of the sacrifices.

Note. A li is a measure of distance, approximately a third of a mile, or about 575 metres.

### • Base line, 9

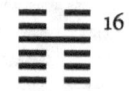

Claps of thunder:
afterwards there is laughing and talking.
Auspicious.

#### Commentary

When thunder comes there is danger and fear. 'Afterwards there is laughing and talking', and everything will be in order. Being alert leads to good fortune.

### • Second line, 6

Roaring thunder:
there is a danger of losing cowrie shells.
One climbs the Nine Hills.
Do not pursue.
One will catch it in seven days.

#### Commentary

When thunder comes with a roar there is danger of losing money or property.
Climbing the Nine Hills: after a quake (thunder in the earth, lower inner trigram Mountain), people flee into the hills, leaving their valuables behind. They should not pursue them, because they will regain it in seven days.

- **Third line, 6**

    Rumbling thunder.
    It thunders:
    in travel there will be no calamity.

 55

#### Commentary

When thunder comes, one trembles with fear. In going somewhere, being cautious and alert will prevent disaster.

- **Fourth line, 9**

    Thunder strikes into the marsh.

 24

#### Commentary

The power of thunder is absorbed in the mud. A strong effort (striking thunder) is smothered.

- **Fifth line, 6**

    Thunder comes and goes.
    Danger.
    There will be no loss.
    There will be activity.

17

#### Commentary

*Thunder comes and goes:* there is danger in movement (travelling). If there is loss (of money or property), it will not be great. Yet there are things to be done.

- *Top line, 6*

   *Rolling thunder:*
   *people look around in fear.*
   *Ominous for an attack.*
   *Thunder does not hit him, it hits his neighbour.*
   *There will be no blame.*
   *Among the wife's kin there will be talk.*

   *Commentary*

When it thunders people are anxious and distracted. Advancing brings disaster. The thunder does not affect his person, but affects his neighbour. There will be no blame. A marriage causes gossip: there is a need for caution.

- *Summary*

Double Thunder means rumbling thunder, indicating shock, shaking, arousing, awe-inspiring, threatening, and fear. Claps of thunder burst in the spring sky, waking up creatures from their hibernation, causing fear and trembling.

   The image of double Thunder indicates great power, but too much strength and movement can be dangerous, and calls for restraint and moderation. Thunder indicates success. When thunder arrives people tremble with fear but afterwards they laugh and talk, and everything will be in order again.
Here someone (a leader) appears who maintains his equilibrium under rather disturbing circumstances.

   Hexagram 50, The Cauldron, Transformation, is followed by hexagram 51, Thunder, Arousing, because after wind and lightning (fire) of hexagram 50, thunder of hexagram 51 follows naturally. After the transformation (hexagram 50) the arousing (hexagram 51) follows.

   Hexagram 51 is about shock and arousing in different stages:

   In the first line there is danger and fear, later there is laughter and talking and everything will be in order. Staying alert leads to good fortune.

In the second line there is danger of losing money or property. Do not pursue it, it will be regained in seven days.

In the third line there is danger and fear, but with caution and awareness one will prevent disaster.

In the fourth line a strong effort is stopped (smothered) in action.

In the fifth line there is danger in coming or going (travelling). There may be loss (of money or property), but not a great loss. One should not fail to do what has to be done.

In the sixth line there is danger, and people are terrified. To advance brings disaster. It will not affect oneself, but one's neighbour. If there is a relationship, it will cause gossip. No blame. There is a need for caution.

# 52. *Gen* / Mountain, Stilling

*gen* / mountain, standing still

*gen* / mountain, stilling, stopping

- **Image**

    Double Mountain.
    Mountains standing together: Stilling, Stillness.
    The noble person does not let his thoughts
    go beyond his position.

- **Judgment**

    Keeping the back still, one does not feel the body.
    If one goes into the courtyard one does not see the people.
    No misfortune.

*Commentary*

Double Mountain means stillness. Stilling means stopping. Stopping when it is time to stop, moving when it is time to move. Movement and rest appear at the proper time. When they are used at the right time, the Way (*Dao*) will be bright and clear.

When keeping the back still (in meditation), one loses the perception of the body. The noble person keeps his thoughts in the present. If one goes into the courtyard one does not notice the people because one is watching one's movements. There will be no misfortune.

- *Base line, 6*

    *Stilling the feet.*
    *No misfortune.*
    *Long-term augury: favourable.*

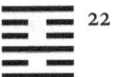

#### Commentary

Keeping the feet still. There will be no misfortune. A prolonged perseverance will be beneficial. One does not stray from the correct path.

- *Second line, 6*

    *Stilling the calves.*
    *Not getting at the marrow*
    *one's heart is not pleased.*

#### Commentary

*Stilling the calves:* stopping one's activities.
*Not getting at the marrow:* not getting at the essence yet, one's heart is not pleased.

- *Third line, 9*

    *Stilling the loins.*
    *Stiffen the spine.*
    *Danger.*
    *Smoke the heart.*

#### Commentary

Keeping the loins still (stopping sexual activity), and stiffening the spine. The heart is suffocated. This will be dangerous.

- **Fourth line, 6**

    Stilling the trunk.
    No misfortune.

*Commentary*

Keeping the trunk still means stilling the whole body. There will be no misfortune.

- **Fifth line, 6**

    Stilling the jaw.
    Words are orderly.
    Trouble will go away.

*Commentary*

Keeping the jaws still: one's speech will be orderly. Regret will disappear.

- **Top line, 9**

    Stilling [the head].
    Auspicious.

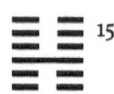

*Commentary*

Keeping the mind completely still will bring good fortune.

- **Summary**

Double Mountain means mountains standing together, indicating stilling, keeping still, stopping, restriction, and control. Its main characteristic is stillness. According to the *Yi Jing* stillness gives rise to movement, and movement follows stillness.

Hexagram 51, Thunder, Arousing, is followed by hexagram 52, Mountain, Stilling, because after strong movement (hexagram 51) everything has to take a rest (hexagram 52). After thunder there is stillness.

This hexagram is related to Daoist and Buddhist meditation, where both body and mind activities are stilled. No misfortune.

This hexagram is about stillness and stilling of body parts in six stages beginning with the feet (first line), and ending with the top of the head (sixth line).

In the first line we should stay where we are, then there will be no misfortune. Prolonged perseverance will be beneficial.

In the second line one stops one's activities. Not able to get at the essence (of the meditation practice), one's mind is not at ease.

In the third line, when the loins are stilled (during meditation), it may lead to heart trouble. If one forcefully stops sexual activity (for instance in celibacy), the heart will be suffocated.

In the fourth line, keeping the whole body still means stopping all activities. No misfortune.

In the fifth line, keeping one's jaws still means that one does not use too many (or arbitrary) words. There will be no regret.

In the sixth line the mind is completely stilled. This highest form of stillness (inactivity) will bring good fortune (Enlightenment).

# 53. *Jian* / Gradual Advance, Wild Goose

 *xun* / wind, wood, gentle, penetrating

*gen* / mountain, standing still, stilling, stopping

- ***Image***

    Wind above Mountain.
    A bird on the mountain: Gradual Advance.
    The noble person, dwelling in worthiness and virtue,
    improves the morals of the people.

- ***Judgment***

    Auspicious for a maiden to be married.
    Favourable augury.

*Commentary*

Gentleness (Wind) and restraint (Mountain) bring advance and achievement. Only when one advances gently and with restraint one gradually attains a position. If one advances with rectitude one is able to correct a situation or the state (nation).

The eldest daughter (Wind) and the youngest son (Mountain) grow up and reach a marriageable age. The marriage of a maiden brings good fortune. Determination will be beneficial.

Note. The image of hexagram 53 is generally interpreted as Wood above Mountain, meaning a tree on the mountain. But it is also Wind above Mountain, meaning a bird flying to a tree on a mountain. A tree is a symbol of stillness, while *gradual advance of the wild goose (bird)* in all the lines indicates movement.

There are bird omens throughout the Yi Jing: li, *the oriole (element fire, hexagram 30)*; ming yi, *the crying pheasant (element earth, hexagram 36)*; hong jian, *the wild goose (element water, hexagram 53)*; feng or luan, *the phoenix (element metal, hexagram 55)*; he, *the crane (element wind, hexagram 61, line 2)*.

In this hexagram it is about the wild goose (a water bird), which signifies gradual advance. It flies from a lower place (water) to a higher one (riverbank, rock, dry land, tree, hill, highland), and is a metaphor for a maiden (wild goose) seeking a husband.

Each line of this hexagram represents a certain kind of marriage (relationship). See the Summary.

- ***Base line, 6***   37

    *The wild goose flies to the riverbank.*
    *The youngest son is in danger.*
    *There will be talk.*
    *No misfortune.*

#### Commentary

The wild goose flies (advances) from the water to the riverbank. The youngest son (Mountain) is in danger (lower inner trigram Water) because of gossip (talk, Wind). No misfortune.

- ***Second line, 6***  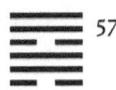 57

    *The wild geese fly to a rock.*
    *They eat and drink at ease.*
    *Auspicious.*

271

*Commentary*

The wild geese fly (advance) from the riverbank to the rocks. They eat and drink together, and enjoy each other's company. Good fortune.

## • *Third line, 9*

*The wild goose flies to dry land.*
*The husband goes on an expedition*
*and does not return.*
*The wife is pregnant, but does not give birth.*
*Ominous.*
*Favourable for fending off robbers.*

*Commentary*

The wild goose flies (advances) to dry land.
The husband goes forth, and does not return, means there will be separation from his own kind.
The wife is pregnant and does not give birth (Mountain, stilling), means that she loses her way. Disaster. It will be beneficial to guard against evil influence for mutual protection.

## • *Fourth line, 6*

*The wild goose flies to the trees*
*and finds a branch to perch.*
*No misfortune.*

*Commentary*

The wild goose flies (advances) to a tree, and finds a place to rest, means that with acceptance (fourth line, *yin*) and gentleness (upper trigram Wind) one obtains a safe position. There will be no misfortune.

- *Fifth line, 9*  52

    *The wild goose flies to the hills.*
    *The wife is not pregnant for three years.*
    *In the end nothing overcomes her.*
    *Auspicious.*

    Commentary

The wild goose flies (advances) to the hills.
*The wife is not pregnant for three years:* there is a delay.
*In the end nothing overcomes her:* she will obtain what she desires. Good fortune.

- *Top line, 9*  39

    *The wild goose flies to the highland.*
    *Its feathers can be used at ceremonial dances.*
    *Auspicious.*

    Commentary

The wild goose flies (advances) to the highland. Its feathers can be used for ceremonial purposes means that things cannot be disturbed, and everything will be in its natural order. Good fortune.

- *Summary*

Wind above Mountain symbolises a bird on top of the mountain, and means gradual advance and development. The eldest daughter (Wind) and the youngest son (Mountain) grow up together.

  *Li* (Fire, upper inner trigram) stands for a bird that leaves the water (*Kan*, lower inner trigram), and flies higher and higher, symbolising a woman looking for a husband. The marriage of a maiden brings good fortune. Determination will be beneficial.

Hexagram 52, Mountain, Stilling, is followed by hexagram 53, Gradual Advance, because after a long period of stillness, movement will start again (Gradual Advance).

This hexagram is about gradual advance, and if the question is about marriage, the six lines stand for six different kinds of marriage. In the first line there is gossip, but the marriage is not unsuitable; the second is a materially successful marriage; the third an unfortunate marriage; the fourth a marriage to a kind person; the fifth a blissful marriage, and the sixth a marriage to a respected person.

In the first line one begins to advance. The youngest son is in trouble because of gossip, but there will be no error.

In the second line they eat and drink together, and enjoy each other's company. Good fortune.

In the third line there will be separation from one's own kind (husband, child, companions), and one may lose one's way. One should guard against evil influence for mutual protection, otherwise there will be disaster.

In the fourth line, with acceptance and gentleness one obtains a safe position. There will be no misfortune.

In the fifth line there will be a delay for three years, but in the end one will obtain what one desires. Good fortune.

In the sixth line there will be no more disorder because everything will be in its natural order. Good fortune.

*Note. In the* Yi Jing *there are six hexagrams about the relationship (engagement, marriage) between male and female: hexagram 31, Feeling, Sensation, Attraction, is about the beginning of a relationship; hexagram 32, Lasting, Enduring, Constancy, is about a long-lasting marriage; hexagram 42, Gain, Increase, is about a marriage which will bring material gain; hexagram 44 Meeting, Contact, Encounter, is about a woman who has relationships with many men (one* yin *line and five* yang *lines); hexagram 53, Gradual Advance, Wild Goose, is about a marriage which improves gradually; hexagram 54 Marrying Maiden, is about a marriageable woman who marries as a second wife.*

# 54. *Gui Mei* / Marrying Maiden

zhen / thunder, shock, moving, growth

dui / lake, still water, pool, marsh, joy, pleasing

- **Image**

    Thunder above Lake.
    Thunder rumbling over the lake: Marrying Maiden.
    The noble person, knowing the cause of error,
    tries to avoid disorder in the end.

- **Judgment**

    A marrying maiden.
    Ominous for an attack.
    Nothing is favourable.

### Commentary

'Pleasing' (Lake) and 'moving' (Thunder) make the Marrying Maiden. Advance brings misfortune (disaster) because a marriage between an older man (Thunder, eldest son) and a young girl (Lake, youngest daughter) will give rise to unfaithfulness, quarrelling, and eventually misfortune.

The Marrying Maiden symbolises the great principle of heaven and earth. If heaven and earth do not interact, the myriad things do not come into being. Marriage signifies the beginning (hexagram 53) and end (hexagram 54) of humankind.

- *Base line, 9* 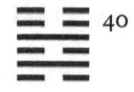 40

  *The marrying maiden becomes a concubine.*
  *The lame can walk.*
  *Auspicious for an attack.*

  ### Commentary

  A maiden ready to marry becomes a concubine of an already married man. (This was a cultural practice in China.)
  *The lame can walk:* she is able to improve her position, but only to one of a relatively inferior status. Advancing brings good fortune.

- *Second line, 9* 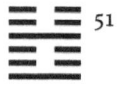 51

  *The one-eyed will be able to see.*
  *Favourable augury for a person in confinement.*

  ### Commentary

  *The one-eyed will be able to see:* in spite of her position (marrying maiden) she is limited in her status and conduct. Perseverance for a secluded person brings good fortune.

- *Third line, 6*  34

  *From a maid, the marrying maiden*
  *will be a secondary wife.*

  ### Commentary

  From a maid servant, the marrying maiden may become a secondary wife.

- *Fourth line, 9*

   *The maiden's marriage is delayed.
   She went late to her new home.*

   Commentary

   The time will surely come for a belated marriage.

- *Fifth line, 6*

   *[King]* Diyi *gives his youngest sister
   or daughter in marriage.
   The sleeves of the mistress
   are not as fine as the sleeves of the secondary wife.
   The moon is almost full.
   Auspicious.*

   Commentary

   The marrying maiden marries. The regal garments of the first wife are not as splendid as those of the secondary wife. Although the first wife is in a higher position, she shows her nobility and better taste by not dressing too grandly.
   *The moon is almost full:* one is realising one's goal. Good fortune.

   Note. The marriage of the marrying maiden as a secondary wife in this fifth line is less beneficial than the marriage of a first wife in the fifth line of hexagram 11, because the marriage in hexagram 54, line 5, changes in hexagram 58 (Lake, Joy, Pleasing), line 5, where confident joy is disintegrating. On king Diyi, see the note of hexagram 11, line 5.

## • Top line, 6

*The maiden holds out a basket
but there is nothing in it.
The young man stabs a sheep, but there is no blood.
There is nothing for which this is favourable.*

### Commentary

The marrying maiden presents a basket, but it is empty. The young husband stabs a sheep, but no blood flows. This marriage will not produce offspring. No goal or destination is favourable.

## • Summary

Thunder above Lake symbolises thunder rumbling over the lake, and indicates a marrying maiden, a woman ready to marry. Advance brings misfortune (disaster). Nothing is favourable.

The eldest son (Thunder, upper trigram) and the youngest daughter (Lake, lower trigram) are married, but their marriage will not last.

Fire (lower inner trigram) is the sun which evaporates the water (upper inner trigram) rising up from the clouds. The thunder announces the coming of rain which may flood the lake.

The strong attraction between the older man (eldest son, Thunder) and the young girl (youngest daughter, Lake) soon gives rise to unfaithfulness, quarrelling, and eventually misfortune.

This hexagram is about marriage, where a young woman (marrying maiden) marries into the home of an already married (older) man, and her position develops from a servant (maid) to a concubine and then to a wife but she will not be the principal wife. In the end the marriage will not bring its expected fruit (offspring), or will not fulfil one's expectations.

Hexagram 53, Gradual Advance, Wild Goose, is followed by hexagram 54, Marrying Maiden, because the marriage of a maiden can be considered a gradual advance (development).

Hexagram 54 is about a maiden ready to marry into a marriage that does not give her full status, in six stages:

In the first line someone is able to improve her position, but only to a relatively inferior status. Advancing brings good fortune.

In the second line someone is limited in her status and conduct (secluded, kept from company), but perseverance brings good fortune. There will be no real change in the ordinary course of events.

In the third line someone may improve her position to a relatively limited status.

In the fourth line someone has to wait before a belated marriage can take place.

In the fifth line someone in a high position shows nobility and modesty by not showing off her status. One realises one's goal. Good fortune.

In the sixth line a marriage or relationship will not be successful. One is left empty-handed. No goal or destination is favourable.

# 55. *Feng* / Abundance, Phoenix

zhen / thunder, shock, moving, growth

li / fire, light, lightning, brightness

- ## *Image*

    Thunder above Fire.
    Thunder and lightning during a storm: Abundance.
    The noble person decides legal cases
    and carries out just punishments.

- ## *Judgment*

    a) *Offering.*
       *The king goes to the sacrifice.*
       *Don't be sad.*
       *Be like the sun at noon.*

    b) *Success.*
       *The king proceeds to the sacrifice.*
       *Do not worry.*
       *Be like the sun at midday.*

*Commentary*

Brightness (Fire) and movement (Thunder) are joined, hence Abundance. Abundance means fullness, greatness, and plenty. The king attains abundance.

*Do not worry. Be like the sun at midday:* such a one should shed light on the world, and benefits and enlightens the people.

After midday the sun begins to decline, when the moon is full it begins to wane. As everything under heaven and on earth waxes and wanes in accord with time, how much more true is this for humans, spirits, and gods? The noble person brings light (Fire, lightning) or intelligence in solving disputes, and strikes terror (Thunder) into the hearts of evil-doers (criminals).

Note. The feng or luan bird (phoenix) signifies prosperity. There are five kinds of birds in the Yi Jing. See hexagram 53, Note Commentary on the Judgment.

### • Base line, 9

62

> He meets his master.
> For ten days there will be no misfortune.
> Going forth will bring reward.

*Commentary*

*He meets his master*: one meets someone with authority, someone of equal rank who may enhance one's development.
*For ten days there will be no misfortune*: if one exceeds a period of ten days it will bring misfortune. To advance will bring esteem (praise).

Note. In ancient China the 'week' consisted of ten days. In general it means a relatively long period.

### • Second line, 6

34

> Full is the screen.
> At midday we can see the pole star.
> If one goes, one will get the risk of illness.
> The captives are aroused.
> Auspicious.

281

*Commentary*

The 'screen' stands for a thing that covers and darkens the light. 'Full is the screen' means that there is abundance of darkness (during the storm), so that at midday one can see the pole star. Advancing will bring doubt and enmity (hostility). With sincerity and confidence there will be good fortune.

*Note. The darkness that made it possible to see the stars during the day in line 2, 3, and 4 is probably caused by a solar eclipse in the year 1070 BCE, but looking at the image of the hexagram – thunder and lightning – the darkness is caused by a storm.*

- *Third line, 9*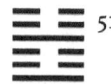

   Full is the covering.
   At midday we can see the Mei star.
   He breaks his arm.
   No error.

*Commentary*

*Full is the covering:* the darkness (during a storm, upper inner trigram Cloud) is such that at midday we can see the *Mei* star (a small and dim star which is only visible in extreme darkness).
*He breaks his arm:* he is incapable to undertake a great task. There will be no error.

- *Fourth line, 9*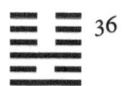

   Full is the screen.
   At midday we can see the pole star.
   He meets his master.
   Auspicious.

*Commentary*

The 'screen' stands for something that covers and darkens the light. 'Full is the screen' means that there is abundance of darkness (during the storm, upper inner trigram Cloud), so that at midday we can see the pole star.
*He meets his master*: one meets someone with authority, someone of equal rank who may enhance one's development. Taking action will bring good fortune.

- *Fifth line, 6*  49

    *The sunlight is visible again.*
    *In the coming period*
    *there will be rejoicing and honour.*
    *Auspicious.*

*Commentary*

After the storm the light of the sun appears again. In the coming, rather long period, there will be blessings and fame. Good fortune.

- *Top line, 6*  30

    *Wide is the roof*
    *thoroughly covering the house.*
    *He peeks through the door: no one is there.*
    *Not seen for three years.*
    *Ominous.*

*Commentary*

Full is his house. There is abundance in his dwelling. He stays hidden in seclusion and keeps the world out. He peeks through the door and sees no one. Looking from outside, people also see no one in the house.

For three years he encounters nobody. By hiding himself and not sharing his abundance with others, he acts against the Way (*Dao*). There will be misfortune.

## • *Summary*

Thunder above Fire means thunder and lightning occurring during a storm and symbolise greatness, abundance, fullness. Thunder and lightning also indicate abundance of light (during lightning) or abundance of darkness when the lightning is over (during thunder).

The upper trigram (Thunder, power) and the lower trigram (Fire, lightning, brilliance) together depict thunder and lightning during a storm or the sun at midday, or a forest in the summer. All are scenes of great brilliance and power. But as the sun at midday also begins to descend, all abundance will change into its opposite, and decline starts. One should not be sad or worried, but be like the sun at midday, and share one's light with others. This will bring success.

Hexagram 54, Marrying Maiden, is followed by hexagram 55, Abundance because a maiden who marries will not only bring forth abundance, but may also attain abundance.

This hexagram is about abundance of either light or darkness in different stages:

In the first line one meets someone with authority who may enhance one's development. For a certain period ('ten days') there will be no misfortune. Exceeding those ten days there will be misfortune. To advance will bring recognition and esteem.

In the second line there is abundance of darkness. Going forward will lead to doubt and enmity (hostility). But with sincerity and confidence there will be good fortune.

In the third line there is so much darkness that one is incapable of undertaking great things. No error.

In the fourth line there is abundance of darkness. One meets someone with authority who may enhance one's development. If one advances or takes action there will be good fortune.

In the fifth line, after abundance of darkness there will be a rather long period of abundance of light again. Blessing and fame are won. Good fortune.

In the sixth line someone has an abundance of knowledge or material goods, but keeps himself hidden. Because he does not share his abundance with others, there will be misfortune.

# 56. Lü / Travelling, The Wanderer

*li* / fire, light, brightness

*gen* / mountain, standing still, stilling, stopping

- **Image**

    Fire above Mountain.
    A fire burns on top of the mountain:
    Travelling, The Wanderer.
    The noble person is clear-minded
    and cautious in imposing punishments
    and does not allow the cases to be delayed.

- **Judgment**

    a) Small offering.
    Augury auspicious for travelling.

    b) Small success.
    Determination brings good fortune to travellers.

*Commentary*

While one travels, resting (Mountain) and clarity of mind (Fire) will lead to small success. Good fortune comes to the determined traveller.
The noble person tries to gain clarity (Fire) over things, is cautious in imposing punishments and does not delay (Mountain) the cases.
The timely occurrence of travelling is of great importance.

- **Base line, 6**

    A traveller dwells on trivial things.
    Disaster.

    *Commentary*

If an (inexperienced) traveller dwells upon trivial things (unimportant matters), it will bring calamity upon himself.

- **Second line, 6**

    A traveller arrives at a lodging.
    He carries his wealth with him.
    He obtains a young servant.
    Augury: auspicious.

    *Commentary*

A traveller arrives at his resting place, still carrying his belongings. He is served by a trustworthy person. Determination will bring good fortune.

- **Third line, 9**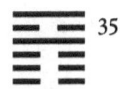

    A traveller burns down his lodging.
    He loses his young servant.
    Augury: danger.

    *Commentary*

Due to carelessness or lack of caution the traveller's lodging burns down. Because of his arrogance he loses the loyalty of the young servant. Determination will lead to danger.

- **Fourth line, 9**

    *A traveller reaches a lodging.*
    *He gets his valuables and an axe.*
    *His heart is not happy.*

    *Commentary*

The traveller arrives at a resting place. He obtains money for his expenses but he is not pleased.

- **Fifth line, 6**

    *Shooting a pheasant, he loses an arrow.*
    *In the end he obtains honour and position.*

    *Commentary*

*Shooting a pheasant, he loses an arrow*: trying to obtain an official rank, but failing in the attempt (a *yin* line in the wrong place). Ultimately one wins praise and attains to office.

- **Top line, 9**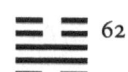

    *The bird's nest burns.*
    *The traveller first laughs*
    *but later weeps and wails.*
    *He loses his ox at* Yi.
    *Ominous.*

    *Commentary*

Due to carelessness and lack of caution the traveller gets his home ('nest') burnt down. First he laughs, but later he will be sad because he has lost his wealth ('ox'). Disaster. He will never hear about it again.

*Note. Yi refers to another state in ancient China where the herdsmen took their cattle.*

## • *Summary*

Fire above Mountain means a fire burns on top of the mountain and symbolises travelling, wandering, a traveller, a stranger, and an exile. The lower inner trigram (Wind, Wood) stands for the trees that grow on the mountain and the wind that spreads the fire. The wind-blown fire and the immovable mountain symbolise the traveller and his place of exile. Determination brings good fortune to travellers, but there will only be small success.

Hexagram 55, Abundance, is followed by hexagram 56, Travelling, The Wanderer, because if abundance reaches its extreme and changes into its opposite (the law of extremes), one may lose one's home and will have to wander.

Hexagram 56 is about travelling, wandering in six stages:

In the first line someone trifling with unimportant matters will draw disaster upon himself.

In the second line someone arrives at a resting place, still carrying his valuables. He obtains the services of a trustworthy person. Determination will bring good fortune.

In the third line someone's carelessness or lack of caution will lead to calamity. Because of arrogance he loses the loyalty of his servant. Determination will bring danger.

In the fourth line someone arrives at a resting place, and obtains the money for his travelling expenses, but he is not pleased.

In the fifth line someone is trying to obtain an official position, but first fails to do so. Ultimately he wins praise and attains to office. One first loses something to obtain something else later.

In the sixth line someone's home is burned, and his wealth is lost. Disaster. First he laughs but later he will be sad. No news of what he has lost will ever be heard of.

# 57. *Xun* / Wind, Penetrating, Gentle

*xun* / wind, gentle, penetrating

*xun* / wood, yielding, submission

- ***Image***

   Double Wind.
   Wind blowing over the woods: Gentle, Penetrating.
   The noble person repeats his orders gently
   and gets works carried out.

- ***Judgment***

   a) Small offering.
      Favourable to have somewhere to go.
      Favourable to see a great man.

   b) Small success.
      Beneficial to undertake something.
      Beneficial to see a great person.

*Commentary*

The trigram Wind is doubled. This means that the orders are repeated gently.
The yielding (Wood) submits to the firm (Wind). The weak is submissive to the strong. Hence small success. It will be favourable to undertake something and to meet a person of wisdom.

- **Base line, 6**

    Advancing and retreating.
    Favourable augury for a warrior.

 9

### Commentary

There is doubt (hesitation) about whether to advance or to retreat. Determination is favourable for a warrior. This means that the will should be firm.

- **Second line, 9**

    Laying out offerings
    below the sacrificial altar.
    Using diviners and sorcerers will be auspicious.
    No misfortune.

 53

### Commentary

Laying out offerings below the sacrificial altar instead of on top, means that the offering is not correctly done, and therefore (due to too much hesitation and submissiveness) will create a negative influence. Employing diviners and sorcerers to avert that negative influence will bring good fortune. No error.

- **Third Line, 9**

    Repeatedly laying out the offering.
    Distress.

 59

### Commentary

Repeated submission will bring distress and exhaustion of our willpower.

- *Fourth line, 6*  44

    *Trouble will go away.*
    *In the hunt three kinds of game are caught.*

    Commentary

Regret vanishes. One achieves merit in three kinds of ways (gratitude, reward, and praise).

- *Fifth line, 9*  18

    *Augury auspicious.*
    *Trouble will go away.*
    *There is nothing for which this is unfavourable.*
    *No good beginning.*
    *There will be an end.*
    *Auspicious for three days before a* geng *day*
    *and three days after a* geng *day.*

    Commentary

Determination will bring good fortune. Trouble will disappear. Nothing is unfavourable. A poor beginning, but a good end. Three days before and three days after a change, a specific event or circumstance, occurring at the fourth day after this consultation of the *Yi Jing*. Good fortune.

Note. Geng *is the seventh day in the ancient Chinese ten-day 'week'.*

- *Top line, 9*  48

    *Laying out offerings*
    *beneath the sacrificial altar.*
    *He loses his valuables and an axe.*
    *Augury: ominous.*

*Commentary*

Laying out offerings below the sacrificial altar instead of on top, means that the offering is not correctly done (due to too much hesitation or submissiveness), and therefore will create a negative influence.
Determination will bring disaster.

## • *Summary*

Double Wind means wind blowing over the woods, symbolising gentleness, penetration, yielding, submissiveness. Trees and grasses (Wood) bend before the wind. In general double Wind, or wind following upon wind, indicates a favourable wind. Small success. In going somewhere or undertaking something, it will be beneficial to have a goal or destination in view.
It is advisable to see a man of wisdom.

Hexagram 56, Travelling, The Wanderer, is followed by hexagram 57, Wind, because when the traveller finds no place to stay, he needs gentleness and compliance ('a favourable wind') to gain entrance.

This hexagram is about hesitation and submission in different stages:

In the first line there are doubts about one's own intentions. It is advised to be determined, and to keep our will firm.

In the second line there is some negative influence, due to hesitation and submissiveness, that can be averted by employing advisors. No error. This will bring good fortune.

In the third line an attitude of repeated submission will bring distress and exhaustion of our willpower.

In the fourth line regret vanishes, and one will have three kinds of result.

In the fifth line there is a poor beginning, but a good end. Regret vanishes, and nothing is unfavourable. One should observe the three days before and the three days after a change that will occur (on the fourth day). Good fortune. (See also hexagram 18, Judgment.)

In the sixth line one loses one's valuables or money. Determination will bring misfortune.

# 58. *Dui* / Lake, Pleasing, Joy

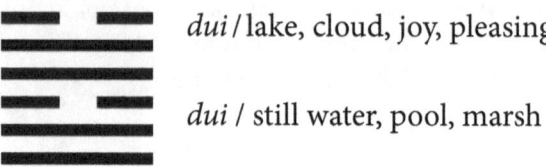

*dui* / lake, cloud, joy, pleasing

*dui* / still water, pool, marsh

- ***Image***

    Double Lake.
    Two lakes coming together: Pleasing, Joy.
    The noble person joins with his friends
    for discussion and practice.

- ***Judgment***

    a) Offering.
       Favourable augury.

    b) Success.
       Perseverance will be beneficial.

*Commentary*

Double Lake indicates joy. Success.
A joyous perseverance will be beneficial. Joy is in accordance with the will of Heaven, and responds to the wishes of men. If the people are joyous they forget about their burdens. If they confront their difficulties with joy, they may even forget their fear of death. There is no greater joy (double Joy) than the joy that encourages the people.

- ***Base line, 9***  47

    *Harmonious joy.*
    *Auspicious.*

*Commentary*

Harmonious joy will bring good fortune. This indicates that one acts without doubt.

- ***Second line, 9***  17

    a) *Joy of a capture.*
    *Auspicious.*
    *Trouble goes away.*

    b) *Confident joy.*
    *Good fortune.*
    *Trouble disappears.*

*Commentary*

Confident joy will bring good fortune. Trouble will disappear. One has full confidence in one's own will.

- ***Third line, 6***  43

    *Coming joy.*
    *Ominous.*

*Commentary*

Expecting joy, but it will not manifest. Disaster.

- *Fourth line, 9*  60

    *Considering joy.
    Not yet peaceful.
    Illness under control.
    There will be joy.*

    #### Commentary

Anticipating future joys. One is not at ease (restless). The illness is overcome. There will be happiness.

- *Fifth line, 9*  54

    *a) Captives at a flaying.
    Danger.*

    *b) Confidence in what is disintegrating.
    There will be danger.*

    #### Commentary

Confident joy in what is deteriorating leads to danger.

- *Top line, 6* 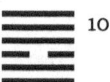 10

    *A drawn out joy.*

    #### Commentary

An extended (forced, alluring) joy, but it is not really satisfying.

## • Summary

Double Lake. Two beautiful lakes conjoined: joyousness, happiness, pleasing. The two lakes represent the beneficial aspects of a lake for human beings, animals, and plants.

The two trigrams also represent two young girls (Lake, youngest daughter) joyously playing together. *Dui* also means mouth. Double Lake indicates discussions.

Joyous perseverance will be beneficial. Success.

Hexagram 57, Wind, Gentle, is followed by hexagram 58, Lake, Joy because proceeding gently (hexagram 57) leads to joyousness.

Hexagram 58 is about joy (increasing joyousness) in six different stages:

In the first line there is a harmonious joy. This will bring good fortune. One acts without doubt.

In the second line confident joy will bring good fortune. One has confidence in what one wants. Trouble disappears.

In the third line one expects joy to come, but it will not manifest. Misfortune (disaster).

In the fourth line, anticipating future joys, one is restless. An illness (something negative) under control leads to happiness (joy).

In the fifth line there is confidence in a situation which is already decaying. This is dangerous, but with the right attitude the danger may be avoided.

In the sixth line there is a forced joy in the form of an allurement, but it does not lead to satisfaction.

# 59. *Huan* / Scattering, Dispersion

xun / wind, wood, gentle, penetrating

kan / moving water, rain, stream, danger

- *Image*

Wind above Water.
Wind blowing over the water: Scattering, Dispersion.
Kings thus made sacrifices to the Lord of Heaven
and built ancestral temples.

- *Judgment*

a) Offering.
  The king proceeds to his temple.
  Favourable to cross the great river.
  Favourable augury.

b) Success.
  The king approaches his temple.
  Beneficial to go on a journey.
  Determination will be beneficial.

*Commentary*

Penetrating (Wind) and danger (Water) are conjoined. Scattering, dispersion brings danger. Success.
*The king approaches his temple:* in time of dispersion (unrest, disorder) the king fulfils his ancestral duties to keep the country and the people together.

It is beneficial to go on a journey. If this journey is done by boat (Wood) it will bring merit (gratitude, reward). Determination will be beneficial.

- **Base line, 6** 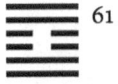 61

    a) Use a gelded horse: health.
    Auspicious.

    b) One is saved by using a strong horse.
    Good fortune.

*Commentary*

*Using a strong horse*: one uses strength to prevent or save the situation from disintegrating. This will bring good fortune.

- **Second line, 9**  20

    It (sacrificial blood)
    rushes over the low table (altar).
    Trouble will go away.

*Commentary*

At the time of dispersion (rushing of sacrificial blood) one hurries to that which supports him. Trouble disappears. One gains what one desires.

- **Third line, 6**  57

    It (sacrificial blood) spills over the body.
    No trouble.

*Commentary*

Dissolving one's selfishness (spilling of sacrificial blood). This means that one's attention is directed to others. There will be no trouble.

## • *Fourth line, 6*

> *It scatters over the crowd.*
> *Very auspicious.*
> *It scatters on the mound.*
> *Not what common people think of.*

*Commentary*

Dispersing one's group ('it scatters over the crowd'), means that one leaves one's companions. Very good fortune.
Dispersing one's property ('it scatters on the mound'), means that dispersion leads to accumulation (of material or immaterial things). This is something beyond what ordinary people understand.

## • *Fifth line, 9*

> *Sweating it out.*
> *A great cry.*
> *Dispersion in the king's residence.*
> *No misfortune.*

*Commentary*

*Sweating it out:* a situation of illness or anxiety.
*A great cry:* a royal (important) statement.
The king disperses his belongings to the people in order to secure his position. There will be no misfortune.

- *Top line, 9*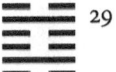

    *Scattering blood.*
    *Going far away.*
    *No misfortune.*

    *Commentary*

*Scattering blood:* fending off the danger.
*Going far away:* keeping injury at a distance. If this is done, there will be no misfortune.

- *Summary*

Wind above Water means the wind is blowing over the water, and symbolises scattering, dispersion, disintegration, dissolution. Wind blowing over the water stirs up the water, causing waves.

Wind above water also means boats (Wood) on the water, which points to travelling ('crossing the great river'). Determination will be beneficial. Success.

The hexagram indicates that it is time for a change (of ideas, home, work) or movement of some kind. Something may be broken up: a separation in the family, or among friends, or a dispersion of property. If one goes on a journey, making use of a boat will bring reward.

Hexagram 58, Lake, Pleasing, Joy, is followed by hexagram 59, Scattering, Dispersion, because after happiness and joyfulness things may break up, and there may be dispersion.

This hexagram is about scattering, dispersion, and dissolution in six stages:

In the first line one may use strong measures to prevent or save the situation from disintegrating. A strong horse symbolises a strong ally to help someone, or a strong effort to pull oneself out of a disintegrating situation. This will bring good fortune.

In the second line one hurries to that which gives strength and support. Regret vanishes. One gains what one wants.

In the third line one dissolves one's selfishness, and attention is directed more to others. No regret.

In the fourth line one leaves one's group of companions. Very good fortune. Dispersion leads to accumulation. This is not what ordinary people understand. Here acts of generosity are advised.

In the fifth line there is a situation of anxiety or illness. Acts of generosity are necessary to secure one's position. There will be no misfortune.

In the sixth line one keeps the danger and injury at a distance. If this is done, there will be no misfortune.

# 60. *Jie* / Restraining, Limitation

*kan* / moving water, rain, danger

*dui* / lake, still water, pool, joy, pleasing

## • *Image*

> Water above Lake.
> Rain falling on the lake: Restraining, Limitation.
> The noble person sets up rules
> and discusses virtuous conduct.

## • *Judgment*

a) *Offering.*
*Bitter restraint.*
*Augury: unfavourable.*

b) *Success.*
*Severe limitation.*
*Persisting is unfavourable.*

### Commentary

Joy (Lake) and danger (Water) are conjoined. There is joy in undertaking what is dangerous.
Success. Harsh limitation should not be persistently applied, because it leads to exhaustion.
When heaven and earth keep to their restriction, then the four seasons will function properly.
If regulations are used in a measured (restrained) way to govern, there will be no damage to property and no injury to the people.

- **Base line, 9**

    He does not go out of the door
    and courtyard.
    No misfortune.

### Commentary

*He does not go out of the door and courtyard:* one knows when movement (progress) will be smooth or obstructed. There will be no misfortune.

- **Second line, 9**

    He does not go out of the door
    and courtyard.
    Ominous.

### Commentary

*He does not go out of the door and courtyard:* one misses the right time (and opportunity). Disaster.

- **Third line, 6**

    No restraint.
    Sighing.
    No misfortune.

### Commentary

Sighing over a lack of restraint. Whose fault is it? If one had controlled oneself, there would have been no misfortune.

- **Fourth line, 6** 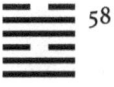 58

    *Offering.*
    *Easy restraint.*

    *Commentary*

Success. Because one accepts restraint, one is able to handle it with ease. Accepting restraint means that one follows the way of an authority.

- **Fifth line, 9**  19

    *Sweet restraint.*
    *Auspicious.*
    *Going will bring reward.*

    *Commentary*

*Sweet restraint*: an enjoyable restraint. Because one accepts this restraint, one can gain its benefits. Because one's position is central (a *yang* line in the middle of two *yin* lines), one abides with the Mean. Not going into extremes (keeping to the middle way) is the kind of restraint that is enjoyable ('sweet'). Good fortune. To advance will bring esteem (praise).

- **Top line, 6**  61

    a) *Bitter restraint.*
    *Augury: ominous.*
    *Trouble goes away.*

    b) *Severe limitation.*
    *Perseverance will bring disaster.*
    *[Stopping it,] trouble disappears.*

*Commentary*

Severe limitation. Perseverance will bring great misfortune (disaster). If this way of severe restraint is stopped, then trouble will disappear.

## • *Summary*

Water above Lake means rain is falling on the lake, and symbolises restraint, limitation, control. Rain on the lake may cause flooding, and therefore limitation and control are needed.

Dangerous (Water) actions are often accompanied with joy (Lake). This asks for restraint.

The lower inner trigram is Thunder (movement, strength), while the upper inner trigram is Mountain (keeping still). Strength (Thunder) should be restrained, otherwise there will be danger (Water).

Success, but one should not persist in harsh restraint because this will lead to exhaustion.

Hexagram 59, Scattering, Dispersion, is followed by hexagram 60, Restraining, Limitation, because a situation of too much scattering or dispersion will lead to danger, therefore restraint follows.

This hexagram is about restraint, limitation, and control in six stages:

In the first line one does not go out because one knows when progress will be obstructed. There will be no misfortune.

In the second line one does not go out, and does not take advantage of an opportunity presenting itself. Misfortune (disaster).

In the third line one sighs over a lack of restraint. But whose fault is it other than oneself? If one had controlled oneself, there would have been no misfortune.

In the fourth line one accepts restraint, and is therefore able to handle it with ease. Accepting restraint means that one follows the way of some authority. Success.

In the fifth line one appreciates the limitation (of keeping to the middle way), and by doing so one gains its benefit. Good fortune. To advance brings praise.

In the sixth line, continuing with severe restraint will bring disaster. When this way of restraint is stopped, regret will disappear.

# 61. *Zhong Fu* / Inner Trust, Confidence

*xun* / wind, wood, gentle, penetrating

*dui* / lake, still water, pool, joy, pleasing

- **Image**

    Wind above Lake.
    Wind blowing over the lake: Inner Trust, Confidence.
    A noble person is careful in his judgment of criminal cases and moderate in his penalties.

- **Judgment**

    a) A young pig and a fish.
    Auspicious.
    Favourable to cross the great river.
    Favourable augury.

    b) A piglet and a fish.
    Good fortune.
    Beneficial to go on a journey.
    Perseverance will be beneficial.

*Commentary*

Joy (Lake) and gentleness (Wind) together constitute an inner trust which is capable to transform the realm.
*A piglet and a fish:* inner trust affects all creatures. Good fortune.
*Favourable to cross the great river:* it is beneficial to go on a journey. If this journey is done by boat (Wood), it will bring merit (gratitude, reward).

Perseverance accompanied with confidence or inner trust will be beneficial because they correspond to the will of heaven.

- **Base line, 9**

    *a) A yu burial ritual.
    Auspicious.
    Unexpected disturbance.
    Not calm.*

    *b) To be at ease.
    Good fortune.
    There will be unexpected disturbance.
    Restlessness.*

    *Commentary*

In repose ('ease' and confidence) there will be good fortune. There will be an unexpected disturbance caused by others. This will give rise to anxiety. One's purpose remains unchanged.

*Note. A yu burial ritual is a ritual of repose, performed on the way when mourners are going home.*

- **Second line, 9**

    *A crane calls on a shady slope.
    Its young respond.
    I have a fine goblet and will empty it with you.*

*Commentary*

*A crane calls on a shady slope. Its young respond:* someone reaches out to others and receives a favourable response. This is in answer to the heart's desire of those who follow.
*I have a fine goblet and will empty it with you:* something valuable is shared with others.

- **Third line, 6**

    *Getting an enemy.*
    *Some beat drums, some rest.*
    *Some weep, some sing.*

 9

*Commentary*

*Getting an enemy:* one has an inharmonious relationship or a hostile confrontation with someone.
*Some beat drums, some rest. Some weep, some sing:* one is uncomfortable with the situation and therefore unstable and erratic in one's behaviour.

- **Fourth line, 6**

    *The moon is almost full.*
    *A pair of horses: one goes away.*
    *No misfortune.*

 10

*Commentary*

*The moon is almost full:* a situation is approaching completion.
*A pair of horses: one goes away:* one rises above one's own kind. No error.

- *Fifth line, 9*  41

    a) There are captives all tied together.
       No misfortune.

    b) Confidence pulls people together.
       No misfortune.

    *Commentary*

    Someone's confidence is drawing people together. No error.

- *Top line, 9*  60

    The sound of flapping wings
    rises up in the sky.
    Augury: ominous

    *Commentary*

    *The sound of flapping wings rises up in the sky:* one is over-confident (pride, boasting). Persistence will bring disaster. How can this last long?

- *Summary*

Wind above Lake means the wind is blowing over the lake, and symbolises inner trust, inner truthfulness, confidence, sincerity.

The upper trigram (Wind, eldest daughter, gentleness), and the lower trigram (Lake, youngest daughter, joy) are in harmony with each other. The upper inner trigram (Mountain, youngest son, stilling), and the lower inner trigram (Thunder, eldest son, movement) balance each other.

This hexagram represents harmony in the family, among friends, and in society. Therefore there is inner trust, confidence, sincerity. Good fortune. It will be advisable to go on a journey. If the journey is done by boat (Wood) it will bring reward. Perseverance accompanied with confidence will be beneficial.

Hexagram 60, Restraining, Limitation, is followed by hexagram 61, Inner Trust, Confidence, because when restraint is established, people will be trustworthy. Thus after restraint, confidence and sincerity follow.

Hexagram 61 is about trust and confidence in different stages:

In the first line an attitude of repose will bring good fortune. Some unexpected disturbance caused by others will give rise to anxiety, but our purpose remains unaltered.

In the second line someone reaches out to others and receives a favourable response. Here one is able to share something valuable with others.

In the third line one has an inharmonious relationship or a hostile confrontation with someone. Due to the situation one's behaviour will be unstable. One has lost confidence in the other.

In the fourth line, just before something is completed, one goes away to serve a higher purpose. No error.

In the fifth line one's confidence or inner trust is such that it draws people together. No error.

In the sixth line one is over-confident. Persistence will bring disaster. It may not last long.

# 62. *Xiao Guo* / Excessiveness of the Small

*zhen* / thunder, shock, moving, growth

*gen* / mountain, standing still, stilling, stopping

- *Image*

   Thunder above Mountain.
   Thunder rumbling over the mountain:
   Excessiveness of the Small, Small Excess.
   The 'noble' person shows too much reverence
   or humbleness in his conduct,
   too much grieve in his bereavement
   and is too stingy in his spending.

- *Judgment*

  a) Favourable augury.
     Good for small things, not good for big things.
     A flying bird leaves a sound.
     It is not right to go up, it is right to go down.
     Auspicious.

  b) Persistence is beneficial.
     Small things can be done, but not great things.
     A high flying bird leaves behind its sound.
     It is not fit to go up, but fit to stay down.
     Good fortune.

*Commentary*

Movement (Thunder) and stillness (Mountain) oppose each other: excessiveness of the small. Persistence is beneficial for the small, and in accord with the time. Small matters can be undertaken, but not great ones.
*A high flying bird leaves behind its sound*: the flying bird leaves a sign (message): it is not appropriate to strive upward, but to remain below. To ascend is not appropriate, to descend (staying low) is in accord with the time. Good fortune.

### • *Base line, 6*

 55

*A flying bird.*
*Ominous.*

*Commentary*

*A flying bird*: disaster. Nothing can be done about it.

### • *Second line, 6*

32

*He passes [the tablet of] his forefather*
*and faces [the tablet of] his foremother.*
*He does not reach the ruler, but meets the minister.*
*No misfortune.*

*Commentary*

By seeking out the lesser positioned of the two ('foremother'), he avoids harm.
By not reaching the highest rank ('ruler', superior), and only meeting the lower rank ('minister') means that one should not be dissatisfied, because one attained what one should have. No error.

*Note. The tablet is an image in the temple of the ancestors.*

## • Third line, 9

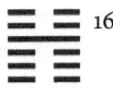

*He does not pass him.
He prevents him.
Someone following injures him.
Ominous.*

#### Commentary

If one fails to take precautions to protect oneself, someone will do harm. Disaster.

## • Fourth line, 9

*He does not pass him, but meets him.
Going brings danger.
One must be cautious.
Do not prolong in this determination.
No misfortune.*

#### Commentary

*He does not pass him, but meets him:* someone is humble enough to face the situation. Continuing will entail danger. One must be cautious. Do not persist too long with this encounter. No error.

## • Fifth line, 6

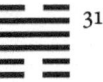

*Dense clouds, but no rain
from our western outskirts.
The duke shoots a bird with a string-arrow
and takes it from a cave.*

*Commentary*

*Dense clouds, but no rain from our western outskirts:* there will be progress but no result yet. This result will come from the western direction. (See hexagram 9, Judgment.)

*The duke shoots a bird... : success; ... and takes it from a cave:* but this success will only be in small matters.

- ***Top line, 6***

    *He does not meet him, but passes him.*
    *A flying bird is caught in a net.*
    *Ominous.*
    *Calamity.*

 56

*Commentary*

*He does not meet him, but passes him:* someone feels himself too superior (arrogant).

*A flying bird is caught in a net:* this indicates disaster and calamity.

- ***Summary***

Thunder above Mountain means thunder rumbling over the mountain, and symbolises excessiveness of the small.

The upper trigram (Thunder, strength, movement) and the lower trigram (Mountain, strength, stillness) oppose each other. There is an excess of strength, but it cannot be executed because of the opposing tendencies of movement and stillness. This indicates a slight (small) excess or small mistake that can prevent the achievement of great things.

Persistence will be beneficial for the small. Small things can be done, but not great things. It is advisable to keep a low profile.

Hexagram 61, Inner Trust, Confidence, is followed by hexagram 62, Excessiveness of the Small, Small Excess, because when there is too much confidence (hexagram 61, line 6), all extremes are changing into its opposite (hexagram 62 is the opposite of hexagram 61), and excessiveness of the small will follow.

This hexagram is about excessiveness of the small (excessive humbleness, stinginess, arrogance, lack of purpose) in different stages:

In the first line ascending brings disaster. Nothing can be done to avoid this misfortune.

In the second line he stays low and avoids harm. By not reaching what one aimed for, one still attains what one needs. No error.

In the third line, there is the possibility that *if* one fails to take precautions to protect oneself, there will be injury, disaster.

In the fourth line, instead of passing him by, one confronts someone because one is humble enough to face the situation. But continuing with this will entail danger. One must be cautious. Do not persist with this encounter too long. No error.

In the fifth line there is progress but no result yet. If there is success, it will only be in small matters. One should not expect too much, and be satisfied with small success.

In the sixth line one feels himself superior ('flying bird'). This superiority and arrogance will lead to calamity and deliberate injury.

# 63. *Ji Ji* / Already Completed

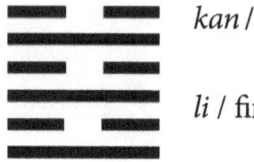

kan / moving water, rain, stream, danger

li / fire, light, brightness, clinging

- *Image*

    Water above Fire.
    Fire boils the water: Already Completed.
    The noble person perceives danger
    and takes precautions to fend it off.

- *Judgment*

    a) Offering.
    Somewhat favourable augury.
    Auspicious in the beginning, disorder in the end.

    b) Success.
    Some perseverance is beneficial.
    Good fortune in the beginning, disorder in the end.

### Commentary

Water and Fire oppose each other, but they also keep each other in balance. Success. It is beneficial to have some perseverance.
Because in this hexagram the firm and the yielding, the hard and the soft and the strong and the weak are in the right positions, there is success and good fortune in the beginning.
As everything is changing, and the way of completion eventually runs out, there will be disorder in the end.

• **Base line, 9**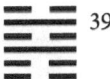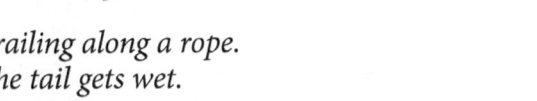

> *Trailing along a rope.*
> *The tail gets wet.*
> *No misfortune.*

#### Commentary

Dragging along a rope spanned over the water, the rear part gets wet. This means that one should be cautious, otherwise there could be misfortune.


• **Second line, 6**

> *The lady loses her carriage curtain.*
> *Do not seek for it.*
> *She will get it in seven days.*

#### Commentary

If something is lost, do not search for it. It will be regained in seven days. This could also mean, that if a situation of completion and success is disturbed, one should not try to restore it. Staying on the middle path, it will be recovered after a certain period ('seven days').

*Note. In ancient China important ladies were travelling in carriages with veiled windows. If the lady loses her carriage curtain she will be exposed to the eyes of the ordinary people. This means a shameful situation.*


• **Third line, 9**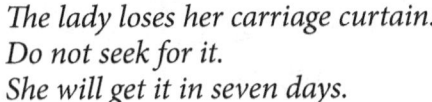

> *The High Ancestor*
> *attacked the Demon Territory*
> *and conquered it in three years.*
> *The small man should not attempt this.*

*Commentary*

Completion and success is achieved only at a high cost, and after a long period ('three years') of tiredness, weariness, and exhaustion. Ordinary men or men of mean attainments could not accomplish this.

*Note. The 'High Ancestor' was the* Shang *king* Wu Ding. *The region of the Northwestern border tribes was called the 'Demon Territory',* Gui Fang.

- ***Fourth line, 6***

  *A tunic lined with worn-out silk.*
  *Be cautious all day long.*

 49

*Commentary*

Things or persons are not what they appear to be. There is reason for doubt. Be cautious throughout the day.

- ***Fifth line, 9***

  *The neighbours to the east slaughter an ox.*
  *The neighbours to the west*
  *with their* yue *sacrifice*
  *really receive the blessing.*

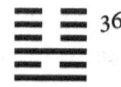 36

*Commentary*

The sacrifice of the neighbour to the east is not as timely as that of the neighbour to the west, who really receives the blessing. Success lies in being in accord with the time, and not in the greatness of the sacrifice. There will be unexpected or unsought good fortune.

Note. In general the yue sacrifice is mentioned as a summer sacrifice, but according to the Chinese seasonal calendar this is an autumn sacrifice. The neighbour to the east refers to the Shang and the neighbour to the west refers to the Zhou.
See also the notes of hexagram 45, line 2 and hexagram 50, Image and Judgment.

- **Top line, 6**

    The head gets wet.
    Danger.

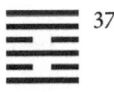

*Commentary*

*The head gets wet*: completion and success is at its end, and danger and disorder threaten. But how can this trouble last long?

- **Summary**

Water above Fire means fire boils the water, and symbolises completion, fulfilment, and success. Good fortune in the beginning, disorder in the end. Perseverance will be beneficial.

This state of completion and success is symbolised by a young man (Water, middle son) and a young woman (Fire, middle daughter) living harmoniously. But according to the law of change, as a full moon must wane, so all completion and success may decline.

The outer trigrams and inner trigrams are both Water and Fire, but in an opposite combination. As fire and water oppose each other, one has to keep a careful watch so that they will stay in balance. If the fire is too big the water will evaporate. If there is too much water, it will put out the fire.

In this hexagram all the *yin* and *yang* lines are in the correct places: straight lines in the strong positions, and broken lines in the yielding positions, indicating balance and harmony in all things.

Hexagram 63 and hexagram 64 are actually two states of the so-called end of the *Yi Jing*. Because every end is also a new beginning, hexagram 63 is called Already Completed, and hexagram 64 is called Before Completion. It is also indicated by the fact that several lines contain similar subjects (line 1 and 6 of both hexagrams, line 3 of hexagram 63 and line 4 of hexagram 64, line 1 of hexagram 63 and line 2 of hexagram 64).

Hexagram 62, Excessiveness of the Small, Small Excess, indicates a situation of excess. It is followed by hexagram 63, Already Completed because those who exceed others may be able to fulfil their goals (hexagram 63).

This hexagram is about situations of completion, fulfilment, and success in a changing condition, manifesting in different stages:

In the first line one should be cautious, otherwise there could be misfortune.

In the second line, if a situation of completion and success is disturbed, one should not try to restore it. Staying on the middle path, it will be recovered after a certain period ('seven days'). If one loses something, it will return by itself.

In the third line completion and success is achieved only at a high cost and with great fatigue and exhaustion. Men of mean attainments cannot accomplish this.

In the fourth line things or persons are not what they appear to be. Doubt and suspicion prevail. One should be cautious.

In the fifth line success lies in doing things in accord with the time, and does not depend on the greatness of one's efforts. It also depends on one's attitude, sincerity or devotion. Those to the west are more likely to receive the unexpected good fortune than those to the east.

In the sixth line completion and success is at its end, and danger and disorder threaten. This trouble will not last long.

# 64. *Wei Ji* / Before Completion

*li* / fire, light, brightness, clinging

*kan* / moving water, rain, stream, danger

### • *Image*

Fire above Water.
The sun rising above the water: Before Completion.
The noble person distinguishes between things
and puts them in the right order.

### • *Judgment*

a) Offering.
The small fox, almost across the river, gets its tail wet.
Favourable for nothing.

b) Success.
The young fox, not quite across the stream, gets its tail wet.
There is nothing for which this favourable.

*Commentary*

The sun (Fire) rising above the water (Water) indicates a new beginning: Before Completion. Success.
*The young fox, not quite across the stream...:* one has not yet passed the middle (halfway) of the subject concerned.
*...gets its tail wet:* one is not able to bring things to completion. There is nothing for which this is favourable.

Note. In hexagram 64 'offering' is translated into 'success', but it is not the kind of success as in hexagram 63, where things are completed. In hexagram 64 things are not completed (yet).

- **Base line, 6**

    *Its tail gets wet.*
    *Distress.*

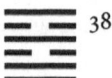 38

*Commentary*

*Its tail gets wet:* there is danger and trouble which leads to distress.

- **Second line, 9**

    a) *Trailing along a rope.*
       *Augury: auspicious.*

    b) *Dragging along a rope over the river.*
       *Determination brings good fortune.*

 35

*Commentary*

*Dragging along a rope over the river:* struggling over difficulties. Determination will lead to good fortune.

- **Third line, 6**

    *Not yet crossed over the stream.*
    *Ominous for an attack.*
    *Favourable for crossing the great river.*

50

*Commentary*

*Not yet crossed over the stream:* one has not yet accomplished one's goal.
*Ominous for an attack:* advancing or moving forward will bring misfortune but it is still beneficial to go on a journey ('crossing the great river').

- *Fourth line, 9*

   a) Augury: auspicious.
   Trouble goes away.
   Zhen *attacked the Demon Territory.*
   *In three years he was rewarded*
   *in the great state (of* Shang*).*

   b) Determination brings good fortune.
   Trouble disappears.
   Zhen *attacked the Demon Territory,*
   *and in three years he was rewarded*
   *with a large state (by the* Shang *king).*

*Commentary*

Determination brings good fortune. Trouble disappears.
Zhen *attacked the Demon Territory, and in three years he was rewarded:* after a difficult period one is able to realise one's goal.

Note. Zhen *is another name for the duke of* Zhou, Ji Li. *The region of the Northwestern border tribes was called the Demon Territory,* Gui Fang.

- *Fifth line, 6*

   a) Augury: auspicious.
   No trouble.
   Glory for the nobles.
   There is a capture.
   Auspicious.

   b) Determination brings good fortune.
   There will be no trouble.
   Glory for the noble person.
   There is confidence.
   Good fortune.

*Commentary*

Determination brings good fortune. There will be no trouble. The light of the noble person, being confident and sincere, will bring good fortune.

- *Top line, 9*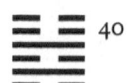

   a) There is a capture while drinking wine.
   No misfortune.
   The head gets wet.
   There are captures.
   Losing a spoon.

   b) There is confidence while drinking wine.
   There will be no misfortune.
   The head gets wet.
   There is more confidence.
   He will lose a spoon.

*Commentary*

The time of incomplete fulfilment (Before Completion) is at its end, and the time of fulfilment (completion) is approaching. There is confidence, and one is optimistic and celebrates it ('drinking wine'). No error. But if one is over-confident ('there are captures'), and lacks restraint ('the head gets wet'), one loses the trust and respect of others ('losing a spoon').

*Note. The spoon was important at feasts and ancestral sacrifices. Losing it indicates a bad omen.*

## • *Summary*

Fire above Water means the sun rising above the water, and symbolises Before Completion (a new beginning). Success. It signifies a time of great effort or concentration, just before something is completed. But one is not yet halfway of the subject concerned, and one may not be able to bring things to completion. There is nothing for which this is favourable.

The outer and inner trigrams of hexagram 63 and 64 are the same, but because their structure is totally opposite, they have opposite meanings.

While in hexagram 63 the lines are in the correct position, in hexagram 64 they are not. Here the *yang* lines are in yielding positions, and the *yin* lines are in strong positions.

As in hexagram 63 the relation between the male (Water, middle son) and female (Fire, middle daughter) is in harmony and balance, in hexagram 64 it is not. Here the female is above the male, showing that the wife is in a strong position, and the husband is yielding to the wife (traditionally seen as an unbalanced relationship).

Even though completion or success is not yet there, this hexagram shows hope for the future. It is a time for a new beginning and a new undertaking.

Hexagram 63, Already Completed, is followed by hexagram 64, Before Completion, because both hexagrams are two states of the same end of the *Yi Jing*, and according to the *Yi Jing* every end (hexagram 63) is followed by a new beginning (hexagram 64).

Hexagram 64 is about 'before completion', a time of incomplete fulfilment, in different stages:

In the first line one's attempt to bring something to completion fails. This leads to distress.

In the second line, struggling against difficulties, one's determination will lead to good fortune.

In the third line one has not yet accomplished one's goal. Advancing or undertaking something will bring misfortune, but it is still beneficial to go on a journey.

In the fourth line determination will bring good fortune, and trouble will disappear. After a difficult period ('three years') one will be able to realise one's goal.

In the fifth line determination will bring good fortune. There will be no trouble. The confidence and sincerity of a noble person will bring good fortune.

In the sixth line one is optimistic and celebrates. But if one is over-confident and lacks restraint, one may lose the trust and respect of others. A bad omen.

# THE TWELFTH WING
## Reflections on the Yi Jing

*Reflections on The Book of Change
may lead to understanding of its inner structure and workings.
But only reflections on the changes obtained from the Book
may lead to insight in the inner workings of destiny
and perhaps to the hidden wisdom of the* Dao.

# Introduction

This is a collection of articles, written as a spin-off when preparing this new translation of the *Yi Jing*.

These articles are reflections on the inner structure and ways of working of the *Yi Jing* that are essential to its understanding. They are an attempt to answer the basic questions concerning the *Yi Jing*, such as:

What are the main principles underlying the *Yi Jing*?
What are the components of the process of Change?
What is its relation to the concept of Time?
Are the methods to consult the *Yi Jing* based on Chance?
How does the *Yi Jing* really work?
Are there inconsistencies in the theoretical framework of the *Yi Jing*?
What are the ways of wisdom in the *Yi Jing*?
Is there some kind of formal order in the sequence of the hexagrams?
What are the various methods used to consult the *Yi Jing*?

These articles are named The Twelfth Wing because there are Ten Wings attached to the classic *Yi Jing*. Then there is *The Eleventh Wing: an exposition of the dynamics of I Ching for now*, written by Khigh Alx Dhiegh, and because there are twelve articles in this present exposition.

Reflections on the *Book of Change* may lead to understanding of its inner structure and workings, but only reflections on the changes obtained from the book may lead to insight in the inner workings of destiny, and perhaps to the hidden wisdom of the *Dao*.

# Eight main principles in the Yi Jing

In the *Yi Jing* there are eight main principles which form the foundation of its theoretical framework.

These principles are:
1. Reality is One: everything is related to everything else;
2. Reality is Information: everything has meaning;
3. The Whole is in the parts: everything is potentially present in every part of Reality;
4. Impermanence: everything is continuously changing;
5. Change is Time and Time is Change;
6. Extremes change into their opposites;
7. Parallelity;
8. Cause and Effect

## 1. Reality is One

Because Reality is basically One, everything is related to everything else. Our ordinary waking reality, our dream reality, and any other reality in between or beyond, all belong to the One Reality. This implies that they are all related to each other, and that whatever happens in one relative reality may also happen in another, or at least has some effect on it.

The *Yi Jing* can be regarded as a framework over Reality, as a whole through which information can be obtained about events occurring in any of the relative realities. This can be done by means of different methods of divination (prediction). The *Yi Jing* covers all worlds, all the different kinds of realities, whether here or beyond, whether waking, dreaming, the past or future. Thus by stimulating one event in the present reality, such as throwing coins to answer a question, one can know something about a future reality by looking up its meaning in the *Yi Jing* text.

## 2. Reality is information

Everything in Reality can be regarded as information. Whatever people perceive or experience in Reality may have a certain meaning either for them or to others. Many people are usually not aware that most of the time a lot of information passes by without being recognised. For information has no meaning if it is not observed by a subject and recognised as meaningful. Still there are some people who can read the weather from signs in the morning clouds, or the outcome of an enterprise from an event that happened at its beginning.

This information can be more or less accurate, but it is generally not available to everyone. The *Yi Jing*, as a tool of prediction, is able to give meaning to every little hunch, sign, dream, idea or something interesting that is noticed by anyone. Information may then become meaningful – becomes knowledge, and this knowledge may give one the power to effect changes and influence one's fate.

But information alone is not yet knowledge, and having knowledge does not imply that one has the power to change things. And even if one has that power, it may still not be wisdom – the wisdom to do the right thing at the right time and right place. A wisdom the *Yi Jing* is only slowly pulling us into.

## 3. The Whole is in the parts

From the idea of the Oneness of Reality follows the idea that the Whole is in the parts, or that each and every part of the Whole contains that Whole, at least potentially. This does not only mean that the question we have, already contains the answer, but that actually the question *is* the answer. This can already be noticed from the fact that any question guides its answer.

When we do not know anything about a subject matter, we are usually not only unable to ask the right questions, but also not able to interpret the answer correctly.

As the Whole is in the parts and the parts contain the Whole, then all things that are part of us – whatever is close to us, all things around us – may give an indication, may say something about us, and even what may happen to us. With the help of the *Yi Jing*, our birth date or our identity number – even our phone number – can be translated into information about us. Even our *dao* – what we have to do in this life – is contained in the *Book of Change*. Everyone is opening it at a different page (see *Yi Jing numerology*, p. 392).

## 4. Impermanence

Everything in Reality is continuously changing, nothing stays the same, everything is impermanent. Considering the fact that everything is in constant flux, it would be principally impossible to make a prediction about anything in the future because, theoretically, the next moment many conditions and circumstances may have changed in such a way that the previous outcome would immediately contain an error. At the same time the use of the *Yi Jing* – as long as 3000 years – shows, that based on the same idea of change, it is not only possible but actually very realistic to make any prediction in the future with great accuracy.

## 5. Change is Time and Time is Change

People are aware of Time mainly because of the perception that everything is continuously changing, and Change is noticed also due to the indication of Time. *Change is Time and Time is Change*. When we know one, we will be able to know the other. So when we look at our watch, we know the whereabouts of the sun, and when we look at the sun, we can approximately say what time it is. Within the framework of the *Yi Jing* the relationship between the concepts of Time and Change are fundamental.

With the help of the *Yi Jing* we can know a whole life's changes, up to its minute details from its time of birth (Time is Change). And, if necessary it may be possible to trace someone's exact birth date from the life hexagram that appears after consulting the *Yi Jing* (Change is Time).

As time changes everything, all changes have their own time. This idea about Change is also considered very important in the *Yi Jing*, because all changes that people or situations have to go through always have their own time. They cannot be accelerated or slowed down without disturbing the process of change.

## 6. Extremes change into opposites

When the sun stands at midday it begins to set, and when the moon is dark it begins to wax. The fullness and emptiness of heaven and earth wane and wax according to the times. When something reaches its highest or lowest point it always changes into its opposite. This principle can be applied to the whole of Reality, and is also one of the basic ideas about change in the *Yi Jing*.

## 7. Parallelity

*Parallelity* is the principle on which the system of divination of the *Yi Jing* is supposed to work (see *Parallelity and the Yi Jing*, p. 353). According to this principle, two events occurring in Reality are related to each other, in the sense that their meaning is perceived from the perspective of the observer. It is about a *meaningful* co-incidence in the sense that two incidents (events) occurring in Reality run parallel to each other. That two events are related to each other is mainly based on the idea of the One Reality in which everything is related to everything else. Without a subject noticing the signs or omens and perceiving a certain meaning from them, everything in Reality is just related to everything else, and has no significant meaning attached to it.

This principle of Parallelity is about the relation between two events occurring in Reality, but *not* on the basis of Causality, where one event causes the other and precedes it in time. Here events do not have a causal relationship, and could happen at the same time, or at different times – in one reality (ordinary reality) or in different ones (inner and outer realities). This parallelistic relation between two events goes beyond the concept of Time, because Time is an illusion, and only apparent within the realm of ordinary reality (duality), where everything is continuously changing. Within the realm of duality – where everything is changing – Time manifests as past, present and future, but in the One Reality there is actually only the present which contains both past and future.

By throwing yarrow stalks, coins or dice at a particular time (the present) – with the help of the *Yi Jing* – one can know its meaning in relation to other events that will take place at another time (the future), and run parallel to it. Or by consulting the *Yi Jing* about one event in the present, another event in the future can be connected with it through the meaning looked up in the *Book of Change*. Thus the meaning of the relationship of two events occurring in Reality can be found in the *Yi Jing*.

## 8. Cause and Effect

The principle of Cause and Effect can be seen as one of the fundamental principles of the *Book of Change*, because the use of the book is based on the idea of the Cause and Effect of actions, in the sense that all actions (deeds, words and thoughts) have their effects. This is the Law of Karma, which says that one always has to face the consequences of all one's actions.

By consulting the book one may know the changes (effects of intended actions), and may thus have the choice to advance or retreat in certain situations. By means of divination human beings may have some idea about the effects of their actions – may therefore influence their karma, and thus their fate and destiny.

# The Yi Jing *and the process of Change*

## Introduction

The *Yi Jing* or the *Book of Change* is a book of divination based on the changes in Reality. It is founded on the idea of Impermanence: *everything in Reality is in constant change, nothing stays the same.*

Change can be defined as something in Reality becoming different than it was before. The process of change is about alteration, modification and transformation.

Reality is One and Many: in Reality there is Unity and Duality. It is only in Duality that Change manifests itself, and it does so in relation to Time. Change is based on Time: because time passes change is perceived. Time is based on Change: because changes (in nature and life) are perceived time is conceived. *Change is Time and Time is Change.*

The development in Reality from Unity to Diversity comes in different steps. First there is Oneness (the One Reality), then there is two (Duality, *yin* and *yang*). As Reality is actually One, *yin* and *yang* are not only opposites but complementary. Together they make up the Oneness of Reality.

Then there is three (Tri-unity, the trigrams), because opposites can only exist on the basis of their difference (a third aspect). If there is no difference one cannot perceive them.

Then there is five (the five 'elements' or the *five states of change*), and from these five 'elements' everything (the many) comes into being.

## Aspects of change

All the changes in Reality are manifesting in accordance with the Process of Change, that is again based on the Law of Change. Within the theoretical framework of the *Yi Jing*, this Law of Change or principle according to which change manifests, is not singular, but has several different aspects:

1. the Law of Extremes; 2. the changes of the trigrams; 3. the Five States of Change; 4. the changing hexagrams.

The Process of Change is assumed to have certain aspects and phases or certain characteristics and stages of development. As the *Yi Jing* is the *Book of Change*, the 64 hexagrams and 384 lines are assumed to be the aspects and phases of the Process of Change.

### 1. The Law of Extremes

When the moon is full it will begin to wane, and when the moon is dark it will begin to wax. The Law of Extremes says, that if something comes to an extreme (high or low) it will change into its opposite. According to this law, when something becomes too *yang* it will change into its opposite (*yin*) and if that becomes too *yin* it will again change into its opposite (*yang*). This can be clearly seen in the hexagrams where a changing *yang* (whole) line changes into a *yin* (broken) line in the new hexagram, and a changing *yin* line changes into a *yang* line. *Extremes changing into its opposite is the basic pattern of change.*

### 2. The changes of the trigrams

In the *Book of Change yin* and *yang* are expressed in lines: a broken line is *yin* and a whole line is *yang*. Two of these lines on top of each other make a bigram, and three lines create a trigram. The trigrams develop in a natural way from Unity to Duality, from the subtle to the dense.

Out of the Absolute Unity of *Tai Ji* (the Whole, lit. the Great Ultimate) the two main principles of Duality, *Yin* and *Yang*, appear represented by a *yin* (broken) and a *yang* (whole) line. From these two principles the four symbols (bigrams) appear, represented by great *yin* (two *yin* lines), lesser *yang* (a *yang* line on top of a *yin* line), lesser *yin* (a *yin* line on top of a *yang* line), and great *yang* (two *yang* lines). From the four symbols the eight trigrams in the Early Heaven Arrangement (EHA) appear: *heaven, lake* (or *cloud*), *fire, thunder, wind, water, mountain,* and *earth*.

The Early Heaven Arrangement of trigrams, which came forth from the natural development of trigrams, is based on the sequence of events as manifesting in heaven (the sky). Its sequence and order are derived from the observation of natural phenomena such as the weather:

1. *heaven* (a clear summer sky) – 2. *cloud* (due to heat, hot air rises and clouds are formed) – 3. *fire* (heavy clouds bring forth lightning) – 4. *thunder* (after lightning thunder always follows) – 5. *wind* (wind follows thunder) – 6. *water* (after the wind comes the rain) – 7. *mountain* (the rain falls first on the mountain) – 8. *earth* (the rain falls on the earth). *This sequence of the eight trigrams as manifesting in heaven (the sky) can be considered a natural pattern of change.*

### 3. The Five States of Change

The eight trigrams are based on the five elements. These elements, Earth, Water, Fire, Wood and Metal, are also represented by five of the eight trigrams. Each element may represent one or more trigrams:

Earth (*earth* and *mountain*), Water (*water/rain*, and *lake/cloud*), Fire (*fire*), Wood (*wind* and *thunder*), and Metal (*heaven* and *lake*).

These elements are actually *states of change or transformation* as they are manifesting on earth. The 'elements' are related to one another in that they follow specific patterns of change. The relationships of the trigrams as 'elements' play a role in the meanings of the hexagrams.

These relationships are:

- *producing*: Earth produces Metal, Metal produces Water, Water produces Wood, Wood produces Fire, Fire produces Earth;
- *exhausting* (the opposite of producing): Earth exhausts Fire, Fire exhausts Wood, Wood exhausts Water, Water exhausts Metal, Metal exhausts Earth;

- *injuring*: Fire injures Water, Water injures Earth, Earth injures Wood, Wood injures Metal, Metal injures Fire;
- *destroying*: Water destroys Fire, Fire destroys Metal, Metal destroys Wood, Wood destroys Earth, Earth destroys Water.

These relationships of the elements help decide the good fortune or misfortune aspects within each hexagram.

The main pattern of change, in regard to the elements as states of transformation, is the one which is *producing*: Earth produces Metal (rocks), Metal produces Water (water flows out of rocks), Water (rain) produces Wood (plants), Wood (if burned) produces Fire, and Fire produces Earth (ashes). *This sequence of the trigrams as States of Change manifesting on earth can also be considered a natural pattern of change.*

## 4. The changing hexagrams

Two trigrams make a hexagram or six-line image, and combinations of the eight trigrams make up the 64 hexagrams that together are assumed to represent the 64 aspects in a continuous Process of Change in Reality. Within the hexagram structure of six lines, the *yin* and *yang* lines are related to each other in very specific ways, and are assumed to represent its six phases of change.

Based on the premise that the 64 hexagrams are aspects and stages of an ongoing process of transformation (Change), they must have a specific sequence and order. The order of the text used today has been accepted since the earliest beginnings of the *Yi Jing*. But there does not seem to be a consistent logic behind this ordering.

See for a discussion on different kinds of sequence of the hexagrams p. 358, *Inconsisitencies in the Yi Jing: 3. The sequence and order of the hexagrams.*

## Conclusion

Taking into consideration that the Process of Change in the *Yi Jing* is based on the Law of Change, because it manifests according to it, this Law of Change has several aspects.

The Law of Change, which is the basis of the Process of Change, seems to have been observed from the fact that all extremes change into their opposites (Law of Extremes); the order of the trigrams (Early Heaven Arrangement) follows the changes of weather phenomena as manifesting in the sky; and the Five States of Change follow the order of natural phenomena as manifested on earth.

These aspects of the Law of Change in some way seem to suggest that the 64 hexagrams and the 384 lines are the aspects and phases of the Process of Change. They are characteristics and stages of development in that process indicating a natural pattern of change. But the inconsistencies in the actual sequence of the 64 hexagrams are not very supportive of this idea.

And if one looks at the lines of the hexagrams, they are not always phases in the process of change within a hexagram. They could also represent events in the theme of that particular hexagram.

Therefore, the 64 hexagrams and the 384 lines are *not* aspects and phases of the Process of Change, but only an orderly system from which the changes can be known (read).

As the Law of Change can be regarded as the foundation (source) for the remarkable predictions of the *Book of Change* for many hundreds of years – the connected meanings between the hexagrams show some kind of development – one may only say that the sequence and order of the 64 hexagrams does somewhat reflect the Process of Change.

# The Yi Jing *and the concept of time*

Time is usually seen as going into effect at the beginning of the creation of the universe, and continuing until the universe comes to an end. According to Newton, there is Absolute Time within an Absolute Space, where Time develops from a beginning to an end in a linear manner. This Time is divided into the past, the present, and the future, where the present is just a thin line between the past and the future. In the so-called passage of Time everything is 'becoming'.

According to Einstein with his Theory of Relativity, Time is relative. Depending on the position and the speed of the subject, there are differences in time and the passage of time. There is a past, a present, and a future, but the present is not the same everywhere.

Time and Space are apparent only on the ordinary dense level of Reality. Once one touches the deeper levels of matter (sub-atomic), or the subtle levels of consciousness (dreams), Time/Space changes drastically and may even disappear.

Time and Space seem to be in the world objectively, but they may only be means to enable human beings to structure the world. Moreover, in the passage of time there is both objective and subjective time. The time that is experienced in dreams (for instance, hours) can vary with the objective time (minutes).

Thus there is objective time and relative time, but as Reality is both Absolute (Emptiness, Unity) and Relative (Form, Duality), Time is both objective and relative. In Reality only the present is real, for there is no past (the past is gone), and there is no future (the future has not arrived). This present also contains both the past and the future, but this is not always apparent to everybody.

Time does not have to be linear, it can also be cyclic – as seen with the seasons of the year, where every end is a new beginning. Time can even be without a beginning or an end – as when one asks the question about the duration of the universe.

In the *Yi Jing* or *Book of Change* Time plays an important role. Change is the basis for Time, but one can also say that Time marks the birth of all changes. Time is usually perceived in connection with the changes noticed in nature and life, and also Change is perceived by one's awareness of time. *Change is Time and Time is Change*. On the basis of this important principle the matter of timing, or doing the right thing at the right time, can be regarded as the essence of the *Yi Jing's* wisdom.

## Change is Time and Time is Change

The *Yi Jing* is based on the principle of Change as the foundation of Time. *Change is Time and Time is Change*. This can firstly be noticed from the fact that each hexagram has six lines, and that in most hexagrams the lines follow each other as if they represent changes in time. This *division into six units* can be found in our present sense of time, which has many divisions of six: 60 seconds = 1 minute, 60 minutes = 1 hour, 24 hours (4x6) = 1 day, 30 days (5x6) = 1 month, 12 months (2x6) = 1 year. It can also be found in the Chinese 60 years' cycle, and their 12 months' lunar calendar.

Secondly, time changes everything, and all changes have their own time. When we know one, we will be able to know the other. For example, when we look at our watch (Time), we will more or less know the position of the Sun in the sky (Change). And when we look at the Sun (Change), we can approximately say what time it is.

In the same way, when we know someone's date of birth (Time), we can translate this into a life-hexagram (Change), and get some information about the changes in that person's life.

All this can be done by means of the numerology of the *Yi Jing* (see *Yi Jing numerology*, p. 392).

Knowing the hexagram of a certain day, one may consider the good or bad fortune of that particular day as a birth time of changes to come. Thus one may decide whether to take action or to refrain from doing so.

A hexagram derived from a date can function as a day-hexagram from which we may know what is in store for us that particular day. This hexagram is obtained by totalling the numbers of the day, month, and year in a numerological way, and calculating the changing line from the day.

In the same manner, by taking the day and month of our birth, and adding the present or another year to it, we shall obtain a year-hexagram for that particular year. This will inform us about what to expect, or give an insight into what already happened during that particular year.

We can also calculate our life-hexagram by adding up the day, month and year of our birth. This will give information about our karmic pattern and the kind of life we will live.

By knowing the time of an event we may therefore know the changes in store.

If someone does not know his or her exact date of birth, but only the month and the year, one could nevertheless consult the *Yi Jing*. From the hexagram received as an answer (Change), it may be possible to figure out the exact date of birth (Time).

## The matter of timing

By contemplating life's changes as derived from consulting the *Book of Change*, or from dates obtained with the numerology of the *Yi Jing*, one may decide whether to advance or retreat in certain situations.

This brings us to the *matter of timing* – doing the right thing at the right time – as the essence of the wisdom of the *Yi Jing*. As all changes have their own time, a small effort at the right time (timing) will have a greater chance of success than a great effort at the wrong time.

The *Yi Jing*'s numerology can help one decide at which point of the day, of the year, or of one's life to initiate certain actions in order to activate the best chances for manifestation. Similarly one can know when to refrain from actions that would cause an indicated misfortune to manifest.

Thus the use of numbers (dates) in relation to symbols (hexagrams) brings forth information on which to contemplate in order to stay in the *Dao*. The matter of timing is the essence of the *Yi Jing's* wisdom.

This system of numerology and prediction is based on the changes on Earth, and not on changes in Heaven, or on the influences of planets, as in astrology. It is based on the patterns of change manifesting on Earth, related to Time as we ordinarily know it, namely objective time.

# The Yi Jing *and the theory of chance*

Consulting the *Yi Jing* can be done by means of yarrow stalks, coins or even dice. These methods of consulting the *Yi Jing* are generally associated with Chance, therefore their outcome will be based on chance.

According to the Theory of Chance, all the hexagrams should have the same chance to appear as an answer to a question: their occurrence should be without design. This is also the case with the different lines of the hexagrams. The different changing and stable lines should have the same chance to appear.

According to the Theory of Chance, the appearance of the hexagrams and the lines should be based on Randomness, or having the same chance to appear. But it seems that some hexagrams appear more often than others – more often than can be expected from the Theory of Chance.

The answers given by the *Book of Change*, the hexagrams and the different lines, do not appear at random, as they should according to the Theory of Chance.

The answer to this problem could be:
1. the *Yi Jing's* independent wisdom influences the appearance of the answers (hexagrams);
2. the personal problems and condition of the persons consulting the *Yi Jing* influence the appearance of the answers (hexagrams);
3. the methods used for consultation influence the appearance of the lines;
4. the qualities of the stable or changing lines influence their appearance.

## 1. The influence of the *Yi Jing*'s independent wisdom

The *Yi Jing* is generally known as a book of divination, but it is also a book with its own independent intelligent wisdom.

*The first indication* for such an independent intelligent wisdom is the fact that if a person consults the book without enough of a respectful attitude – for example by asking the same question several times while he has already received an answer – the book will give in response the fourth hexagram indicating immaturity and youthful folly.

*The second indication* is that when someone consults the *Yi Jing* with the intention to harm someone, or perform an immoral or unethical act the *Yi Jing* does not go along with the inquirer's motivation, but will always point to the incorrectness of his intention.

*The third indication* is that if one consults the book, by definition one can not receive the same answers (hexagram and lines) for the same question asked again after a lapse of time. The reason is that theoretically, the changes which have occurred during any lapse of time, should always lead to a different answer. But if the situation asked about is still the same, it is possible that the *Yi Jing* will give exactly the same answer.

*The fourth indication* is that sometimes the book answers with a hexagram having no changing line. This generally means that there is no change in the situation or process inquired about.
It can also mean that the inquirer cannot really 'hear' the answer, because he is not ready, prepared or ripe for it.

The various indications point to the fact that the *Yi Jing* does have its own independent intelligent wisdom which directs the answer to each question asked, and therefore influences the appearance of the hexagrams.

## 2. The personal influence of the consultant on the appearance of an answer

One is advised to consult the *Yi Jing* only with a quiet and balanced mind. If one is emotionally involved during a consultation, the answer will most likely not be clear or adequate. If one has desires or fears, the answers will usually be biased. This indicates that the personal condition, problems and interests of the inquirer in a way influences the appearance of the hexagrams.

According to the Theory of Chance, every hexagram should have the same chance as any other to appear as an answer. But the hexagrams as answers seem to be influenced by the personal condition of the inquirer.

### 3. The influence of the methods used for consultation

As hexagrams are composed of six lines, their appearance is directly dependent on the chance of appearance of the different lines during the consultation of the oracle. The methods of consulting the *Yi Jing* differ in their quality, because they give different chances of appearance to the stable or changing lines. Among the yarrow stalks, coins or dice, the stalks is the best method.

|  | Yarrow stalks | Coins | Die |
|---|---|---|---|
| stable line | 12/16 or 3/4 or 60/80 | 6/8 or 3/4 or 60/80 | 8/10 or 4/5 or 64/80 |
| changing line | 4/16 or 1/4 or 20/80 | 2/8 or 1/4 or 20/80 | 2/10 or 1/5 or 16/80 |
| stable *yang* | 5/16 or 25/80 | 3/8 or 6/16 or 30/80 | 4/10 or 32/80 |
| stable *yin* | 7/16 or 35/80 | 3/8 or 6/16 or 30/80 | 4/10 or 32/80 |
| changing *yang* | 3/16 or 15/80 | 1/8 or 2/16 or 10/80 | 1/10 or 8/80 |
| changing *yin* | 1/16 or 5/80 | 1/8 or 2/16 or 10/80 | 1/10 or 8/80 |

From this calculation of the chances we can see that the method of consultation seems to influence the chance of appearance of the different lines.

### 4. The influence of the qualities of the stable or changing lines on their appearance

The chance of appearance of the different lines is also dependent on the quality of the line. According to the theory of the *Yi Jing*, a *yang* line by its nature (active, doing), should have a greater chance to appear than a *yin* line (receptive, being). This is the case with a changing *yang* line, but not with a stable *yang* line. Still the qualities of the stable and changing lines influence the chance of their appearance. This again influences the possibility of appearance of the hexagrams.

In an experiment to determine whether the *Yi Jing* was functioning on the basis of Chance (Randomness) or not, the oracle was consulted on one question by using two similar methods simultaneously. One method was based on random numbers, and the other on numbers acquired from six different persons.

In this experiment six people were asked to think about the same question and to mention a number from 0 to 9. The other method was to generate six numbers, 0 to 9, from a *random number generator* (RNG). The even numbers (0, 2, 4, 6, 8) would give a *yin* line, and the odd numbers (1, 3, 5, 7, 9) a *yang* line. The changing lines were *yin* (6) and *yang* (9). With these numbers two hexagrams (answers) were formed. The experimenter was the only person who already knew the answer.

As the outcome of this experiment, the answer acquired from the random number generator gave a hexagram *without a changing line*, and was therefore less specific than the answer received from the persons *which had a changing line*.

The answer based on the method of using persons was more adequate and precise, despite the spreading of the numbers amongst six persons.

In conclusion, we would say that there are so many internal and external influences during the consultation of the oracle, that the hexagrams and lines do *not* have any chance to appear at random, and *the Yi Jing does therefore not function on the basis of Chance*.

In spite of the fact that binary logic is the basis for modern computing – and one may say that computers operate on a similar symbolic language as the *Yi Jing* (for instance 0 and 1, *yin* and *yang*) – the computer consultation method based on a random number generator is not adequate because *Yi Jing* consultations are *not* based on randomness or chance.

All the methods or consultation based on random numbers of a computer program are therefore totally inadequate.

# *Parallelity and the* Yi Jing

The *Yi Jing* or *Book of Change* is mainly known as an old Chinese book of divination. It is a text of 64 hexagrams or images, each composed of six lines in a way representing the different aspects and phases of the continuous process of Change. By means of various methods of consultation such as the use of yarrow stalks, coins or dice, one may receive an answer to any question about any subject, object or event, the truth of which may be revealed in time. Actually, the *Yi Jing* is a book containing 64 codes of meaning that can be consulted in relation to anything occurring in Reality.

The *Yi Jing* is a book of divination because it is a book totally based on signs and omens. Signs are things perceived as indicating a (future) state or occurrence, and omens are occurrences or objects regarded as portending good or evil.

Signs and omens are actually events occurring at a particular time (present or past) which may give an indication as to what may happen at another time (future), or give meaning to a present situation. These events could happen in the external, ordinary reality, but they could also be internal psychic events, such as intuitions, dreams and visions.

These events are called signs and omens only if there is a *subject* (human being) giving a particular meaning to them. Without a subject noticing the signs or omens, and giving meaning to them, they hold no significance whatsoever.

Thus by looking at the early morning sky some farmers are able to predict the weather of the coming day. And from an event occurring at the beginning of an enterprise, some people can read its final outcome.

In the *Yi Jing* the idea of signs and omens is worked out extensively. Within the system formulated by this ancient book, all kinds of signs and omens are explained in a sophisticated way. These meanings are described in 64 hexagrams as the 64 stages in a process of continuous change, and in 6 lines as the phases of change within each hexagram.

How consultation of the *Yi Jing* works is theoretically not quite clear. One could say that it works according to the *principle of synchronicity*. This principle concerns the relation between two events occurring in Reality – though not on the basis of Causality, where one event causes the other and precedes it in time.

Synchronicity comes from the word 'synchronise' which has to do with events occurring *at the same time*. This principle was proposed by Carl Jung to explain the relationship between meaningful events that could not be explained by the *principle of causality*.

Causality is the principle where two events in Reality are meaningfully related to one another, in the sense that one event can be regarded as the cause of the other (the effect), and precedes it in time. In the case of causality the cause always has to come before the effect, but at the more subtle levels of Reality (the subatomic level or the level of dreams), it may happen that the effect precedes the cause. In these cases the principle of causality is not adequate to explain the relationships between two meaningfully related events.

In the *Yi Jing* the principle of causality plays an important role, as the use of the book is based on the idea that all actions have their effects. By consulting the book one may know the changes – the effects of intended actions – thus having the choice to advance or retreat in certain situations. By means of the *Yi Jing* human beings may get some idea about the effects of their actions, and may therefore have some influence on their fate and destiny.

To explain how the *Yi Jing* itself works, Jung proposed the *principle of synchronicity*. According to Jung, synchronicity means the simultaneous occurrence of a certain psychic state with one or more external events which appear as meaningful parallels to the momentary subjective state of the observer. Or, the simultaneous occurrence of two meaningful, but not causally connected events (Jung: *Synchronicity*, p. 36).

Synchronicity frequently involves several events which – though radically different in form (an idea or a physical object) – are tied together by a common pattern or theme. On a more profound level such themes seem bound together by a common sense of meaning (id., p. 31).

According to the *principle of synchronicity*, two events occurring in Reality at a specific time (moment), are meaningfully related to each other, in the sense that their meaning is *perceived by an observer*. Because the two events do not always have to happen *at the same time*, this phenomenon can better be described as *parallelity*. Here events run parallel to each other in the great Reality beyond ordinary reality, where time and space are transcended.

*Parallelity* is about a *meaningful co-incidence*, in the sense that two incidents (events) occurring in Reality are perceived as being meaningfully related by an observer noticing it. These events do not have a causal relationship, and could happen at the same time or at different times – in one reality (ordinary reality), or in different ones (inner subjective, and outer objective realities).

That these two events are related to each other is based on the idea of the One Reality. Because Reality is basically One, everything is interconnected and thus related to everything else. Without a subject noticing these events and giving meaning to them, however, everything in Reality is merely related to everything else, while having no special significance.

Reality can also be regarded as having different levels: the ordinary, dense level of Reality: the level of Duality and Causality, where Time and Space are apparent, and the more subtle level of Reality: the level of Oneness, Unity and Non-duality, where Time and Space are not so apparent, and may even disappear.

Causality belongs to the separate, dualistic aspect of Reality. Synchronicity and Parallelity belong to the interconnected, non-dualistic aspect of Reality but are observed in duality because one needs *two events* to synchronize or run parallel. In this sense, mind (the inner reality) and matter (the outer reality) are two separate realities from the dualistic point of view, but in the One Reality they are an integral unity.

In the One Reality everything is related to everything else, because everything is connected with everything else. The meaning given to two events occurring in Reality could be causal or synchronistic (a-causal) – all dependent on an observer who is noticing them.

Modern physics and psychology have also attained to the insight that the observer, not being separate from the events observed, is always influencing them. Therefore, all meaning given to events is totally dependent on the observer.

Because *Synchronicity and Parallelity* belong to the non-dualistic level of Reality, such a relation between two events goes beyond the concept of Time. Time is an illusion, apparent only within the realm of ordinary dualistic reality, where everything is continuously changing. Time is noticed mainly because of the perception that everything is changing continuously and change is also perceived due to the indication of time. *Time is Change and Change is Time*. Within the realm of ordinary reality (Duality), time manifests as past, present and future. In the One, Non-dual Reality, there is actually only the present, which contains both past and future.

Based on the idea that the observed meaningful events do not always happen at the same time, but basically run parallel to each other within the One Reality – where past, present, and future are one – *parallelity* is a more adequate concept to explain the predictions about the future made with the *Yi Jing*. Because in the One Reality – where past, present, and future are one – it is as with a predictive dream, where one event (the dream) that happens in the present runs parallel with the event that takes place somewhere in the future.

With the creation of one event (by throwing stalks, coins or dice) at a particular time (the present), one is able to know its meaning (by reading the hexagram and lines in the book) in relation to another event, which will take place at another time (the future). The event that leads to the information is related to the event that will happen in the future, in the sense that in the One Reality it runs parallel to it.

Like the old fortune tellers of China, one of the authors has consulted the *Yi Jing*, several times a day, every day, and for many years. In this case he consulted the *Yi Jing* four times each day, for the four sections of the day (from midnight to 6:00 h., from 6:00 to 12:00 h., from midday to 18:00 h. and from 18:00 h. to midnight.).

By doing this he obtained four hexagrams for the four sections of the day with their specific changing lines. Because each section was divided into six hours, each changing line was precisely at a certain hour of a particular section.

So through the years he noticed that, whether he was travelling on a train (which suddenly slowed down at about 21:00 h., when hexagram 57 line 3 – about exhaustion of power – was on); or seeing something on television (a big accident at midnight due to the weather, when hexagram 62, line 6 – about a calamity – was on); or in a dream (at around 2:00 h. in the morning where he was travelling when hexagram 56, line 2 – about arriving at a house and meeting a young woman – was on); or in a meditation retreat (where one day the meditation went quite well at about 16:00 h., when hexagram 52, line 4 – about stilling the whole body – was on): the prediction (as one event) was always connected to the other real event in the future. Of course only when there was an observer to notice and interpret its meaning.

Thus by consulting the *Yi Jing* about one event in the present, another event in the future that is connected with it can be known through the meaning looked up in the book.

Bibliography

Aziz, R.: *Jung's Psychology of Religion and Synchronicity,* SUNY, New York, 1990.
Bohm, David: *Causality and Chance in Modern Physics,* Routledge and Kegan Paul, London, 1957.
Combs, Allan & M. Holland: *Synchronicity: science, myth, and the trickster,* Floris Books, Edinburgh, 1994.
Hacker, Edward: *The I Ching Handbook,* Paradigm Publications, Brookline, MA, 1993.
Hamlyn, David W.: *The Theory of Knowledge,* Doubleday, New York, 1970.
Jung, Carl G.: *Synchronicity: an acausal connecting principle,* Pantheon, New York, 1955.
Koestler, Arthur: *The Roots of Coincidence: an excursion into parapsychology,* Random House, New York, 1972.
Main, Roderick: *Jung on Synchronicity and the Paranormal,* Princeton University Press, 1997.
Main, Roderick: *Synchronicity as a Form of Spiritual Experience,* Lancaster University, Department of Religious Studies, Lancaster 1995.
Mansfield, V: *Synchronicity, Science and Soul-Making,* Open Court, Chicago, 1995.
Peat, F. David: *Synchronicity, the Bridge between Matter and Mind,* Bantam, New Age Books, Toronto 1988.

# Inconsistencies in the Yi Jing

Consistency is the assumption that all theoretical frameworks should be consistent, or in conformity with earlier principles of thought, and not be contradictory to them. All the way through the theoretical framework certain ideas and concepts should have the same meanings and be used in the same way.

This has to do with Language, where words should have a clear and definite meaning, and not be ambiguous or multi-interpretable. It also has to do with Logic, namely a two-valued logic, where something is either true or not true (only one possibility is true). A more-valued logic where there is more than one possibility for truth (both possibilities can be true) does not apply.

Consistency is applied to theoretical frameworks as abstractions of Reality while Reality itself may actually be much less consistent than we assume it to be.

The *Yi Jing* or *Book of Change* is a Chinese text containing 64 hexagrams or six-line images, and is mainly used for the purpose of divination or prediction of future events. It can be regarded as the foundation of Chinese civilisation because many decisions that decided the course of Chinese history, and many inventions that made a change in Chinese culture, have been made on the basis of consulting the *Yi Jing*.

Assuming consistency for all theoretical frameworks, the *Yi Jing*, as a theoretical framework about Impermanence and the process of Change contains many inconsistencies. Nevertheless, despite all its inconsistencies the *Yi Jing* is able to predict events quite accurately, and has been used for this purpose for some three thousand years.

The inner structure of the *Yi Jing*, as the foundation of its theoretical framework, consists of 64 hexagrams or six-line images, which are constructed from the combination of eight trigrams which are again composed of *yin* (broken) and *yang* (whole) lines representing Duality in Reality. Both in its inner structure and its theoretical framework or text the *Yi Jing* contains many inconsistencies.

These inconsistencies relate to:

1. the *Yin-Yang* division; 2. the order and meanings of the trigrams; 3. the sequence and order of the hexagrams; 4. the position and meaning of the individual lines.

## 1. The *Yin-Yang* division

In the Chinese theory of Reality everything is divided into *yin* and *yang*. This is not an ordinary dichotomy. *Yin* and *yang* are not only *yin* or only *yang*, they also complement each other. The image symbolising *yin-yang* is a circle, *Tai Ji* (the Whole, lit. the Great Ultimate), with a black and a white section: in each section is a small dot of the opposite quality ☯ .
This indicates that both 'opposites' are complementary to each other, because there is always something of *yin* in the *yang* and vice versa.

In a listing of the qualities of *yang* and *yin*, *one can clearly see an inconsistency*. One may begin with certain qualities, such as light and dark, hot and cold, sun and moon, heaven and earth, day and night, fire and water, energy and matter, spirit and body, action and rest, life and death – but by continuing, one may end with its opposites qualities. For example, if one takes the '*yang* and *yin* style' in martial arts – being hard and soft, having angular and round movements, and thus square and circular, earth and heaven – one arrives at *yin* and *yang* instead of *yang* and *yin*.

The presence of some *yang* in the *yin* and some *yin* in the *yang* implies that no quality, event or object in Reality is only of one kind: there is always something of its opposite in it. This can clearly be seen in the 'good fortune' and 'misfortune' division of the *Yi Jing*: in every good fortune there is always some misfortune, and in every misfortune there is always some good fortune, as is usual in actual Reality.

## 2. The order and meanings of the trigrams

The trigrams are three-line images formed by combining *yang* (whole) lines and *yin* (broken) lines. Some of the trigrams represent the so-called Western elements such as: Earth, Water, Fire, Air (Wood), and Ether (Metal), but in the *Yi Jing* they are actually regarded as *states of change* or *transformation*. The eight trigrams are formed out of the five trigrams representing the 'elements': Earth (*earth* and *mountain*), Water (*water/rain*, and *lake/cloud*), Fire (*fire*), Wood (*wind* and *thunder*) and Metal (*heaven* and *lake*).

The order of the eight trigrams is said to be derived from the *He Tu* and *Lo Shu* patterns of dots found on sacred animals, but they can also be derived from natural phenomena, such as the weather and the seasons.

In the Early Heaven Arrangement (EHA) of trigrams, the sequence of events in the sky (heaven) can be taken as the ideal. In the Later Heaven Arrangement (LHA) the order of the seasons on earth can serve as the model.

In the EHA the sequence of the trigrams is consistent with the sequence of events in the sky:

1. *heaven* (a clear summer sky) – 2. *cloud* (due to heat, hot air rises and clouds are formed) – 3. *fire* (heavy clouds bring forth lightning) – 4. *thunder* (after lightning thunder always follows) – 5. *wind* (wind follows thunder) – 6. *water* (after the wind comes the rain) – 7. *mountain* (the rain falls first on the mountain) – 8. *earth* (the rain falls on the earth).

But in the LHA the sequence of trigrams is not consistent with the sequence of events on earth (the seasons): 1. *water* (rain) and 2. *earth* (rain falls on the earth mainly in the winter) represent the winter; 3. *thunder* and 4. *wind* (thunder and wind stand for growth of plants) represent the spring; the number 5 is missing; then it should be followed by *fire* (but this trigram has number 9) representing the summer; 6. *heaven* and 7. *cloud/lake* represent autumn, and 8. *mountain* (stillness is also an attribute of the winter).

On earth the trigrams as elements follow the sequence of *the five states of change (or transformation)*: Water (rain) produces Wood (plants grow); Wood produces Fire (wood is burned); Fire produces Earth (ashes); Earth produces Metal (rocks are formed), and Metal produces Water.

Based on this order, the LHA of the trigrams on earth could actually be: 1.*water* (Water, rain, winter) leads to 2. *thunder* (Wood, spring, growth) and

3. *wind* (Wood), leading to 4. *fire* (Fire, summer), which again leads to 5. *earth* (Earth), and 6. *mountain* (Earth), leading to 7. *heaven* (Metal, autumn), and 8. *lake* (Metal/Water, autumn), which again leads to *water*.

In the course of time, besides the elements and natural phenomena, many other attributes were attached to the eight trigrams, such as family members (father, mother, daughter, son), numbers, shapes, colours, sounds, tastes, body parts, places, directions, months, hours.

The various attributes of the trigrams play an important role in the meaning of the hexagrams which are composed of the different trigrams *but these attributes are not used consistently throughout the text.* In some hexagrams one attribute of a trigram is used, in another the other attribute is chosen. The same attribute may also have different meanings.

## 3. The sequence and order of the hexagrams

Based on the premise that the 64 hexagrams are aspects and stages of an ongoing process of transformation (Change), they must have a specific sequence and order. The sequence and order of the hexagrams used today has been accepted since the beginning of the *Yi Jing*. But there does not seem to *be a consistent logic behind this ordering.*

The sequence of the hexagrams is *not* based on a *specific mathematical order*, except for the numbering of the hexagrams progressively from 1 to 64. The sequence has also *no* basis in *some kind of formal order* that is independent from the meanings of the hexagrams (Hacker: *The I Ching Handbook*, p. 104).

The sequence is *not* based on the *inner structure of the hexagrams,* namely the changing combinations of the trigrams that compose them. After hexagram 1 (double Heaven) and hexagram 2 (double Earth) as 'opposite hexagrams' (all lines are opposites), there are eight 'reversed hexagrams' (the hexagrams turn upside down) hexagram 3 to 10. Then comes another pair of opposite hexagrams (11 and 12), followed by fourteen reversed hexagrams (13 to 26). Then come two pairs of opposite hexagrams (27 and 28, 29 and 30), followed by thirty reversed hexagrams (31 to 60). The sequence ends with another pair of opposite hexagrams (61 and 62, 63 and 64).

The sequence is also *not* based on the *Round and Square charts of the 64 hexagrams* of *Shao Yong* (Liu: *I Ching Numerology*, p. 127-129).

The sequence of the hexagrams is also *not* based on the *order of events according to weather phenomena* (in relation to the EHA of the trigrams). For example, the *wind* above *heaven* in hexagram 9 (Small Cultivation), may lead to the *cloud* (*lake*) below *heaven* in hexagram 10 (Treading, Conduct), and the *thunder* and *rain* (*water*) in hexagram 40 (Release, Liberation) cause the *lake* in hexagram 41 (Loss, Decrease) to be overflown, which can easily make the *mountain* crumble into it.

Of the 63 possible follow-up combinations of the hexagrams in relation to the EHA of trigrams – *ordered according to the weather and other natural phenomena* – there are only 12 pairs that can be considered following each other.

The sequence of the 64 hexagrams is also *not* based on the *order of hexagrams arranged according to the number of yang lines* in each hexagram. This arrangement shows a perfect, changing pattern of dark (*yin*) and light (*yang*), but the numbers of the hexagrams are not in the order of the present *Yi Jing* text.

The sequence of the 64 hexagrams is also *not* based on the *order of hexagrams called 'the mandala of hexagrams'* (Boering, et al.: *De Mandala van Kernhexagrammen*, the mandala of inner hexagrams). See also, *A Mandala of Hexagrams*, p. 394.

This mandala has hexagrams 1 ,2, 63, 64 in the centre, the hexagrams 44, 28, 43, and 24, 27, 23 and 38, 54, 40, and 39, 53, 37 in the inner circle and the rest of the hexagrams in groups of four hexagrams making up the outer circle. This mandala comes into creation by finding the inner hexagram of each hexagram, and again the nuclear hexagram of those inner hexagrams until one ends up with the four centre hexagrams 1, 2, 63, 64. This mandala suggests that all hexagrams emerge from the four centre hexagrams 1, 2, 63 and 64, but it does not match with the present sequence of hexagrams.

The sequence is also *not* based on the *movements of the trigrams as elements* – where *fire, heaven, wind* and *thunder* move upwards, and *earth, mountain, lake* and *water* move downwards – to create a visual image of hexagrams (Govinda: *The Inner Structure of the I Ching*). In this structure, three pairs of hexagrams (3 and 4, 21 and 22, 35 and 36) are required to change places to attain the perfection of the visual image.

The sequence and order of the hexagrams may not be consistent, but they are close to Reality itself. If the 64 hexagrams are put in a specific grid or framework of hexagrams, they match a framework containing components of the DNA genetic code (Walter: *Tao of Chaos*, p. 166-168).

The only possible reason for the present sequence of the 64 hexagrams is the one based on the *sequence of connected meanings* between the successive hexagrams. (See also: *The order and sequence of the hexagrams*, p. 371.) These meanings are related to:

- *Ideas*: when Heaven (hexagram 1,) and Earth (hexagram 2,) unite, they give birth to hexagram 3 (Beginning, Difficulty), and this is naturally followed by hexagram 4 (Growing, Immaturity)
- *Themes*: for example, situations of excess (hexagram 28) will naturally lead to situations of danger (hexagram 29).
- *The law of extremes*: if something comes to an extreme, high or low, it will always change into its opposite. For example Water doubled (hexagram 29) is followed by Fire doubled (hexagram 30).
- *Natural phenomena* related to the EHA of trigrams based on the weather: for example, *thunder* and *rain* (hexagram 40, Release, Liberation) causes the *lake* to be overflown, which can easily make the *mountain* crumble into it (hexagram 41, Loss, Decrease).
- *Some continuing stories* as a connecting element between the hexagrams based on the attitude or behaviour of the noble person or 'superior man'.

Even the explanations in the *Sequence or Order of the Hexagrams* – the Ninth Wing (one of the ten commentaries, or 'Wings', added to the classic Yi Jing) – are not consistent. *(R. Wilhelm, I Ching, p.260.)*

### 4. The position and meaning of the individual lines

The meanings of the individual lines of the hexagrams are derived from the meanings of the trigrams composing the hexagram – whether the relationships between the trigrams composing the hexagram are positive or negative – and from the positions and the relationships of the lines in the hexagram. Lines in good positions should have good fortune and not misfortune.

*In some instances the meanings of the lines are not consistent with the inner structure* (the position of the lines or the meanings of the trigrams):

1. The first lines of hexagram 11 and 12 mention the same pulling out of grass with its roots indicating good fortune and success. Both hexagrams are constructed of the trigrams *heaven* and *earth,* but in different positions on top of each other. Hexagram 11, line 1 is a *yang* line in a correct position, and hexagram 12, line 1 is a *yin* line in a wrong position. Hexagram 12, line 1 should bring misfortune, but it does not.
2. Hexagram 11, line 4, and hexagram 15, line 5, both mention that wealth is not shared with the neighbours, which indicates something negative. Because line 4 of hexagram 11 is a *yin* line in a correct place, its meaning should be positive (which is not in some texts), while the meaning of line 5 of hexagram 15 – which is also a *yin* line but in an incorrect place – should be negative (as it is in most texts).
3. In Hexagram 13, line 2 is a *yin* line in a *yin* position (correct position) and it is about a gathering of people of the same clan. Here it should be good fortune, but it is misfortune and brings distress.
   If we compare this with hexagram 8, line 2 – also a *yin* line in a *yin* position – it will bring good fortune, but only if one joins with *those of one's own circle or kind.*
4. In hexagram 20 (Observing, View, Contemplation), the meanings of lines 5 and 6 are placed differently in different translations. In one translation line 5 says that the noble person is looking over and watching the lives of others. Another translation says that he is looking at and contemplating his own life.
   Line 5 is a *yang* line in a correct position, and line 6 is also a *yang* line but incorrectly placed. Because line 5 is the place for someone in a position of worldly power (who is capable of watching over the lives of others) and line 6 is the position for a sage (who is away from the world to contemplate his own life) – the one who is watching over others has to be on line 5, and the one contemplating his own life has to be on line 6.
   Also seen within the context of the lines 1, 2, 3 and 4 of hexagram 20 (Observing, View, Contemplation), line 5 has to be about watching the lives of others, and line 6 about observing one's own life.

5. In hexagram 28 (Great Excess), for example, line 2 is about a young woman, and regarded as positive (nothing is unfavourable), and line 5 is about an old woman, and regarded as less positive (no blame, no praise). Line 2 is a *yang* line in a wrong position, and it is part of the trigram *wind* which stands for the eldest daughter (an older woman), and line 5 is a yang line in a correct position, and it is part of the trigram *lake* which stands for the youngest daughter (a young woman).

Despite the wrong positions of the lines, and the incorrect meanings of the trigrams – in the experience of working with the *Yi Jing* – the answers received about relationships are always connected with the correct lines. If a young woman is involved in the inquiry, one will receive line 2 (an earlier position of the lines in a hexagram), and if an older woman is involved, one will receive line 5 (a later position). This is an example of a very strong inconsistency.

Assuming the inner structure of the *Yi Jing* as the basis for its theoretical framework, it should be consistent with the text and its network of meanings. But as shown in this chapter, there are many inconsistencies, both in the inner structure and in its theoretical framework. That nonetheless the *Yi Jing* has worked through the ages as a tool for prediction of future events, indicates that the prerequisite of consistency does not always apply for a theoretical framework as the *Yi Jing*.

This is especially true in relation to the idea, that for the *Yi Jing* to work it has 64x6 (lines) + 64x1 (a hexagram without a changing line) = 384+64 = 448 possible answers, which have to be multi-interpretable (dependent on the question, context, level, etc.), otherwise it would not be able to cover the whole of Reality. The hexagrams and lines should have more than one meaning to cover Reality as a whole, and that is probably the reason why the *Yi Jing's* theoretical system is not as consistent as it should be.

# The Yi Jing's *ways of wisdom*

### Several ways of wisdom

One way of defining wisdom is *to have the knowledge and experience together with the power to apply them practically and correctly*. Information alone is not yet knowledge: only after information is ordered it becomes knowledge. Knowledge itself is not yet power: if one knows something, it does not mean that one is able to change things.

Power is not yet wisdom: one may have the power to change things, but the result may not necessarily be right. Knowledge is also not yet wisdom: only when knowledge is combined with experience may it lead to wisdom – as having the knowledge and power to do the right thing at the right time and place.

The *Yi Jing* is not only a book of divination where, by means of prediction, one is able to know something about the future and be prepared for it. The *Yi Jing* is also a book of wisdom. The *Yi Jing's* wisdom mainly refers to that 'special wisdom' based on insight into the nature of Reality.

This is the wisdom that *everything is continuously changing (Impermanence)* and that *everything is related to everything else*. Because of that, *all actions have their consequences (the Law of Cause and Effect or Karma)*. Founded on *the wisdom of the Mean* and *the wisdom of the* Dao, the *Yi Jing's* special wisdom is based on action expressed in different ways of conduct.

The *wisdom of the Mean* or the *Middle Way* is considered an ideal attitude that leads one to be careful in speech and action, avoiding extremes.

This is an aspect of the wisdom of the *Dao*: to follow the sequence of events, to go with the flow of things. One does not resist anything in life: like water flowing over, under or around all the obstacles or hindrances it encounters. It is the wisdom of spontaneously doing the right thing at the right time and place.

With the help of the *Yi Jing* a wise person may observe the changes and decides what actions to take. He is therefore able to influence his fate and his destiny for the better. This does not mean that he fully controls his destiny, for some things cannot be avoided, because they just have to happen. *Real wisdom is to stay with the flow of things, instead of trying to control them.* It implies that sometimes he chooses for those things that should ordinarily be avoided, because he knows that they belong to him.

When first starting to consult the *Yi Jing* for prediction, people usually follow the good fortune, and discard the misfortune. Later on when people grow in wisdom, they realise that in all good fortune there is always some misfortune, and in all misfortune there is some good fortune. So one may sometimes choose for misfortune in the beginning, when the whole sequence of events will be heading towards good fortune in the end.

But at the highest stage of wisdom, the duality of good fortune and misfortune is transcended, and the ideal is simply *to do the right thing at the right time and place*. Attention to the right timing of every action is the extraordinary wisdom the *Yi Jing* tries to teach its practitioners.

This special wisdom – doing the right thing at the right time and place – is then no longer a way of action, but actually one of non-action: *doing without doing* (wu wei), *where everything goes naturally and spontaneously.* Here one lives in the natural flow of things (*Dao*).

## The *Yi Jing*'s independent wisdom

The *Yi Jing* is generally known as a book of divination that teaches several ways of wisdom. Less widely recognised is the fact that it is a book with its own independent, intelligent wisdom.

*The first indication* of an independent, intelligent wisdom is seen when someone consults the book without proper respect. For example someone asks the same question several times after having already received an answer. In such cases the book will give the fourth hexagram, indicating immaturity and youthful folly.

*The second indication* of the *Yi Jing's* independent wisdom is that when a person consults the book with the intention to harm another or to do something immoral or unethical, the *Yi Jing* does not go along with the inquirer's intention, but always points to the incorrectness of the motive.

*The third indication* comes when the book answers with a hexagram without a changing line. This generally means that there will be no change in the situation or process of the inquiry. It can also indicate that the inquirer is not able to 'hear' the answer, because he is not ready, prepared or ripe for it.

*The fourth indication* is that, in principle, one cannot receive the same answer (hexagram and line(s)) to a question after a lapse of time. The changes that have occurred during the passage of time should always lead to a different answer. But if the situation has remained the same it is possible that the *Yi Jing* will give exactly the same answer (hexagram and line(s)) as previously.

All the different indications affirm that the *Yi Jing* does have its own independent, intelligent wisdom – directing the right answer to the right question – and that the *Book of Change* can not be manipulated by something outside of itself. It may also give an indication that the wise answers given by the *Yi Jing* are based on a larger picture of the events and their consequences and not on limited, short-term thinking.

The *Yi Jing's* way of wisdom implies that it knows how to act at the right time and place, because the fruits of wisdom will always be within the *Dao*.

## Wisdom

By means of the *Yi Jing* one may know about future events before they happen. The *Yi Jing* as an oracle is such a great tool for prediction, that with its help one may even know about anything in the world. Knowing the future makes it possible to take measures. If one knows something about the future, one could prepare for it and adjust one's action to it.

One could either prevent bad events from happening, or support good events to take place. While in most cases one may have to go through the coming events predicted, in some cases one may even be able to avoid it. But to do all this does not mean that the actions taken – based on the consultations of the *Yi Jing* – are necessarily wise.

Somehow, negative (bad) events are necessary to happen to people because they have to go through them to force people to make changes in their lives. They should therefore not always be known beforehand and be avoided.

These unknown and unexpected negative events could be regarded as warnings not to continue too long on their present course, or are meant as tests about the quality of one's consciousness.

Being able to know anything about the future is therefore not always a blessing. This can be noticed from psychic people who come to know about future things they do not really want to know. In a way it is a good thing that most people do not know anything about the future.

Suppose that one comes to know how bad one's karma will be in this life – when all the accidents, illnesses or disasters will come, when or how one will die. To most people this would cause a great disturbance, because they could not deal with it properly. That knowledge may even lead to a self-fulfilling prophecy, and may prevent them from doing what they could have been doing in their life if they did not know about it.

Wisdom is therefore also *how to deal with the pros and cons of knowing something about the future.* One can not and should not always say what one knows about the future to others, for it may disturb the natural way of how things could develop. All the knowledge about the future that one could obtain from the *Yi Jing* should actually be contained. That may also be one of the main reasons why for most people the language of the *Yi Jing* is so difficult to understand.

## Wisdom of the *Dao*

The *Dao* can be regarded as the natural order of events, such as the order of the seasons on earth (spring – summer – autumn – winter), or the cycle of life on earth (birth – growth – decay – death). It can also be seen as being in the flow of things, where everything happens at the right time and place.

Translated to the events in someone's life, one could say that a man or woman of wisdom will always be in the *Dao*, because everything in his/her life will happen at the right time and place. This means that s/he will always have what s/he needs – will always meet the right persons at the right time and place, will have enough time to be able to do the things that has to be done in this life, etc.

Being in the *Dao* may even mean that if one goes out of the house, and it is raining, the rain will stop – when one is under cover (in another house or car), that it may start again, and when one is outside in the open again, the rain will again stop.

Does this mean that whatever a man or woman of wisdom wants will be manifested, as it may happen with magic? If there is enough personal power this is possible, but that may not necessarily be in the *Dao*. For the natural order of events (being in the *Dao*) is decided from the larger Whole, and not from a small personal self (ego), as magical acts usually are.

With the help of the *Yi Jing* we can know about future events, so that we can decide whether to advance or retreat in certain situations, and stay in the natural order of events (the *Dao*). Reflecting on the changes obtained from the *Yi Jing* may therefore lead to the insight in the inner workings of destiny and the hidden wisdom of the *Dao*.

# The order and sequence of the hexagrams

The process of change expressed in the *Yi Jing* is a process of becoming and the sequence of hexagrams is about that process. From the union of hexagram 1 (Heaven) and hexagram 2 (Earth) all aspects (hexagrams) and phases (lines) of life's changes come into existence. The sequence of the hexagrams is basically dependent on the meanings of the different hexagrams. These meanings are either ideas, themes, or some continuing stories connecting several hexagrams together. These ideas and stories are again founded on the meanings and the relationships of the trigrams composing the specific hexagrams. In spite of the existence of an order of meanings, one cannot say that it is a very consistent order, for there are many weak connections in the sequence (see *Inconsistencies in the Yi Jing*, p. 358).

## A description of the sequence

- Hexagram 1 (Heaven) and hexagram 2 (Earth) are the beginning of the sequence, because out of the union of these two hexagrams (double *heaven* and double *earth*) all other hexagrams emerge. When Heaven and Earth unite there is a new beginning, the birth of something new. This is always accompanied with difficulties.
- Hexagram 3 (Beginning, Difficulty) – composed of the trigrams *thunder* below *water*, or thunder and rain – is about the chaos that creates something new when Heaven and Earth have intercourse.

- Hexagram 4 (Growing, Immaturity) is composed of the trigrams *water* below *mountain,* or a spring (danger) at the foot of a mountain (youngest son), indicating immaturity. After a new beginning in hexagram 3 (Beginning), hexagram 4 (Growing) follows naturally.
- Hexagram 5 (Waiting, Getting Wet, Inaction) is composed of the trigrams *water* above *heaven,* or rain in the sky, indicating that because of the rain one must wait, otherwise one gets wet. As hexagram 4 is about youth and immaturity it is followed by hexagram 5 (Waiting), because youth is often depicted in situations of idle waiting, or hanging around and waiting for something to happen.
- Hexagram 6 (Conflict, Dispute, Lawsuit) – composed of the trigrams *water* below *heaven* – is the reverse of hexagram 5 (*water* above *heaven*) and is about heavy rain threatening in the sky: conflict. *Heaven* (strength, power) and *water* (danger) may lead to conflict. It follows hexagram 5 (Waiting), because one can imagine that in a situation of idle waiting and doing nothing (hexagram 5) conflicts can arise.

- Hexagram 7 (The Army, Multitude) is composed of the trigrams *water* below *earth,* or water (danger) collecting in the earth. When there is a situation of conflict – a dispute (hexagram 6) of a local ruler of a town of 300 households with the king – the army (hexagram 7) is put into action to deal with it.
- Hexagram 8 (Joining, Union, Alliance) is composed of the trigrams *water* above *earth,* or water moistens the earth, indicating water nourishing the earth. Hexagram 8 (Joining, Union) follows hexagram 7 (the Army) because in hexagram 8 (Joining, Union) the king tries to create a greater union of local rulers under his authority.
- Hexagram 9 (Small Cultivation) is composed of the trigrams *wind* above *heaven,* or wind blowing across the sky, accumulating clouds which will eventually bring rain. It is about the cultivation of virtues, because after the creation of an alliance (hexagram 8), the values and norms of the society are established (hexagram 9).
- Hexagram 10 (Treading, Conduct), composed of the trigrams *lake* below *heaven,* or a cloud (lake) below the sky – indicating the youngest daughter (lake) following the father (*heaven*) – is about how to act in relation to the ruler or superior. Hexagram 9 (Small Cultivation)

was about the cultivation of virtues, and thus hexagram 10 is about conduct in society.
- Hexagram 11 (The Great, Peace) is composed of the trigrams *heaven* below *earth*, or *heaven* and *earth* acting together. Hexagram 10, which is about conduct in society, is followed by hexagram 11 ('the Great Way'), because in this hexagram the ruler or king tries to manifest the way of heaven and earth. Hexagram 11 (*heaven* below *earth*) is about the Great Way because here heaven and earth intermingle, while in hexagram 12 (*heaven* above *earth*) heaven and earth move away from each other.
- Hexagram 12 (The Small, The Petty) is composed of the trigrams *heaven* above *earth*, or heaven and earth do not act together. Hexagram 11 is followed by hexagram 12 (The Small, The Petty) because – according to the Principle of Extremes in the *Yi Jing* – when something comes to an extreme, high or low, it always changes into its opposite (the hexagrams are opposites).

The structure of hexagram 12 (*heaven* above *earth*) is completely opposite, reversed, and inverted to hexagram 11 (*heaven* below *earth*). Because all the lines are opposite, the hexagram is also about the values of small, petty men, which are totally opposite to the values of the great way of heaven and earth in hexagram 11.

- Hexagram 13 (Assembling People) is composed of the trigrams *fire* below *heaven*, or fire going up to the heaven, suggesting men's tendency to associate with others. It follows hexagram 12, because one can imagine that out of the situation where petty, bad people dominate (hexagram 12), a movement could emerge, lead by a noble person, to counter this negative influence.
- Hexagram 14 (Great Possession) is composed of the trigrams *fire* above *heaven*, or the sun shining brightly in the sky. This hexagram is about power and material things. Assembling people to accomplish great things will often lead to great possession.
- Hexagram 15 (Modesty) is composed of the trigrams *mountain* below *earth*, indicating a mountain (wealth) hidden within the earth. Hexagram 14 (Great Possessions) is followed by hexagram 15 (Modesty), because as one's ability grows greater (hexagram 14), one becomes more humble and modest (hexagram 15).

- Hexagram 16 (Enthusiasm) emerges out of the combination of hexagram 14 (Great Possessions) and hexagram 15 (Modesty). This hexagram is composed of the trigrams *thunder* above *earth*, or thunder rolling over the earth, indicating great enthusiasm to undertake new things.
- Hexagram 17 (Following, Pursuit) is composed of the trigrams *thunder* below *cloud*, indicating that thunder always follows the cloud. After beginning new undertakings with great enthusiasm in hexagram 16, one has to be aware of making the right choices in hexagram 17 ('following what is right').
- Hexagram 18 (Decay, Deterioration) is composed of the trigram *wind* below *mountain*, or the wind blowing strongly at the foot of the mountain leading to erosion and decay. This hexagram is about the mistakes of the past, and it follows hexagram 17, because it is about the results of the choices made in hexagram 17.

- Hexagram 19 (Approaching, Wailing) is composed of the trigrams *lake* below *earth*, or a lake under the earth, and because the earth moves down into the lake, it indicates approach. Hexagram 19 (Approaching, Wailing) follows hexagram 18 (Decay), because hexagram 19 is about wailing at a funeral ceremony gathering where people approach each other and reminisce about the past of the deceased.
- Hexagram 20 (Observing, View, Contemplation) is composed of the trigram *wind* above *earth*, or the wind blowing over the earth, or a bird flying over the land, indicating observation. This hexagram is about observation, because in approaching others (hexagram 19), people may generally look, observe, view (hexagram 20) before they act to find a worthy one to contact. It is also about the ruler keeping a watch over the people in the different regions.
- Hexagram 21 (Biting and Chewing, The Law) is composed of the trigrams *thunder* below *fire*, or thunder and lightning, and picturing a mouth with something to chew. After hexagram 20 (Observing) – keeping a watch over the people in the different regions – the former kings set up rules and established laws in hexagram 21.
- Hexagram 22 (Beautifying, Adornment) is composed of the trigrams *fire* below *mountain*, or the sun at the foot of the mountain. It is beautiful, but the sun is setting and nightfall is near. Setting up rules and establishing

laws in hexagram 21, the former kings – desirous to ensure the good functioning of the state – attempt to beautify and decorate it in hexagram 22.
- Hexagram 23 (Stripping Away, Flaying) is composed of the trigrams *mountain* above *earth*, or a mountain standing alone on the earth which can crumble down. Hexagram 22 (Beautifying) is followed by hexagram 23, because in this hexagram the position of the ruler is threatened by petty men surrounding him.
- Hexagram 24 (Return, The Turning Point) is composed of the trigrams *thunder* below *earth*, or thunder rumbling inside the earth, indicating return. In hexagram 23 the position of the ruler was undermined, thus in hexagram 24 the ruler closed the border passes, and abstained from visiting his territories to prevent his position being attacked.

- Hexagram 25 (The Unexpected) is composed of the trigrams *thunder* below *heaven*, or thunder roaring in the sky, indicating the unexpected. Here the ruler unexpectedly brings prosperity to the people to prevent his position being undermined (hexagram 23), and losing his mandate from heaven.
- Hexagram 26 (Great Cultivation) is composed of the trigrams *heaven* below *mountain*, or heaven within a mountain, indicating the storing of great knowledge and power. Hexagram 25 is followed by hexagram 26 because – after bringing prosperity to the people (to secure his mandate from heaven) – the ruler nourishes his virtue (with the words and conduct of the wise men of the past), and attempts to bring the cultivation of the great virtues of the sages to others.
- Hexagram 27 (Nourishing) is composed of the trigrams *thunder* below *mountain*, or thunder rumbling at the foot of the mountain, and indicates nourishment because it will rain soon. It follows hexagram 26, because in hexagram 27 the noble person – trying to teach the great virtues of the wise to others – encounters persons seeking spiritual nourishment of various quality: from those unworthy and not ready, to those very eager and well qualified.
- Hexagram 28 (Great Excess) is composed of the trigrams *lake* above *wood* or a forest (trees) submerged in water, and indicates a flood (excess). It follows hexagram 27, because – having done his task of teaching

the old virtues to spiritual seekers of different quality (in hexagram 27) – the noble person withdraws from the world without regret.

- Hexagram 29 (Water, Danger, Pitfall) is composed of two trigrams *water* (double danger), symbolising water flowing on and on into the depth. It follows hexagram 28 (Great Excess), because excessive situations usually lead to danger.
- Hexagram 30 (Fire, Light) is composed of two trigrams *fire*, or fire rising in two flames, symbolising light, brightness – illuminating the four quarters of the earth. It follows hexagram 29 (Water, Danger), because in hexagram 28 (Great Excess) the noble person – after withdrawing from the world without regret – continuously practised the higher virtues (in hexagram 29), and teaching it to others. With these actions the noble person spreads his light (high virtues) to the four corners of the world.

- Hexagram 31 (Feeling, Sensation, Attraction) is composed of the trigrams *lake* above *mountain*, or a lake on top of the mountain. A joyous young woman (*lake*) and a young man (*mountain*) are strongly attracted (sensation, stimulation) to each other. Hexagram 31 follows hexagram 30, because in hexagram 30 the noble person's character and high virtues illumines the four corners of the earth, and in hexagram 31 the noble person in doing so, influences and stimulates others.
- Hexagram 32 (Lasting, Enduring, Constancy) is composed of the trigrams *thunder* above *wind*, or thunder followed by wind – where thunder and wind work together. It follows hexagram 31 (Feeling, Attraction), because in hexagram 31 a young man (*mountain*) and a young woman (*lake*) were very attracted to each other, and in hexagram 32 the older man (*thunder*) and older woman (*wind*) are having an enduring and lasting marriage.
- Hexagram 33 (Withdrawal, Retreat) is composed of the trigrams *mountain* below *heaven*, or a mountain beneath the sky. It follows hexagram 32 (Lasting, Enduring), because – according to the Law of Change – something may last long (endures for long), but it cannot last forever. Therefore when endurance comes to an extreme – according to the Law of Extremes – things will be withdrawn (retreat).
- Hexagram 34 (Great Strength, Power) is composed of the trigrams *thunder* above *heaven*, or thunder in the sky. Hexagram 33 (Retreat) is followed by hexagram 34 (Great Strength, Power), because it is in situations

of retreat that great power can be collected.
- Hexagram 35 (Advancing, Progress) is composed of the trigrams *fire* above *earth*, or the sun rising over the earth. The sun (*fire*) advances through the sky over the earth. Hexagram 35 (Progress) follows hexagram 34 (Great Strength, Power), because only with strength and power can progress be made.
- Hexagram 36 (Darkening Light) is composed of the trigrams *fire* below *earth*, or the sun is sinking under the earth. Hexagram 35 (Progress) is followed by hexagram 36 (Darkening Light), because progress will often meet with resistance and hindrances. This may lead to darkening of the light, or injury and damage.

- Hexagram 37 (The Family) is composed of the trigrams *wind* above *fire* or air (wind) rising from fire. The family is composed of the trigrams *wind* (eldest daughter), the trigram *fire* (middle daughter), and the upper inner trigram *fire* (another middle daughter): all indicating that women are the important members of the family, who also keep the fire of the household burning. Hexagram 36 (Darkening Light) is followed by hexagram 37 (The Family), because if a person is injured on the outside (the world), he will draw back into his family (a safe place) to recover.
- Hexagram 38 (Opposition) is composed of the trigrams *fire* above *lake* or a fire above a marshy lake. Hexagram 37 (The Family) is followed by hexagram 38 (Opposition), because the women of the family (*fire*, a middle daughter, *lake*, a youngest daughter, and another middle daughter) are opposite in character, and their wishes do not accord. Thus they become totally opposite to one another.
- Hexagram 39 (Trouble, Obstruction) is composed of the trigrams *water* above *mountain*, or a river running down the mountain. Hexagram 38 (Opposition) is followed by hexagram 39 (Trouble, Obstruction), because situations of opposition (trigrams *fire* and *water* of hexagram 38, and inner trigrams *fire* and *water* of hexagram 39) will naturally lead to obstruction and trouble.
- Hexagram 40 (Release, Liberation) is composed of the trigrams *thunder* above *water*, or thunder and rain, indicating that with thunder comes rain. Hexagram 39 (Trouble) is followed by hexagram 40 (Release), because in hexagram 40 the troubles and difficulties of hexagram 39 are

dissolved and bring release.
- Hexagram 41 (Loss, Decrease) is composed of the trigrams *lake* below *mountain*, or a marshy lake at the foot of the mountain. Hexagram 40 (Release) is followed by hexagram 41 (Decrease), because after thunder and rain (hexagram 40) the lake will be overflown, and the mountain may crumble into it.
- Hexagram 42 (Gain, Increase) is composed of the trigrams *wind* above *thunder*, or a forest of blooming trees in spring. Hexagram 41 (Decrease) is followed by hexagram 42 (Increase), because after thunder and rain (hexagram 40) there is abundant water (hexagram 41), and the forest will grow and bloom again.

- Hexagram 43 (Decisiveness, Resolution) is composed of the trigrams *lake* above *heaven*, or a cloud heavy with rain in the sky. Hexagram 42 (Gain, Increase) is followed by hexagram 43 (Resolution), because thunder and wind (hexagram 42) are followed by clouds heavy with rain in the sky (hexagram 43) which could burst. If increase (hexagram 42) continues it may become too much, and result in a breakthrough (hexagram 43).
- Hexagram 44 (Meeting, Contact, Encounter) is composed of the trigrams *wind* below *heaven*, or the wind blowing beneath the sky. Hexagram 43 (Resolution) is followed by hexagram 44 (Meeting), because the heavy clouds in the sky (hexagram 43) may be accompanied by strong winds (hexagram 44). With enough resolution one is sure to encounter opportunities.
- Hexagram 45 (Coming Together, Gathering) is composed of the trigrams *lake* above *earth*, or a lake where streams come together. Hexagram 44 (Meeting) is followed by hexagram 45 (Gathering), because – when strong winds blow below heaven (hexagram (44) – clouds gather above the earth (hexagram 45). When people meet (hexagram 44) it results in a gathering (hexagram 45).
- Hexagram 46 (Climbing, Rising) is composed of the trigrams *earth* above *wood*, or trees growing upward from the earth. Hexagram 45 (Gathering) is followed by hexagram 46 (Rising), because the small streams gathering at the lake (hexagram 45) moisten the roots of the trees, growing rapidly from the earth (hexagram 46). In circumstances of gathering (hexagram 45) there are always possibilities to raise (hexagram 46) one's position.

- Hexagram 47 (Adversity, Exhaustion) is composed of the trigrams *water* below *lake*, or a lake drained by a moving stream – water flowing away from the bottom of the lake. Hexagram 46 (Rising) is followed by hexagram 47 (Adversity, Exhaustion), because the trees that grow out of the earth (hexagram 46) will be exhausted due to lack of water that is drained from the lake (hexagram 47). When advancing goes on without stopping it will soon lead to exhaustion.
- Hexagram 48 (The Well) is composed of the trigrams *water* above *wood* or water contained by wood – a well lined with wood. Hexagram 47 (Exhaustion) is followed by hexagram 48 (The Well), because the water that is drawn from the lake (hexagram 47) appears in another place as a well (hexagram 48).

- Hexagram 49 (Radical Change, Revolution) is composed of the trigrams *fire* below *lake*, or a fire within a lake – a fire that dries up the lake. Hexagram 48 (The Well) is followed by hexagram 49 (Radical Change) because the water in the well coming from the lake is dried up, and the city has to be moved (a radical change) because of lack of water.
- Hexagram 50 (The Cauldron, Transformation) is composed of the trigrams *fire* above *wood*, or wood within the fire. The wind is blowing into the fire. Hexagram 49 (Radical Change) is followed by hexagram 50 (The Cauldron), because in hexagram 49 (Radical Change) the old is abolished and hexagram 50 (The Cauldron, Transformation) is about transformation, where the new is established.
- Hexagram 51 (Thunder, Arousing) is composed of two trigrams *thunder* or claps of thunder. Hexagram 50 (The Cauldron) is followed by hexagram 51 (Thunder), because after lightning (*fire*) and wind (hexagram 50) thunder (hexagram 51) follows. When the new (hexagram 50) comes it is usually accompanied by shock (hexagram 51).
- Hexagram 52 (Mountain, Stilling) is composed of two trigrams *mountain* or standing still, stilling, stopping. Hexagram 51 (Thunder, Arousing) is followed by hexagram 52 (Mountain, Stilling), because after thunder there is stillness. After strong movement (hexagram 51) events have to take a rest (hexagram 52).
- Hexagram 53 (Gradual Advance) is composed of the trigrams *wind* above *mountain*, or a bird on the mountain. Hexagram 52 (Stilling) is followed

by hexagram 53 (Gradual Advance), because after a long period of stilling movement will start again, and gradual development (hexagram 53) starts again.

- Hexagram 54 (Marrying Maiden) is composed of the trigrams *thunder* above *lake*, or thunder rumbling over a lake. Hexagram 53 (Gradual Advance) is followed by hexagram 54 (Marrying Maiden), because the marriage of a maiden can be considered a gradual advance (hexagram 53).

- Hexagram 55 (Abundance) is composed of the trigrams *thunder* above *fire*, or thunder and lightning during a storm. Hexagram 54 (Marrying Maiden) is followed by hexagram 55 (Abundance), because a maiden who marries will bring abundance.
- Hexagram 56 (Travelling, The Wanderer) is composed of the trigrams *fire* above *mountain*, or a fire burns on top of the mountain. Hexagram 55 (Abundance) is followed by hexagram 56 (Travelling), because if abundance reaches its extreme it will change into its opposite. One may loose one's possessions or home, and will have to wander (hexagram 56).
- Hexagram 57 (Wind, Penetrating, Gentle) is composed of two trigrams *wind*, or wind blowing over the woods. Hexagram 56 (Travelling) is followed by hexagram 57 (Wind, Gentle), because when the traveller finds no place to stay, he needs gentleness, and a favourable wind (hexagram 57) to gain entrance.
- Hexagram 58 (Lake, Pleasing, Joy) is composed of two trigrams *lake*, or two beautiful lakes conjoined. Hexagram 57 (Wind, Penetrating, Gentle) is followed by hexagram 58 (Joy), because proceeding gently (*wind*) generally leads to joy.
- Hexagram 59 (Scattering, Dispersion) is composed of the trigrams *wind* above *water*, or the wind blowing over the water. Hexagram 58 (Joy) is followed by hexagram 59 (Dispersion), because after happiness and joy things may break up, and there will be dispersion.
- Hexagram 60 (Restraining, Limitation) is composed of the trigrams *water* above *lake*, or rain (water) falling on the lake. Hexagram 59 (Dispersion) is followed by hexagram 60 (Restraining), because too much dispersion will lead to danger. Therefore restraint (hexagram 60) follows.

- Hexagram 61 (Inner Trust, Confidence) is composed of the trigrams *wind* above *lake*, or the wind blowing over the lake. Hexagram 60 (Restraining) is followed by hexagram 61 (Inner Trust), because when restraint is established people will be trustworthy. Thus after restraint (hexagram 60) confidence and sincerity (hexagram 61) follows.
- Hexagram 62 (Excessiveness of the Small) is composed of the trigrams *thunder* above *mountain*, or thunder rumbling over the mountain. Hexagram 61 (Inner Trust, Confidence) is followed by hexagram 62 (Excessiveness of the Small), because when there is too much confidence (hexagram 61, line 6), all extremes are changing into its opposite (hexagram 62 is the opposite of hexagram 61), and excessiveness of the small (hexagram 62) will follow.
- Hexagram 63 (Already Completed) is composed of the trigrams *water* above *fire*, or the fire boiling the water. Hexagram 62 (Excessiveness of the Small) indicates a situation of excess. It is followed by hexagram 63 (Already Completed), because those who exceed others may be able to fulfil their goals.
- Hexagram 64 (Before Completion) is composed of the trigrams *fire* above *water*, or the sun rising above the water. Hexagram 63 (Already Completed) is followed by hexagram 64 (Before Completion), because both hexagrams 63 and 64 are actually two states of the same so-called 'end' of the *Yi Jing*. And, because – according to the *Yi Jing* – every end is followed by a new beginning, hexagram 63 (Already Completed) is followed by hexagram 64 (Before Completion).

# Yi Jing *methodology*

## How various methods give meaning to signs and omens

When we consult the *Yi Jing* we are advised to do so only once. If we consult the *Book of Change* more than once concerning the same question, the *Yi Jing* may give us hexagram 4 (Immaturity) as an answer. This is an indication of the *Yi Jing's* independent wisdom that may point to our disrespectful attitude towards the oracle.

Still, it would be interesting to find out how the various methods used to consult the oracle produce different answers, especially in relation to the meanings assigned to signs and omens. To do this we need a genuine sign or omen, or some event that could be regarded as a sign or omen, and we have to consult the *Yi Jing* by means of the various consultation methods.

These methods are: 1. The Early Heaven Formula (EHF), First Variation; 2. The EHF, Second Variation; 3. The EHF, Third Variation; 4. The Later Heaven Formula (LHF); 5. Yarrow stalks; 6. Beads; 7. Coins; 8. Dice; 9. A Computer Method (usually based on a *random number generator*, RNG).

All of these consultation methods are based on numerology (numbers).

The first four methods (the Early Heaven and Later Heaven formulas) are different from the other four in that they *transcend the ability of the* Yi Jing *to control the answer*. Because these methods are based on a formula, they always have one changing line. They cannot have more than one changing line or be without a changing line.

The next four methods (stalks, beads, coins and dice) are fully under the *Yi Jing's* control. *With them we cannot transcend the* Yi Jing's *decision to give a particular answer.*

The method with the computer is the most unreliable method, because consultation of the oracle is *not* based on chance, therefore *Yi Jing* methods should not be based on randomness (see p. 352).

## The omen

Signs are things perceived as indicating a future state or occurrence.
Omens are occurrences or objects regarded as portending good or evil.
Signs and omens are events occurring at a particular time (present or past) which may indicate what could happen at another time (future). These events are only called signs and omens *if* there is a subject (human being) who observes and gives them a particular meaning. The meaning of an event that is regarded as an omen can be obtained from consulting the *Yi Jing*.

"One morning at around 10:30 h., while watering the plants, one of the authors standing behind a glass window, saw a bird flying against the window with force. Looking out the window of the adjacent room, he saw the bird shakily resting on a branch of a tree."

As this is not such a common event, it could be regarded as a sign or omen. If the observer looked at the event as an omen, and considered the bird's crash into the window to be a misfortune, the event has to be seen as an *omen of misfortune*. To determine the event's true meaning, we consulted the *Yi Jing* using nine diffrent methods.

## The methods

### 1. The Early Heaven Formula, First Variation

In this numerological method one takes the time of the event (between 9:00 and 11:00 h. gives number 6). This forms the upper trigram of the hexagram.

From the date of the event one calculates a number (in this case 16 from the Chinese calendar dates). Adding time and date number gives 22, from which as many times as possible eight trigrams are subtracted (in this case 2x8 = 16); 22−16 = 6. This forms the lower trigram of the hexagram.

In the Early Heaven Arrangement of trigrams number 6 is *water*, and double *water* forms hexagram 29 (Danger).

To figure out the line, one takes again the time and date, and subtracts as many times six lines from it as possible (6+16 = 22−18 = 4). The outcome is hexagram 29 (Danger), with a changing line 4, changing into hexagram 47 (Adversity).

This method and the ones in formulas 2, 3, and 4 are extensively described in Liu: *I Ching Numerology*, and Huang: *The Numerology of the I Ching*.

## 2. The Early Heaven Formula, Second Variation

In this numerological method one takes a statement, i.e., *a bird flies against the window*, and the time and date of the event, and translates it into numbers. The letters of the statement *a bird flies against the window* give a total of 26 and the total of the time and date is 22.

From these numbers one subtracts as many times as possible eight trigrams (26−24 = 2 (*lake*), and 22−16 = 6 (*water*)), and arrives at hexagram 47 (Adversity).

To figure out the line one does the same as in the first variation of the EHF and arrives at line 4. Thus the outcome is hexagram 47 (Adversity), with a changing line 4, changing into hexagram 29 (Water, Danger). This answer is the opposite of the answer of the first method, but in essence it is the same.

## 3. The Early Heaven Formula, Third Variation

In this numerological method one takes two statements, i.e., *a bird*, and *flies against the window*, and translates them into numbers.

The first statement gives the number 5, and the second statement the number 21−16 (2x8 trigrams) = 5. Translating these numbers into trigrams one arrives at double *wind* or hexagram 57 (Wind, Penetrating, Gentle), with a changing line 4, changing into hexagram 44 ( Meeting, Contact).

## 4. The Later Heaven Formula

In this numerological method one takes the two main objects of the event (bird and window), and translates them directly into trigrams.

This method is much more difficult because one has to choose the right trigram on the basis of the attributes of the trigrams.

A bird stands for *wind* (or *wood*) and the glass window stands for clarity or *heaven*. Combining these two trigrams, one arrives at hexagram 9 (Small Cultivation), with a changing line 4, changing into hexagram 1 (Heaven, The Creative).

### 5. Yarrow stalks

Using yarrow stalks as a method of consultation one gets hexagram 33 (Withdrawal, Retreat), with the changing lines 2, 4 and 6, changing into hexagram 48 (The Well).

### 6. Beads

Using sixteen beads as a method of consultation one gets hexagram 42 (Gain, Increase), with the changing top line changing into hexagram 3 (Beginning, Difficulty).

### 7. Coins

Using three coins one arrives at hexagram 33 (Withdrawal, Retreat), with the changing lines 1, 2 and 4, changing into hexagram 9 (Small Cultivation).

### 8. Dice

Using a ten-sided die one arrives at hexagram 24 (Return, The Turning Point) without a changing line. But if one 'squeezes out' a changing line by means of calculating the time and date, one gets hexagram 24 (Return), with a changing line 5, changing into hexagram 3 (Beginning, Difficulty).

### 9. The Computer Method (RNG)

Using the computer, which is generally based on a *random number generator* (RNG), one arrives at hexagram 56 (Travelling, The Wanderer), with the changing lines 2 and 6, changing into hexagram 32 (Lasting, Enduring).

## The results

From consulting the *Yi Jing* with these nine different methods, one could see that two of them, EHF variation one (hexagram 29(4)47), and EHF variation two (hexagram 47(4)29), give an indication of what happened 'objectively':

385

hexagram 29 (Danger) and hexagram 47 (Adversity) fitting perfectly with the misfortune of a bird flying against a glass window and getting hurt.

These two methods are based mainly on the time the event occurred. For the observer they not necessarily give a predictive meaning to the omen.

The other seven methods show a tendency to give some predictive meaning to the omen. For the consultant who was also the observer of the event, they could be interpreted as an omen.

The coins (hexagram 33(1, 2, 4)9), and stalks (hexagram 33(2, 4, 6) 48) give closely related answers, and have hexagram 33 line 2 and 4 in common. Line 2 is about a powerful determination for withdrawal, and line 4 says that if the noble person withdraws it will be good fortune, while for the inferior man it means misfortune. The answer indicates that the *observer (consultant) has to withdraw from something.*

The LHF method (hexagram 9(4)1), and the coin method (hexagram 33 (1, 2, 4)9) have in their answer hexagram 9 and changing line 4, where owing to confidence, bloody and terrible deeds are avoided. This could mean that *if the observer (consultant) has confidence, he could avoid a terrible misfortune.*

Hexagram 9(1, 2) also says something about a return (line 1 about returning to the path, and line 2 about compelling oneself to go back) – as is the dice method (hexagram 24, Return, with changing line 5, changing into hexagram 3, Difficulty). So something or somebody (the bird) is returning to the observer, and is in difficulty. This can also be related to the answer of the beads method (hexagram 42, Gain, with changing line 6, changing into hexagram 3, Difficulty), which says that *someone or something will strike him (hexagram 42, line 6), and this will lead to difficulty.*

The answer derived from the computer method (hexagram 56, Travelling with changing lines 2 and 6, changing into hexagram 32), could say something about the bird as 'a traveller who arrives at a lodging' (line 2), 'burns his own nest (home)', and 'loses an ox (wealth)' (line 6).

It could also say something about the observer (consultant), *giving him a warning that he will burn his own home, and may lose something of wealth.*

The answer form the Early Heaven Formula (variation three), hexagram 57(4)44, seems to give a predictive meaning which is quite erroneous because it mentions good fortune ('three kinds of game are caught in the field'), while the event is clearly one of misfortune.

Considering all the answers, *the omen indicates that something or someone is returning to the observer (consultant), that he has to withdraw from something, and if he has enough confidence he will be able to avoid a terrible misfortune.*

As during the rest of that day nothing significant happened which could be linked to that omen of misfortune, the observer (consultant) decided to wait, and watch for the occurrence of a significant event related to that omen in a future time period.

## The accident

About one month later, while working in the garden, one of the authors obtained a head wound. Tired from the work, he forced himself to finish the job. While carrying old branches, he hit his head against a thick pointy branch. Looking into the glass frame of the door to the garden, he saw his wound bleeding profusely. Luckily it was only skin deep. This accident could refer to the similarity in information of the LHF method (hexagram 9 *(4)* 1) and the coin method (hexagram 33 *(1, 2, 4)* 9), where hexagram 9, line 4 says that with confidence, bloody and terrible deeds can be avoided. Apparently this did not happen.

Thinking about the accident, he was at first reluctant to connect it with the omen. Yet the bird hit its head against the window, and he hit his head against a pointy branch. Common sense suggests that the bird's misfortune could as well be an omen of his own accident.

## Conclusion

Each of the answers obtained by the different consultative methods is an aspect of what the omen could mean to the observer. Only two answers (LHF and Coins) contained information that could apply to the accident one month later.

Can we say that there is a best answer to the question, and therefore point out the most appropriate method? As there was no best answer, these consultations did not bring forth a most appropriate method to use.

Consulting the *Yi Jing* nine times with nine different methods, we obtained some meaning for the omen, but it did not really match with the reality of what happened to the observer (consultant) afterwards.

Perhaps asking the same question over and over again may lead to confusion rather than to clarity. The different answers may also become meaningless. This supports the idea that *it is not advisable to consult the* Yi Jing *more than once on the same subject*. Even if it is done with nine different methods instead of only one. That may also be why the *Yi Jing* regards more than one consultation on the same subject to be a sign of disrespect, and may then give hexagram 4 (Immaturity) as an answer.

# Consulting the Yi Jing with a die

In China there were two systems of prediction, symbolic and numerical.
The symbolic, which is older, made use of tortoise shells and later on bones. The shells were exposed to fire until different patterns of cracks appeared, like broken jade, roof tiles, and the cracks in dry land. From these patterns good fortune and misfortune were predicted. The patterns of cracks lead to the *yin/yang* lines, the images of the trigrams and hexagrams.

The numerical system is the basis of all the methods of consultation in the *Yi Jing*, and the ancient one made use of yarrow stalks. Later on, during the time of the Warring States (480–221 BCE), when quick decisions had to be made, and the elaborate method with the yarrow stalks was too time consuming, the coin method was developed.

This method is not as adequate as the stalks, because the different lines of a hexagram (the stable and changing lines) do not have the same chance to appear as with the yarrow stalks.

In our modern times, when everything seems to go even faster, the use of the ten-sided die has been developed. This method is as good as the use of the coins, but the yarrow stalks method remains the best.

The coin method was developed to predict events faster. Of the many kinds of coin prediction over the course of time, the use of the three coins was found to be most appropriate and popular. The basis for the coins is numerical but they were developed from the symbolic system.

When using the coins, the hexagram is constructed from the bottom to the top; each throw of the coins determines one line. To obtain a hexagram, the coins are thrown six times: the first throw determines the bottom or base

line, and the sixth throw the top line. For each toss of the coins there are four possible combinations:
a. one head (*yang*) and two tails (*yin*) stand for a 'young *yang*' (a whole line);
b. one tail (*yin*) and two heads (*yang*) stand for a 'young *yin*' (a broken line);
c. three heads (*yang*) stand for 'old *yang*' (a changing whole line);
d. three tails (*yin*) stand for an 'old *yin*' (a changing broken line).

Combinations *a* and *b* are based on what is called 'minority rule': one head or one tail becomes a *yang* or a *yin* line. This is based on the nature of the trigrams, where the *yang* trigrams (*thunder* and *mountain*) have more dark lines (one *yang* and two *yin* lines), and the *yin* trigrams (*wind* and *cloud* or *lake*) have more light lines (one *yin* and two *yang* lines).
People also use a system of combinations based on what is called 'majority rule', where two tails give a *yin* line and two heads a *yang* line.
Although both systems can be used, the one based on the 'minority rule' has a more adequate foundation.

To avoid the choice for one or the other system, the recommended method for consultation is a *ten-sided die* (decahedron), containing the numbers 0 to 9. The even numbers are *yin*, and the odd numbers are *yang*:

a. 1, 3, 5, 7 = 'young *yang*' (a whole line ▬▬ );
b. 0, 2, 4, 8 = 'young *yin*' (a broken line ▬ ▬ );
c. 9 = 'old *yang*' (a changing whole line ▬●▬ );
d. 6 = 'old *yin*' (a changing broken line ▬x▬ ).

One has to throw six times to obtain a hexagram, starting with the bottom or base line.
The die method is the most simple and easy to perform: it uses only one object instead of fifty yarrow stalks or three coins, and one can see the correct line immediately.
Because numerology is at the basis of the *Yi Jing* methods of consultation this die method is the most appropriate method for consulting the book. The only drawback is, because it gives an answer quickly, the inquirer could become less attentive during the consultation.

As we all know when consulting the *Yi Jing*, one needs to take time (as one actually should with everything in these modern times).

The methods of consulting the *Yi Jing* differ in their quality, because they give different chances of appearance to the stable or changing lines. The best of the three main methods – yarrow stalks, coins or die – is the one using the stalks.

The possibility for the occurrence of a stable or changing line with a die is equivalent to the stalks and coins. But the chance for a changing line is smaller than with the other methods (1/5 instead of 1/4). Thus we can see that the die is as good a method as the stalks or coins. See also the table on p. 351.

# Yi Jing *numerology*

Besides the numerical methods of prediction with the stalks, coins or dice there also exists a system of numerology. The numerological system of *Yi Jing* prediction was developed by a philosophical school called the School of Symbol and Number (*Xiang Shu Bai*).

The symbols are the images of the hexagrams, and the numbers are the ciphers 0 to 9 of the numerical system. One of the most known exponents of this school was *Shao Yong* (1011–1077), who developed several numerological formulas to consult the *Yi Jing* in his *Plum Blossom Numerology* (*Guan Mei Shu*).

According to the School of Symbol and Number, anything in Reality can be transcribed into numbers, which in turn can be translated into symbols or hexagrams and their meanings. For this purpose the hexagrams have been assigned numbers from 1 to 64. In their view the future develops in accordance with fixed laws and according to calculated numbers. If the numbers are known, future events can be calculated with great accuracy. (See Wilhelm: *The I Ching*, Wing 5/6, *Ta Chuan*: the Great Treatise, I.v.8, p. 300.)

The *Yi Jing* numerology is based on the principle of Time and Change. Time is based on Change: it is because changes (in nature and life) are perceived, that time is conceived. Change is based on Time: because time passes, change is perceived.

*Time is Change and Change is Time*. Time changes everything, and all changes have their own time. When we know one, we will be able to know the other. For example, when we look at our watch (Time), we will more or less know the position of the Sun in the sky (Change). And when we look at the Sun (Change), we can approximately say what time it is. In the same way when we know someone's birth date (Time), we can translate this into a life hexagram (Change), and get some information about that person's life.

This numerology was originally based on the translation of Chinese calendar dates into hexagrams with one changing line, but nowadays the universally used Western calendar is a more adequate foundation for this system of numerology. The Chinese calendar dates can still be used to attain some complementary information.

By knowing the hexagram of a certain day, one may consider the good or bad fortune of that particular day as a birthtime of the changes to come and may thus decide whether to take action or refrain from doing so. By contemplating life's changes as derived from the dates, one may decide whether to advance or retreat.

A hexagram derived from a date can function as a *day-hexagram* from which we may know what is in store for us on that particular day. All this will inform us about what may happen on that day, or indicate the result of what we may initiate on that day, such as a marriage, a journey, business or a court case.

This hexagram is obtained by totalling the numbers of the day, month and year in a specific way, and calculating the changing line from the day.

For example: 24 December 1998 becomes 24+12+1+9+9+8 = 36+27 = hexagram 63(6)37 or hexagram 63 with changing line 6, which changes into hexagram 37.

This is done by adding the day (24) to the month (12) and the year (27): its total gives the number of a hexagram. In case the total is higher than 64 (the number of hexagrams), one should subtract 64 to attain the number of the hexagram. In the year 2000 the number of the year will be 20, in 2001 it will be 21, and in 2010 it is also 21.

To attain the line, one always takes the number of the date, and subtracts as many times as possible the number of the lines (six), to arrive at the number of the changing line.

For example: date 2 gives line 2; date 9 gives 9–6 = 3; date 12 gives 12–6 = 6; date 16 gives 16–12 (2x6) = 4; date 23 gives 23–18 (3x6) = 5.

By taking the day and month of our birth, and adding the present or another year to it, we shall obtain a *year hexagram* for that particular year. This will inform us what to expect or what happened during that particular year.

We can also calculate our *life-hexagram* by adding up the day, month and year of our birth – to know something about the kind of life we will live and its karmic pattern.

All hexagrams having six lines. The *day-hexagram*, *year-hexagram* and *life-hexagram* can be divided into six periods of four hours, two months, or six periods of a certain number of years, respectively.

In the *day-hexagram* line 1 runs from 00:00 to 04:00 hours, line 2 from 04:00 to 08:00 hours, line 3 from 08:00 to 12:00 hours, and so forth.

In the *year-hexagram*, line 1 covers January and February, line 2 March and April, line 3 May and June, etc.

In the *life-hexagram*, line 1 covers the first ten, eleven or more years depending on the person's span of life expectancy. In ancient China each period of the life-hexagram was ten years, because the life cycle then was about sixty years. In our time each period may be eleven, twelve or thirteen years.

With the numerology of the *Yi Jing* one can make a decision at which point of the day, the year, or of one's life one should initiate certain actions in order to give them the best chances for manifestation.

When choosing a day for a particular purpose one should *match the purpose with the content of the hexagram* to attain the best results. Similarly, we are cautioned when to avoid certain things – by refraining from actions we could prevent the predicted misfortune to manifest. Thus the calculation of numbers in relation to symbols will bring forth information on which one can contemplate when it will be the right time to act. This is because a small effort at the right time will have a greater chance of success, than a great effort at the wrong time. Thus it will help us to continue being in the *Dao*.

This system of numerology and prediction is based on the changes on Earth, and not on changes in Heaven, or the influences of planets as in astrology. It is based on the patterns of change manifesting on Earth.

Although by means of ordinary numerology one may get information about the hidden nature of Reality, the *Yi Jing* numerology is special because – besides the numerological information – it also has access to the very specific knowledge and wisdom of the *Yi Jing*.

If we consult the *Yi Jing* by posing a question, its answer will not necessarily manifest, because by knowing the future we may alter our attitude or actions.

But if we acquire our information from the *Yi Jing* by means of numerology its outcome will surely manifest. The only thing we can do is to carefully watch the circumstances and secondary causes in order to lessen its impact.

With the numerology of the *Yi Jing* one is able to know one's *Dao*, one's purpose in life, and the patterns of its unfoldment. We can also know our fate, destiny, and negative *karma*. As some people will not be able to deal with it adequately, the *Yi Jing* does not necessarily give this information.

Because we transcend the power of the *Yi Jing* to decide whether it will give us an answer or not, it is advisable to use the numerological method of prediction with wisdom.

*Note. Those who may argue that a numerology based on the Christian Western calendar dates is an arbitrary one, may be surprised at its accuracy. For example, someone had a year-hexagram 36 with line 5, which says that he will 'suffer injury' that year. This person had an accident with his leg ('wounded in the left thigh') in the month of March, when the second line of hexagram 36 was active.*

*Another person who had a life-hexagram 55, line 1, changing into hexagram 62 had a life-threatening experience or accident every nine years since his birth because of the 'ominous' augury of the first line of hexagram 62. And in the period of his life when the third line of hexagram 55 was active (the line says 'he breaks his arm'), the person was shot in his right upper arm.*

Bibliography

Huang, Alfred: *The Numerology of the I Ching*, Inner Traditions, Rochester, Vermont, 2000.
Jou, Tsung-Hwa: *The Tao of I Ching*, Tai Chi Foundation/Tuttle, New York, 1984.
Liu, Da: *I Ching Numerology*, Routledge & Kegan Paul, London, 1975.
Nielsen, Bent: *A Companion to Yi Jing Numerology and Cosmology*, Routledge Curzon, London, New York, 2003.
Sandifer, Jon & Wang Yang: *The Authentic I Ching*, Watkins Publishing, London, 2003.
Sherrill, Wallace A. & Chu, Wen-Kuan: *An Anthology of I Ching*, Routledge & Kegan Paul, London, 1977.
Wilhelm, Richard: *The I Ching or Book of Changes*, Routledge & Kegan Paul, London, 1980.

# A mandala of hexagrams

A *mandala* (Sanskrit: 'circle' or 'disc') is a structural matrix, and consists of a number of concentric forms which are related to each other in such a way that it suggests a passage between different dimensions. All the hexagrams of the *Yi Jing* can be positioned in some kind of mandala structure, which contains three layers of hexagrams: the *source hexagrams*, the *inner cause hexagrams*, and the *karmic hexagrams* (see also p. 339, *Cause and Effect*).

This idea has been developed and worked out by four Dutch *Yi Jing* students and they called the three layers, the 'cosmic hexagrams', the 'karmic hexagrams', and the 'worldly hexagrams' (see Boering, *e.a.*: *De Mandala van Kernhexagrammen*).

To arrive at this *mandala*, these authors have explored the idea that within each hexagram there is an inner hexagram, and within that inner hexagram there is a nuclear hexagram. For example, hexagram 55 has hexagram 28 as its inner hexagram, and hexagram 28 has hexagram 1 as its nuclear hexagram. (On the inner hexagram see also *Introduction*, p. xxiv and xxxiii.)

The *source hexagrams* are the centre cluster of the *mandala*, and consists of four hexagrams (1, 2, 63 and 64).

The *inner cause hexagrams* are the middle cluster of the *mandala*, and consists of 12 hexagrams (44, 28, 43, 38, 54, 40, 24, 27, 23, 39, 53, 37).

The *karmic hexagrams* are the outer circle of the *mandala*, and consists of the remaining 48 hexagrams in 12 clusters or groups of four hexagrams. See the image of the *mandala* on p. 399.

Each source hexagram (1, 2, 63 and 64) can be found in three inner cause hexagrams. For example hexagram 1 is the source of the inner cause hexagrams 44, 28 and 43. Each inner cause hexagram (44, 28 and 43) can be found in four karmic hexagrams. For example hexagram 28 is the inner cause hexagram of the karmic hexagrams 55, 30, 56 and 62.

The karmic hexagrams at the outer circle can be regarded as the *life-hexagrams* of persons obtained through the Numerology of the *Yi Jing* (see the previous chapter), and can be seen as the *karmic patterns of life* of those persons. This karmic hexagram tells what karma will be manifested in the world in a particular lifetime.

The inner cause hexagram tells us out of what kind of situation this karmic pattern comes: what the inner cause of this particular karma in someone's life is.

The source hexagram tells us what the source of that situation is.
For example, karmic hexagram 55 (Abundance) comes out of a situation of excess (hexagram 28, Great Excess), and the source of that situation is hexagram 1 (The Creative). This is a clear example of the Creative, which knows no limitation in its ability to create, and may therefore bring forth in an excessive way (hexagram 28), which will again lead to abundance (hexagram 55).

Because all sixty-four hexagrams can be *life-hexagrams*, the source hexagrams and the inner cause hexagrams can also be karmic hexagrams. Thus looking at our karmic hexagram we can see what its inner cause is, and out of what source it all originated.

The source hexagram can be regarded as the basic source out of which the karmic pattern comes. People with hexagram 1 as their source hexagram have an urge for creative things (*heaven* quality), and people with hexagram 2 have an urge for receptive and caring things (*earth* quality).
Those with hexagram 63 as their source hexagram have an urge to complete things, and those with hexagram 64 have it too (because both hexagrams are actually two parts of one end hexagram), only they may stay in the phase before completion (hexagram 64).

The inner cause hexagram can be regarded as the situation out of which the karmic pattern comes, but it can also be seen as the main quality or attitude that is expressed in the manifestation of the karma. For example all the four karmic hexagrams (55, 30, 56 and 62) of the cluster that belong to the inner cause hexagram 28 (Great Excess) can be regarded as having something excessive in it.

The karmic hexagrams within one cluster are strongly related to each other in the way that they change either their first or their last line.

For example, hexagram 55 with line 1, changes into hexagram 62 – hexagram 62 with line 6, changes into hexagram 56 – hexagram 56 with line 1, changes into hexagram 30 – hexagram 30 with line 6, changes into hexagram 55 again.

This means that the person with a certain karmic pattern in that cluster (hexagram 55) may meet the other karmic patterns (30, 56 and 62) in real persons with those karmic hexagrams, and will thus have a strong karma with them that may have to be worked out. Or s/he will encounter the other three karmic patterns (30, 56 and 62) in her/his own life to work out.

With the information from the mandala of hexagrams one will have another tool to gain insight into one's own karmic pattern, but also in one's karmic relations to others (family, friends, associates etc.). How all this will manifest also depends on the specific line of the life-hexagram or karmic hexagram.

*Mandala of Hexagrams*

*The right thing
at the right time
and place:
the only one thing
the* Yi Jing *expresses
in its continuous
cycles of change.*

# Appendix 1

## The working method

Based on historical and archaeological findings of the last century one cannot say that the *Yi Jing* is a homogeneous text with fixed meanings. This concerns its basic structure, its historical development, and its theoretical framework of meanings.

The basic structure of the *Yi Jing*, consisting of the order and sequence of its 64 hexagrams, knows several variations, and is not based on a consistent logic.

The so-called traditional history of the *Yi Jing* with its development from *Fu Xi's* trigrams to king *Wen's* hexagrams and *Kong Fu Zi's* commentaries may not be its actual history. The book's theoretical framework is also an evolving body of material that has changed its meaning in a constant process of re-interpretation through the centuries. As the authors believe there is a coherent *Yi*-tradition underlying the various manifestations of the book, they tried to construct what they see as *the basic Yi Jing*, one that is as close as possible to the essence of the *Yi*-tradition.

Translating the *Yi Jing* the authors based their working method on four pillars – *text, context, experience* and *structure* – on which the truth of the statements in the *Yi Jing* could be established.

### Text

As the Chinese text is not homogeneous, and has evolved in different ways through the centuries, the authors could not only rely on the text.

The work of others (for instance, Kunst, Rutt, Lynn, Blofeld, R. Wilhelm, Ritsema & Karcher, Karlgren), who have done much for the translation of the old Chinese language of this text, proved to be very helpful.

## Context

Because much of the old Chinese cultural phenomena – that could function as the context to ascertain the truth of the statements in the text – were not always conclusive, the authors could also not fully rely on the context. The main reason was that many of the historical and archaeological findings related to the *Yi Jing* were also not always conclusive.

## Experience

The main thing the authors could rely on was their long-time experience of working with the *Yi Jing* in advising others. Through experience one can ascertain whether the statements in the lines are true (literally or figuratively), or not. This experience consisted, for instance, of at least three consultations a day for about 36 years, and the use of Numerology in relation to the *Yi Jing*. With the use of Numerology one may know someone's life hexagram, and compare the information from the hexagrams and lines with the events in the life that already has passed. Comparing several people with the same life hexagram, one comes to know whether a certain hexagram or line is more or less correct.

The authors reflected on their experience of interpreting answers given by the *Yi Jing* and the use of Numerology, and compared their findings with the experiential findings of others (for instance, Wang Bi, Wu Jing-Nuan, Hua-Ching Ni, Da Liu, Alfred Huang, Henry Wei, Chung Wu).

## Structure

Despite the fact that *the basic structure of the* Yi Jing – *consisting of the order and sequence of its 64 hexagrams* – knows several variations, and is not based on a consistent logic, the authors decided that this basic structure of the *Yi Jing* was the best thing that could be relied on. They also decided this on the suggestion one of the authors received in a dream (see p. 3).

Because *the structure of the* Yi Jing *(hexagrams and lines) is assumed to represent the aspects and phases of the general process of change*, they decided to consider this structure of the *Yi Jing* as the source out of which all the meanings of the hexagram and lines emerge. Therefore all the meanings in the text and lines had to match this structure. Staying with the structure meant staying with the meanings and order of the trigrams (the Early Heaven Arrangement, the Later Heaven Arrangement, and the relationships of the Five Elements or States of Change; see *Introduction* p. xxii-xxiv), and the images and order of the hexagrams, to clarify the meaning of the hexagrams and lines.

The authors also used the structure of the *mandala* of hexagrams – based on the inner hexagrams – as an extra tool to check the meanings of the 64 hexagrams (see *The Twelfth Wing, A mandala of hexagrams,* p. 396). For example, the hexagrams 55, 62, 56, and 30 all have something excessive in them, because they all have hexagram 28 (Great Excess) as their inner hexagram.

As the old Chinese characters of the titles attached to the hexagrams have acquired different meanings through time, they did not pay much attention to them, and left them out. They also tried to bring the text down to its most essential parts, not allowing the later attached additions to distort it. Doing this, they did not accept parts of the old Chinese stories and commentaries.

In this *Yi Jing* the Image (symbol) is put before the Judgment (text) because the authors think it is a more appropriate place for it. The Image is expressing the idea of the hexagram, and the Judgment is the expression of that idea in language.

In their basic text they decided, where necessary, to have two expressions of the Judgment (the main part of the text): *a)* and *b)* – where *a)* is the literal text on the basis of the Chinese words, and *b)* is a clarification of that particular part. The same holds for the separate lines.

They also tried to give an argument for the noble person's attitude, based on the component trigrams of the hexagrams.

In the commentaries on the meanings of the lines, only in some cases did the authors use the explanations related to the meaning of the lines, based on their position and relationships, because they found they were too often used without much ground.

Thus all meanings in the text and lines had to match the structure (the trigrams and the hexagrams), and be supported by the long-time experience of working with the *Yi Jing*.

As there were a number of inconsistencies between the inner structure and their meanings, the authors had to make several corrections (25) in the meanings of the individual lines. They did this by reflecting on it, but also by comparing their experiential findings with others. (See p. 408, *Appendix II, Yi Jing Corections*.)

Working on this **Basic Yi Jing** there were a number of assumptions the authors started with and kept in mind. Exploring these assumptions, and progressing further into the work, the authors found that some of those assumptions (1, 3 and 5) could not really stand:

1. The *Yi Jing* is assumed to be a consistent theoretical system, in the sense that it is in conformity with its earlier principles of thought, and not contradictory to them. (See *The Twelfth Wing, Inconsistencies in the Yi Jing*, p. 358.)
2. It is assumed that there are a number of principles on which the theoretical system of the *Yi Jing* is based. (See *The Twelfth Wing, Eight main principles in the Yi Jing*, p. 335.)
3. The structure of the *Yi Jing* (hexagrams and lines) is assumed to represent the aspects and phases of the Process of Change. (See *The Twelfth Wing, The Yi Jing and the process of Change*, p. 340.)
4. It is assumed that there is a numerical order at the basis of the structure of the *Yi Jing*. (See *The Twelfth Wing, Yi Jing numerology*, p. 392.)
5. All meanings in the text and lines are assumed to match the structure (the trigrams and the hexagrams) of the *Yi Jing*. (See *Appendix II, Yi Jing corrections*, p. 408.)
6. The signs and omens attached to the hexagrams and lines are taken from natural and cultural phenomena of old China. Their meanings are assumed to transcend the original old Chinese intended meanings. (See *Introduction, Signs and omens*, p. xviii.)

Trying to construct the *Yi Jing* as close as possible to the essence of the *Yi*-tradition, the hexagrams in this **Basic Yi Jing** are structured as follows:

- The *Image* (symbol) of the hexagram, composed of two trigrams, expresses the idea of the hexagram. This idea is explored through the specific meanings of the trigrams in a general way. It also expresses

an attitude of the noble person, based on the meanings of the trigrams of the hexagrams.
- The *Judgment* (main text) expresses the signs and omens related to the idea of the hexagram.
- The *Commentary* on the Judgment explores the meaning of the signs and omens expressed in the Judgment – on the basis of the various meanings of the composing outside and inside trigrams of the hexagram.
- Each of the *Six Lines* of the hexagram expresses the idea of the hexagram specifically. These lines indicate the different stages of this idea in six successive moments in time.
- In the *Summary* the meaning of the hexagram and the lines is again described in more explanatory ways. Here the Chinese cultural phenomena are translated in such a way that their universal meanings become apparent.

This description of each hexagram in the book – where the meanings of the hexagram and lines are expressed in successive stages of explanation – is done with the intention that the reader will have an easier understanding and a good overview of the hexagram as a whole.

# Appendix II

# *Yi Jing* corrections

During the translation of the *Yi Jing* there were occasions where the authors made corrections in the hexagrams and the position and meanings of some lines. In some instances they consulted the *Yi Jing* itself to find out if a certain text or line was more or less appropriate or correct than another one.

### Corrections in the hexagrams

1. *Hexagram 8.* In various translations the Judgment of hexagram 8 mentions that a second consultation on the same question may be performed. But there is no reason for a second consultation, because in the Judgment it also says that the original divination (the first manipulation of the stalks) brings sublime success. Therefore in this translation a second consultation is not recommended.

Asking the *Yi Jing* about its opinion, it answered with hexagram 12 (The Small, The Petty) line 4, changing into hexagram 20 (Observing, View, Contemplation). Interpreting the answer, it could mean that those people (the small, the petty) who are really not able to understand the given answer with one consultation – in this special case – may do a second one.

2. *Hexagram 12.* Hexagram 11 and hexagram 12 are composed of the same trigrams, Heaven and Earth. Only in hexagram 11 their movement makes them join each other, while in hexagram 12 the trigrams move away from

each other. As all the lines in the two hexagrams are also totally opposite to each other, the meaning of hexagram 11 (The Great, Peace) is also totally opposite of hexagram 12 (The Small, The Petty).
In hexagram 12 line 1, 'offering' or 'success' is mentioned, but line 1 of hexagram 12 is not as good as line 1 of hexagram 11. If hexagram 11 line 1 mentions 'auspicious', then hexagram 12 line 1 cannot mention 'augury auspicious' and also 'offering', but only 'augury auspicious' or 'perseverance will bring good fortune'. Therefore 'offering' or 'success' is left out in hexagram 12 line 1.

3. *Hexagram 62*. In the text of the Judgment of hexagram 62 (Excessiveness of the Small), three parts ('offering, favourable augury') of the often used *'yuan heng li zhen'* formula (meaning, 'great offering favourable augury') are mentioned. At the end of the Judgment it also says 'greatly auspicious'. Considering the name of the hexagram, Excessiveness of the Small, it seems to be too much of a good thing for this hexagram.

Asking the *Yi Jing* what it thinks about the idea that the Judgment of hexagram 62 has three parts of the formula, its answer was surprisingly hexagram 62 (Excessiveness of the Small) without a changing line. So we changed it into two parts: 'favourable augury' ('persistence is beneficial') and changed 'greatly auspicious' ('great good fortune') into only 'auspicious' ('good fortune').

Depending on the 'flavour' of the hexagram or line, 'augury' has five different meanings. (See p. 420, *The four virtues or qualities*.)

## Correction of the meanings and positions of the lines

1. *Hexagram 11*. In hexagram 11 (The Great, Peace) the meaning of line 4 was not clear because in different books it was interpreted differently. Line 4 is a correct *yin* line in a correct place, and indicates the fourth stage of Peace. The line is about riches not shared *by* or *with* the neighbours. If it was not shared *by* the neighbours, it means that the neighbours did not share their wealth with the person, and the person still has confidence in them and does not question their sincerity. If the wealth was not shared *with* the neighbours, it means that the person did not share his wealth with the neighbours, and the neighbours kept their confidence in him and did not question his sincerity.

Consulting the *Yi Jing* what this line means, its answer was hexagram 38 (Opposition) without a changing line. This only indicated that the person and the neighbours are opposed to each other, and did not indicate who was not sharing his wealth. When a line was 'squeezed out' of the hexagram by means of the time method (see *The Twelfth Wing, Yi Jing methodology,* p. 382) it produced line 3. Hexagram 38, line 3 says that a person's head was branded and his nose cut off, which could mean that the neighbours were not really in favour of him, and therefore did *not* share their riches with him.

This is also supported by the idea that hexagram 11 is about peace and harmony, and thus about the attitude of the noble person, who, in line 4, keeps having confidence, and does not question the sincerity of his neighbours – in spite of the fact that they do not share their wealth with him.

2. *Hexagram 20.* In hexagram 20 (Observing, View, Contemplation), the meanings of lines 5 and 6 are placed differently in different translations. In one book it is said that the noble person is looking over, watching the lives of others, and in the other it is said that he is looking at, contemplating his own life. We know that line 5 is the place for someone at a position of power in the world – so he can watch over other people's lives – but this is also the case for line 6 as the position of a sage, who is usually away from the world but may still be very powerful, and able to watch other people's lives.

To find the correct place for these texts, the question asked was: 'Who is watching other people's lives?' Keeping in mind that line 5 is about someone outside, in the world, in society, and line 6 is about someone inside, away from the world – the answer was hexagram 21(4)27: hexagram 21 line 4 changing into hexagram 27.

The arguments for the fifth line holding the position of watching over other people's lives are stronger than for the sixth line because:

- the changing line *(4)* is located in the upper (outside) trigram. It indicates someone who is outside, in the world, in society, therefore in line 5 someone is watching other people's lives. As line 6 usually stands for the sage, living away from the world – it is he who is more likely contemplating or observing his own life;
- line 5 is a *yang* line in a correct position, and line 6 is also a *yang* line, but it is in an incorrect position;
- within the context of the lines 1, 2, 3 and 4 of hexagram 20, Observing, View, Contemplation, line 5 has to be about watching over other people's

lives, and line 6 about observing one's own.

3. *Hexagram 28.* In hexagram 28 (Great Excess), line 2 is about a young woman, and regarded as positive ('nothing is unfavourable'), and line 5 is about an old woman, and regarded as less positive ('no blame, no praise'). Line 2 is a *yang* line in a wrong position, and it is part of the trigram *wind* which stands for the eldest daughter (an older woman), and line 5 is a *yang* line in a correct position, and it is part of the trigram *lake*, which stands for the youngest daughter (a young woman).

Despite the wrong positions of the lines, and the incorrect meanings of the trigrams, in the long-time experience of working with the *Yi Jing*, the answers received about relationships are always connected with the correct lines. If a young woman is involved in the consultation, one will receive line 2 (an earlier position of the lines in a hexagram), and if an older woman is involved, one will receive line 5 (a later position). While this is an example of a very strong inconsistency, in this translation it is not corrected, because the experience of consulting the *Yi Jing* does not support a correction.

4. *Hexagram 29.* In another example, hexagram 29 line 4 states that food and wine are handed through a hole (window) to a person who has fallen into a dangerous pitfall (hexagram 29), and is stuck in it. This statement could mean two things:

- food and wine are handed through the window from outside to relieve the person's suffering in the pit. This is an action *going inside*;
- food and wine are handed through the window by the person in the pit as an offering to the ancestors or superiors to relieve his suffering. This is an action *going outside*.

Finding the correct meaning of the fourth line with the help of the *Yi Jing* the question asked was: "What is this line about?" Keeping in mind that if the changing line of the answer (hexagram) was in the lower (inside) trigram the action was going inside, and if the changing line would fall on the upper (outside) trigram, the action was going outside. The answer was hexagram 49(2)43, that is hexagram 49 line 2, changing into hexagram 43.

The arguments for the first meaning of the line, that the food and wine were handed from outside (an action going inside), are:

- the changing line 2 of hexagram 49 is in the lower trigram (the inside trigram); therefore the action was *going inside*;
- considering the lines 1, 2 and 3 of hexagram 29 of falling into and being in a pitfall, in line 4 the person is still in the pitfall, but his suffering is relieved by something handed to him from outside (an action *going inside*);
- reading the text of line 2 of hexagram 49 (Radical Change, Revolution) it says that it is a blessing. So there is some help from outside (an action *going inside*).

5. *Hexagram 31*. In another example, hexagram 31 – which is about sensation, stimulation in different parts of the body – line 5 mentions a sensation in the upper back part of the spine. This is generally an indication of tension and anxiety. It also says that one's influence (will) is limited. One cannot impose yet. But line 5 is a central and correct line (a *yang* line at the right place). It should therefore not have a negative connotation.
Consulting the *Yi Jing*, the answer was 46(3)7: hexagram 46 line 3, changing into hexagram 7. Hexagram 46(3) is about an ascending and promotion to an empty office or city, and hexagram 7(3) is about a serious defeat and wagonloads of corpses. The reason for anxiety and tension in line 5 of hexagram 31 is the foreboding of something negative. Because line 5 is central and correct, the line also says that there will be no trouble or regret.

6. *Hexagram 32*. Hexagram 32 is about constancy in a story of a husband (*thunder*, eldest son) and a wife (*wind*, eldest daughter) in an enduring marriage. In many translations line 5 says that constancy of virtue is auspicious to the wife but ominous to the husband. And the commentary says that a woman follows one lord for the whole of her life, but a man has to hold to his public duties. This can be interpreted that men should not be constant in their virtues (be less virtuous), and can have more wives (as was the custom in China), otherwise they will have misfortune.
The correct meaning of this line would be that the virtue here is about the *yin* qualities of a woman who is following her husband and being obedient. If the husband would behave like an obedient and following wife it would bring him misfortune. For a man should have *yang* qualities, such as making decisions and leading the way.

7. *Hexagram 55*. In hexagram 55, line 6, it says that a person is living in a big

house, but looking outside he sees no one. But as this house is big and overgrown, it could also mean that people looking from outside cannot see anyone in the house.

Asking the *Yi Jing* what this line is about, it answered hexagram 15(2, 6)18. As line 2 is in the bottom (inside) trigram, it would indicate that someone looks from *inside* the house and sees no one. But as the answer also mentions line 6, which is the upper (outside) trigram, it indicates that people looking from *outside* also do not see anyone in the house. So this line actually says that looking from inside and looking from outside, nobody is seen.

8. *Hexagram 62*. In hexagram 62, line 4, it says that someone does not pass him, but meets him. No misfortune. Because in some translations (Blofeld, Da Liu) this situation is considered negative, the question is whether this 'not passing' is negative or positive. Asking the *Yi Jing* what this line is about it surprisingly answered hexagram 62(2)32. In hexagram 62, line 2, it says that by passing by there will be misfortune in the sense that one does not reach as high as one hoped. *Passing by is thus considered negative.* This implies that *not* passing by is positive.

So the real meaning of hexagram 62, line 4, is positive in the sense that by not passing him but meeting him one does the correct thing.

Although it is no misfortune, at the same time one is warned not to go on with this encounter too long. This can be seen in the context of the third line (where he does not pass him, but here it is ominous), and the sixth line (where he passes him and does not meet him, and it is really ominous).

## The issue of 'blame' and 'shame'

In the *Yi Jing* there are good and bad omens indicating good fortune and misfortune. These could be specified as trouble, harm, disaster, calamity etc. due to faults, mistakes, or errors. All these terms are neutral, objective terms. But if these terms become more 'coloured' (personal), the terms shame, blame, regret and remorse appear.

Although in both Eastern and Western culture shame and blame exist, one may generally say that the Western cultures are more cultures of blame (due to Christianity), and the Eastern cultures are more shame cultures.

The authors think that shame, blame, regret and remorse are the more personally coloured terms which entered the *Yi Jing* in the commentaries.

In our translation we tried to justify the correct use and place of the terms shame and blame in the text of the lines with two arguments:

- it has to fit in the context of meaning of the other lines of the hexagram;
- shame has to be in a line in the inside (lower) trigram (*shame is directed inwards*), and blame in the outside (upper) trigram (*blame is directed outwards*).

If shame happened to be located in an outside trigram (blame's position) it had to be in the inside line (middle or fifth line) of that upper trigram.
If blame was located in the inside trigram (shame's position), it had to be one of the outside lines (first and third lines) of that lower trigram.
If they are in both positions, than both shame and blame are involved.

1. For example in hexagram 12, line 3, shame is the correct term in the right place, because it fits in the context of the story of small, bad men doing immoral things (using an offering as bribery), and it is located in the lower (inside) trigram.
2. In hexagram 18, line 3, freedom from blame is mentioned in relation to taking responsibility for the mistakes of the fathers ("mildew for a deceased male ancestor"). Line 3 is in the lower trigram (the position for shame), but it is also in the outside line of that trigram, therefore both shame and blame are involved.
3. In hexagram 20, line 2, mentions a secret watch (observation) of women which is considered shameful. The second line is in the lower trigram and the inside line of that trigram, therefore shame is correct.
4. In hexagram 22, line 4, adornment gives rise to doubt and suspicion, but ultimately there is no blame. Line 4 is in the upper (outside) trigram and it is its outside line, therefore blame is correct.
5. In hexagram 26, line 2, there is some misfortune for which one is not to blame. As the misfortune is something we cannot do anything about and the line is on the outside (first line) of the lower trigram (indicating shame), in this case it can be blame.
6. In hexagram 28, line 5, an older woman marries a younger man: "no blame, no praise." Line 5 is in the upper (outside) trigram, therefore

blame is correct. But in the commentary it is also mentioned as shameful. This is because line 5 is also the inside line of the upper trigram.
7. In hexagram 30, line 1, someone is approaching a person with reverence and care to avoid a mistake. Line 1 is in the inside trigram (shame's position), but it is also in the first line, the outside line of the lower trigram (blame's position), therefore both blame and shame are involved.
8. In hexagram 39, line 2, someone meets with difficulty upon difficulty but because it is not his fault, he is not to blame. As the second line is in the middle of the lower trigram, it should actually be shame. But here both blame and shame could be involved.
9. In hexagram 40, line 3, it is said that someone carries things on his back while riding a horse, and attracts robbers. If someone acts in such a way who is to blame? While this is clearly a blame situation, the third line is in the lower trigram, and could also be shame. But because the third line is the outside line of the lower trigram, blame is correct.
10. In hexagram 42, line 3, someone experiences increasing misfortune through unfortunate affairs, but if it is done in service to others there will be no blame. As this line is in the lower trigram, it should be shame but because the line is also the outside line of the lower trigram, blame could also be involved.
11. In hexagram 43, line 1, it is said that when one sets out with too much strength (decisiveness) it will lead to failure, which may bring shame. As the first line is in the lower trigram, it is correctly about shame.
In hexagram 43, line 3, a noble person is travelling alone and firmly determined. If he meets rain and gets wet he will have resentment, but there is no need for shame. This line is in the lower trigram (shame), but it is also the outside line of that lower trigram, therefore there is also no need for blame.
In hexagram 43, line 5, it is said that that if one treads the middle path one could avoid blame. As this line is in the upper trigram, blame would be correct.
12. In hexagram 45, line 6, blame is in the correct place because it is in the upper trigram.
13. In hexagram 51, line 6, blame is also in the upper trigram and therefore also correct.

14. In hexagram 63, line 2, it says that a lady loses her carriage curtain. This is a truly shameful circumstance for her, and because it is in the lower trigram, it is also correct.

# Appendix III

# The Trigrams

### The trigrams, their names, colours and meanings

The colours* of the trigrams in this *Yi Jing* are based on the colours of the five 'elements':

Earth (yellow), Water (white), Fire (red), Wood (green), and Metal (blue).

| 1 | ☰ | qian | heaven | blue, creative, power, *yang*, active, male, father |
|---|---|------|--------|-----------------------------------------------------|
| 2 | ☱ | dui | lake | off-white, still water, cloud, pool, marsh, joy, pleasing, youngest daughter |
| 3 | ☲ | li | fire | red, lightning, light, brightness, clinging, cohesion, middle daughter |
| 4 | ☳ | zhen | thunder | dark green, moving, shock, growth, eldest son |
| 5 | ☴ | xun | wind | green, wood, penetrating, gentle, eldest daughter |
| 6 | ☵ | kan | water | white, moving water, rain, stream, danger, middle son |
| 7 | ☶ | gen | mountain | dark yellow, standing, still, stilling, stopping, youngest son |
| 8 | ☷ | kun | earth | yellow, receptive, compliant, yielding, *yin*, passive, female, mother |

* colours depicted in hard cover version only. Order: www.olivepress.nl

## The sequence of the trigrams

The trigrams are three-line images formed by combining *yang* (whole) lines and *yin* (broken) lines. Some of the trigrams represent the so-called Western elements such as: Earth, Water, Fire, Air (in the *Yi Jing*,Wood), and Ether (in the *Yi Jing*, Metal), but they are actually regarded as *states of change* or *transformation*.

The eight trigrams are formed out of the five trigrams representing the 'elements': Earth (*earth* and *mountain*), Water (*water/rain*, and *lake/cloud*), Fire (*fire*), Wood (*wind* and *thunder*), and Metal (*heaven* and *lake*).

The order of the eight trigrams are said to be derived from the *He Tu* and *Lo Shu* patterns of dots found on sacred animals, but they can also be derived from natural phenomena such as the weather and the seasons. In the Early Heaven Arrangement of trigrams, the sequence of events in the sky (heaven) can be taken as the ideal, and in the Later Heaven Arrangement the order of the seasons on earth can serve as the model

In the EHA the sequence of the trigrams is consistent with the sequence of events in the sky:

1. *heaven* (a clear summer sky) – 2. *cloud* (due to heat, hot air rises and clouds are formed) – 3. *fire* (heavy clouds bring forth lightning) – 4. *thunder* (after lightning thunder always follows) – 5. *wind* (Wind follows thunder) – 6. *water* (after the wind comes the rain) – 7. *mountain* (the rain falls first on the mountain) – 8. *earth* (the rain falls on the earth).

*This sequence of trigrams, based on the events of the weather, can be considered a natural pattern of change.*

But in the LHA the sequence of trigrams is not consistent with the sequence of events on earth (the seasons):

1. *water* (rain) and 2. *earth* (rain falls on the earth mainly in the winter) represent the winter; 3. *thunder* and 4. *wind* (thunder and wind stand for growth in the spring) represent the spring; the number 5 is missing; then it should be followed by *fire* (but this trigram has number 9), representing the summer; 6. *heaven* and 7. *lake* (or *cloud*) represent autumn, and 8. *mountain* (stillness is also an attribute of the winter).

On earth the trigrams as 'elements' follow the sequence of *the five states of change* or *transformation*:

Water (rain) produces Wood (plants grow) – Wood produces Fire (wood is burned) – Fire produces Earth (ashes) – Earth produces Metal (rocks are formed) – and Metal produces Water (water comes out of rocks).

*This order of trigrams, based on the relationship between the 'elements', can also be considered a natural pattern of change.*

Based on this order, the LHA sequence of the trigrams on earth could actually be:

1.*water* (Water, rain, winter) leads to 2. *thunder* (Wood, growth, spring) and 3. *wind* (Wood, plants), leading to 4. *fire* (Fire, summer), which again leads to 5. *earth* (Earth), and 6. *mountain* (Earth), leading to 7. *heaven* (Metal, autumn), and 8. *lake* (Metal/Water, autumn) which again leads to *water*.

Although this sequence of trigrams can also be considered a natural pattern of change – and according to the sequence of the elements, it is more appropriate than the original LHA – it is not used in the *Yi Jing* tradition.

# Appendix IV

# Miscellaneous

## The four virtues or qualities

- *yuan*  great           sublime, sublimity;
- *heng*  offering, sacrifice  accomplishment, success, achievement;
- *li*    favourable      benefit, beneficial, beneficence;
- *zhen*  augury          determination and persistence are *yang* terms; perseverance, steadfastness, and constancy are *yin* terms.

## Other significant terms

- *ji*       auspicious, good fortune, prosperity
- *yuan ji*  very auspicious, very good fortune
- *da ji*    most auspicious, great good fortune, supreme good fortune
- *jiu*      misfortune, error, mistake, fault, blame
- *xiong*    ominous, disaster, inauspicious, threatening
- *hai*      harm, evil
- *hui*      trouble, regret, remorse
- *lin*      distress
- *xiu*      disgrace, shame
- *fu*       capture, captive, sincere, sincerity, confidence, reliable

## 'Favourable' and 'unfavourable'

- Everything is favourable;
  There is everything for which this is favourable;
  There is nothing for which this is unfavourable.
- Everything is unfavourable;
  There is everything for which this is unfavourable;
  There is nothing for which this is favourable.

## Some contemporary coins

The most simple coins which can be used for consulting the *Yi Jing* are those that have on one side a round circle (the sun, *yang*), and on the other a square (the earth, *yin*).

# Appendix v

| trigrams upper→ lower↓ | heaven | lake | fire | thunder | wind | water | mountain | earth |
|---|---|---|---|---|---|---|---|---|
| heaven | 1 | 43 | 14 | 34 | 9 | 5 | 26 | 11 |
| lake | 10 | 58 | 38 | 54 | 61 | 60 | 41 | 19 |
| fire | 13 | 49 | 30 | 55 | 37 | 63 | 22 | 36 |
| thunder | 25 | 17 | 21 | 51 | 42 | 3 | 27 | 24 |
| wind | 44 | 28 | 50 | 32 | 57 | 48 | 18 | 46 |
| water | 6 | 47 | 64 | 40 | 59 | 29 | 4 | 7 |
| mountain | 33 | 31 | 56 | 62 | 53 | 39 | 52 | 15 |
| earth | 12 | 45 | 35 | 16 | 20 | 8 | 23 | 2 |

Chart to identify the hexagrams by number
(This chart is based on the Early Heaven sequence of trigrams.)

# Bibliography

## Books on the *Yi Jing*

Balkin, Jack, M.: *The Laws of Change: I Ching and the philosophy of life*, Schocken Books, New York, 2002.

Blofeld, John: *I Ching: the Book of Change*, E.P. Dutton & Co., New York, 1968 (1965).

Cleary, Thomas: *The Taoist I Ching*, (translation of the *Liu I Ming*), Shambala, Boston & London, 1986.

Chung Wu: *The Essentials of the Yi Jing*, Paragon House, St.Paul, Minnesota, 2003.

Da Liu: *I Ching Coin Prediction*, Routledge & Kegan Paul, London, 1975 (expanded ed., $1984^2$);
— *I Ching Numerology*, Routledge & Kegan Paul, London, 1979.

Hua-Ching Ni: *The Book of Changes and the Unchanging Truth*, Shrine of the Eternal Breath of Tao, Santa Monica, 1992.

Huang, Alfred: *The Complete I Ching*, Inner Traditions, Rochester, Vermont, 1998;
— *The Numerology of the I Ching: a sourcebook of symbols, structures, and traditional wisdom*, Inner Traditions, Rochester, Vermont, 2000.

Huang, Kerson & Rosemary: *I Ching*, Workman Publishing, New York, 1985.

Jou Tsung-Hwa: *The Tao of I Ching: the Way to Divination*, Tai Chi Foundation/Tuttle, New York, 1984.

Karlgren, Bernhard: *Grammata Serica Recensa*, SMC Publishing Inc., Taipei, 1996 (1957²).

Koh Kok Kiang & Tan Xiaochun: *The I Ching: an illustrated guide to the Chinese art of divination*, Asiapac, Singapore, 1993.

Kunst, Richard, A.: *The Original 'Yijing': a text, phonetic transcription, translation, and indexes, with sample glosses*, PhD. thesis, Univ. of California, 1985, UMI Dissertations, Ann Arbor, 1998.

Liu Dajun & Lin Zhongjun: *The I Ching: text and annotated translation*, Shandong Friendship Publishing House, Jinan, China, 1995.

Lynn, Richard, J.: *The Classic of Change: a new translation of the I Ching as interpreted by Wang Bi*, Columbia University Press, New York, 1994.

Marshall S.J.: *The Mandate of Heaven: the hidden history of the I Ching*, Columbia University Press, New York, 2001.

Melyan, Gary. G. & Chu Wen Kuan: *I Ching: the hexagrams revealed*, Tuttle & Co, New York, 1977.

Moore, Steve: *The trigrams of Han: inner structures of the I Ching*, The Aquarian Press, Wellingborough, England, 1989.

Nielsen, Bent: *A Companion to Yi Jing Numerology and Cosmology: Chinese studies of images and numbers from Han (202 BCE-220 CE) to Song (960–1279 CE)*, Routledge Curzon, London, New York, 2003.

Richmond, Nigel: *Language of the Lines: the I Ching oracle*, Wildwood House, 1977.

Ritsema, Rudolf: *Differentiating Terms in the I Ching*, Brill, Leiden, 1970.

Ritsema, Rudolf & Stephen Karcher: *I Ching: the classic Chinese oracle of change*, Element, Shaftesbury, 1994.

Rutt, Richard: *Zhouyi, the Book of Changes: a Bronze Age document*, Curzon Press, Richmond, Surrey, 1996.

Shaughnessy, Edward L.: *I Ching, the Classic of Changes* (translation of the Ma Wang Dui text), Ballantine Books, New York, 1997.

– *The Composition of the Zhouyi*, PhD. thesis, Stanford University, 1983, UMI Dissertations, Ann Arbor, 2002.

Sherrill, Wallace, A. & Chu Wen Kuan: *An Anthology of I Ching*, Routledge & Kegan Paul, London, 1977.

Smith, Richard, J: *Fortune-tellers and Philosophers: Divination in Traditional Chinese Society*, Westview press, Boulder, 1993 (1991); also online at www.questia.com.

– *Fathoming the Cosmos and Ordering the World: The Yi-jing (I-Ching or Classic of Changes) and its Evolution in China*, University of Virginia Press, Charlottesville and London, 2008.
Waley, Arthur: *The Book of Changes*, essay in the *Bulletin of the Museum of Far Eastern Antiquities*, no. 5, p. 121-142, Stockholm, 1933.
Wei, Henry: *The Authentic I Ching*, Newcastle Publishing Co., North Hollywood, CA, 1987.
Wei Tat: *An Exposition of the I-Ching or Book of Changes*, Institute of Cultural Studies, Taipei, 1970.
Whincup, Gregory: *Rediscovering the I Ching*, St. Martin's Press, New York, 1986.
Wilhelm, Helmut: *Change: eight lectures on the I Ching*, Routledge & Kegan Paul, London, 1975, (1960).
Wilhelm, Richard: *The I Ching or Book of Changes*, Routledge & Kegan Paul, London, 1980, (1968³).
Wu Jing-Nuan: *Yi Jing*, The Taoist Center, Washington, D.C., 1991.

The main books consulted were the *Yi Jing* texts of Blofeld, Kunst, Rutt, Lynn, Wilhelm, Da Liu, Huang, Wei, Wu, Hua-Jing Ni, Cleary, Ritsema & Karcher.

## Books related to The Twelfth Wing

Aziz, R: *C.G. Jung's Psychology of Religion and Synchronicity*, State University of New York Press, 1990.
Barbour, Julian: *The End of Time: the next revolution in physics*, Weidenfeld & Nicholson, London, 1999.
Boering, Han, G. Hellinga, D. Langeveld, J. Voigt: *De Mandala van Kernhexagrammen (the mandala of inner hexagrams)*, privately published essay, n.d.
Bohm, David: *Causality and Chance in Modern Physics*, Routledge & Kegan Paul, London, 1957.
Combs, Allan & M. Holland: *Synchronicity: science, myth and the trickster*, Floris Books, Edinburgh, 1994.
Da Liu: *I Ching Numerology*, Routledge & Kegan Paul, London, 1979.

Diegh, Khigh Alx: *The Eleventh Wing: an exposition of the dynamics of I Ching for now*, Dell Publishing, New York, 1974.

Govinda, Lama Anagarika: *The Inner Structure of the I Ching: the Book of Transformations*, Wheelwright Press, San Francisco, 1981.

Hacker, Edward A.: *The I Ching Handbook: a practical guide to personal and logical perspectives from the ancient Chinese Book of Change*, Paradigm Publications, Brookline, MA, 1993.

Hamlyn, David W.: *The Theory of Knowledge: modern introductions to philosophy*, Doubleday, New York, 1970.

Hook, Diana ffarington: *The I Ching and its Associations*, Routledge & Kegan Paul, London, 1980.

Huang, Alfred: *The Numerology of the I Ching: a sourcebook of symbols, structures, and traditional wisdom*, Inner Traditions, Rochester, Vermont, 2000.

Jung, Carl G.: *Synchronicity: an acausal connecting principle*, Pantheon, New York, 1955.

Koestler, Arthur: *The Roots of Coincidence: an excursion into parapsychology*, Random House, New York, 1972.

Lindqvist, Cecilia: *China, Empire of Living Symbols*, Da Capo Press, New York, 2008)

Main, Roderick: *Jung on Synchronicity and the Paranormal*, Princeton University Press, Princeton, 1997.

Main, Roderick: *Synchronicity as a Form of Spiritual Experience*, Lancaster University. Lancaster, 1995.

Mansfield, V: *Synchronicity, Science and Soul-Making*, Open Court, Chicago, 1995.

Moore, Steve: *The Trigrams of Han: inner structures of the I Ching*, The Aquarian Press, Wellingborough, England, 1989.

Peat, F. David: *Synchronicity, the Bridge between Matter and Mind*, Bantam, New Age Books, Toronto 1988.

Progoff, I.: *Jung, Synchronicity and Human Destiny*, Delta Book, New York, 1973.

Schönberger, Martin: *The I Ching and the Genetic Code: the hidden key to life*, ASI Publishers, New York, 1979.

Shchutskii, Iulian, K.: *Researches on the I Ching*, Princeton Univ. Press, Princeton, New Jersey, 1979.

Siu, Ralph G.H.: *The Tao of Science*, M.I.T. Press, Cambridge, Mass., 1957.
Toben, Bob & F.A. Wolf: *Space-Time and Beyond*, Dutton, New York, 1975.
Toulmin, Stephen: *The Philosophy of Science*, Harper Torchbook, New York, 1960.
Walter, Katia: *Tao of Chaos*, Element, Shaftesbury, England, 1994.
Wang Yang & Jon Sandifer: *The Authentic I Ching: three classic methods of prediction*, Watkins Publishing, London, 2003.
Yan, Johnson F.: *DNA and the I Ching: the Tao of life*, North Atlantic Books, Berkeley, CA, 1991.

www.ingramcontent.com/pod-product-compliance
Lightning Source LLC
Chambersburg PA
CBHW020632230426
43665CB00008B/134